BEHAVIOUR THERAPY IN PRIMARY CARE

BEHAVIOUR THERAPY IN PRIMARY CARE
A PRACTICAL GUIDE

RICHARD FRANCE (General Practitioner)
and
MEREDITH ROBSON (Clinical Psychologist)
Yateley Medical Centre, Camberley, Surrey

CROOM HELM
London & Sydney

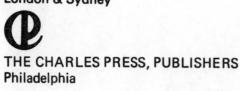

THE CHARLES PRESS, PUBLISHERS
Philadelphia

© 1986 Richard France and Meredith Robson
Croom Helm Ltd, Provident House, Burrell Row,
Beckenham, Kent BR3 1AT
Croom Helm Australia Pty Ltd, Suite 4, 6th Floor,
64–76 Kippax Street, Surry Hills, NSW 2010, Australia

British Library Cataloguing in Publication Data

France, Richard
  Behaviour therapy in primary care: a
  practical guide
  1. Behaviour therapy
  I. Title   II. Robson, Meredith
  616.89'142   RC489.B4

ISBN 0-7099-1080-0

and
The Charles Press, Publishers, Suit 14K,
1420 Locust Street, Philadelphia,
Pennsylvania 19102

Library of Congress Catalog Card Number: 86-70732

ISBN 0-914783-12-2

Phototypeset by Sunrise Setting, Torquay, Devon
Printed and bound in Great Britain
by Billing & Sons Limited, Worcester.

CONTENTS

To Merlin and Paddy
who present the authors with their most difficult problems
and ruthlessly expose their feet of clay.

PREFACE

This book is intended for General Practitioners and other members of the primary health care team including health visitors and district midwifery and nursing sisters interested in practical ways in which they can use behaviour therapy to help in their work. It will also be of assistance in the management of patients who are subsequently referred to clinical psychologists or psychiatrists. Community psychiatric nurses, behavioural nurse therapists and clinical psychologists who are thinking of working in primary care for the first time may also find it helpful.

Although a wide range of topics is covered, we have concentrated on those problems which are most prevalent and easily treated in this setting. There is no attempt to be comprehensive. Most of the material is based on our personal experience in primary care. In a few places, however, we have touched on broader issues (e.g. Behavioural Medicine I) or indicated areas where more extensive research is needed (e.g. Behavioural Medicine II).

We decided to write the text ourselves rather than edit contributions from accepted authorities as we felt that consistency and first hand experience of primary care were advantages that outweighed the inevitable loss of expertise.

No hard and fast rules are laid down as to when referral to specialists is indicated as this decision varies considerably with the experience, resources and enthusiasm of the individual clinician.

References are selected and have been kept to a minimum. Suggestions for further reading and suitable patient handbooks are included, where appropriate, at the end of each chapter.

ACKNOWLEDGEMENTS

Amongst the many people who have given us help and encouragement, we are especially grateful to the following: Ms Gillian Butler, Dr David Clark, Mr Paul Salkovskis and Professor Michael Gelder of the Oxford University Department of Psychiatry who not only allowed us to use and adapt much of their work but who also read and made many helpful comments on the chapter on anxiety-related problems.

Dr Peter Hill of the Department of Child Psychiatry, St George's Hospital, London who read the text of the chapter on children and made invaluable comments.

Dr Margaret Palmer of Yateley Medical Centre who generously read the entire text and made many helpful suggestions.

Miss Sally Read who calmly and expertly prepared the typescript.

Mr Tim Hardwick for his enthusiasm, ideas and encouragement.

Ms Patricia d'Ardenne for her contribution on trans-cultural differences at the end of Chapter 6.

The various authors and copyright holders who have kindly given us permission to quote their material and who are acknowledged in the appropriate parts of the text.

1 INTRODUCTION

A sense of dissatisfaction with the established, largely pharmacological, methods of treating emotional and social problems was probably evident amongst general practitioners (GPs) and their fellow members of the primary health care team even before the news media and academic medicine took up the topic with crusading enthusiasm. It has however proved difficult to find an alternative that provides effective treatment producing reasonably rapid results within the short consulting time possible in general practice.

Various forms of psychotherapy have none the less had their influence on primary care. The most important of these has been the Balint movement which took its name from a Hungarian psychoanalyst who came to England before the second world war. He became interested in the dynamics of the doctor-patient relationship (Balint 1974). The groups that he started with GPs after the war profoundly influenced the modern view of the consultation, and their successors and the society founded in his name still flourish. The rather leisured philosophy of Balint has however never appealed to many GPs. They feel that even its later modifications with their increased emphasis on the short consultation do not conform to the realities of busy present-day general practice. The same may be true of the client centred counselling of Carl Rogers (Rogers 1951) and the transactional analysis model of Eric Berne (Berne 1966) which also have their advocates and their uses.

Compared with all these, drug therapy, despite its manifest drawbacks is often quickly effective, easy to administer, accessible and relatively cheap. Indeed there are those who would argue that the six-minute consultation permits nothing more. These objections, however, are more often raised by those outside general practice than by GPs themselves. It is probable in any case that few doctors stick rigidly to six minutes when faced with a newly presenting emotional problem. Those who do may have more consideration for their timetable than for their patients. Most will give more time to this type of patient in the hope that it can be made up later by savings on simple cases such as sore throats and certificates. Surgery time is, however, always short and must be used economically but it can be stretched by getting the patient to make use of resources outside the consultation.

The Principles of Behaviour Therapy

Behaviour therapy does not provide a panacea for the difficulties faced by the GP or other primary health care worker when coping with psychological problems. There are, however, many ways in which the model fits the existing methods of working in primary care quite closely.

The principles may be summarised as follows:

(1) Whilst originating from theories of learning, present-day methods are based mainly on empirical studies and are not slavishly derived from any one theory of function.

(2) Problems appropriate for management in this way must be current, repetitive and observable. Treatment regimens are aimed at explicit, clearly-defined goals. Progress is carefully monitored and success or failure fed back to the patient.

(3) Current controlling factors are paramount in both assessment and treatment. Past history may be of value in differential diagnosis but is of minor importance in planning management.

(4) An individual 'tailor-made' description is used rather than fitting the problem into diagnostic categories which may be misleading.

(5) Treatment plans should always emphasise the increase of the positive, if possible, rather than the suppression of the negative.

(6) The patient collaborates fully in assessment and treatment.

(7) Measurements should always be made and the treatment plan modified if necessary in the light of these measurements.

The concept of trying to solve the current solvable problem rather than becoming involved with deep abstract theories will be welcomed by the GP who spends his life doing this anyway. The specification of goals and measurement of progress will be less familiar but still require no great conceptual leaps.

History

As with so many modern disciplines, sporadic references to the concepts later incorporated in behaviour therapy can be traced back to antiquity. In spite of these it has essentially developed within the twentieth century and largely within the last 30 years.

The work of Pavlov on the conditioned reflex (Pavlov 1927) and Thorndike (1913) on the psychology of learning in the earlier part of this century laid the theoretical foundations. Both worked with animals and Pavlov's dogs salivated to the production of meat and the sound of a bell, subsequently producing the conditioned response of salivating to the bell alone. This is still quoted as the typical example of classical (antecedent induced) conditioning.

Watson in 1920 produced the first clinical application of treatment based on learning theory when he tried to overcome the conditioned fear of Little Albert for a white rat and other furry objects (Watson and Rayner 1920). This must be one of the most famous incomplete experiments as Little Albert left the hospital before any conclusions could be reached. Later work by Jones (1924), Watson, Mowrer (Mowrer and Mowrer 1938) and others was more successful in the treatment of neuroses. By the Second World War a trickle of reports of early behavioural treatments was appearing. After the war this trickle grew steadily into a torrent.

In the 1950s Wolpe introduced systematic desensitisation in the treatment of phobias (Wolpe 1954). The subject learned to relax and then was gradually exposed to the feared stimulus with resultant reduction of fear. In 1953 Skinner (q.v.) published *Science and Human Behaviour* introducing the concept of operant (consequence induced) conditioning to explain many aspects of human behaviour. The novel *Walden Two* based upon the same ideas had appeared some years previously. This must be an almost unique example of a work of fiction introducing a major advance in scientific thinking. In the 1960s the Maudsley hospital group of Marks (1969), Gelder (Gelder *et al.* 1967) and Rachman (1966) extended the use of behavioural therapy in sexual disorders and were responsible for the introduction and use of flooding, i.e. rapid exposure as opposed to gradual exposure, into the treatment of phobias. The 1970s saw a massive extension of behaviour therapy into previously unexplored areas such as the management of depression. A considerable increase in the associations and scientific journals connected with the approach followed. Equally important, however, was the introduction of the cognitive or information processing element into the model. According to the original workers, behaviour had to be *externally* observable and measurable in order to have significance and the human subject was controlled by a 'black box' programmed to give a specific response to a given stimulus. Workers such as Mahoney (1974) and Seligman (1975) recognised and expressed the inadequacy of this concept. They began to study and modify internal or information processing behaviour leading directly to the rapid development of the cognitive therapy movement led by Beck (1976) and Meichenbaum (1977). Although still not universally accepted, it is this movement that dominates clinical therapy in the late 1980s.

At the same time as the post-war developments described above were taking place, the emerging profession of clinical psychology was looking for a role in treatment to supplement the one that it had already acquired in assessment. It was soon clear that behaviour therapy promised to meet that need and, ever since, clinical psychologists have been the foremost practitioners of this method of treatment and the behavioural approach has, in turn, provided the framework of most, although not all, psychologists' treatment methods. Some early work was rather too dependent on the research psychologist's laboratory approach and some types of aversive therapy which were neither particularly attractive nor effective gave the model a dubious reputation which it took some time to live down. Gradually, clinical psychologists moved out from the research centres and provided services which were first based at district departments of child and adult psychiatry. A milestone in Britain was the founding of a separate Division of Clinical Psychology by the British Psychological Society in 1966. Since 1972 research reports show that clinical psychologists have become increasingly involved in primary care and in many instances have been responsible for introducing behaviour therapy into surgeries and health centres. Here the principles and methods have attracted the attention of other workers, notably health visitors, social workers, counsellors and GPs themselves. In recent years small numbers of behaviourally trained nurse therapists and some community psychiatric nurses with appropriate experience have also begun to offer behaviour therapy in the community in the UK, thus improving the availability of treatment. Resources of all kinds are however very scarce and are likely to remain so as there are only about 1500 British psychologists in the entire clinical branch, most of whom are heavily committed to hospitals and institutions. It seems, therefore, that if behaviour therapy is to be more widely available in primary care it will have to be offered by other members of the team.

The Place of Behaviour Therapy in Primary Health Care

The GP sees many short term problems related to life events and transitions which none the less may be extremely disturbing and disabling while they last. He is accustomed to using a practical, problem-solving approach with limited time available. A knowledge of behaviour therapy sets this approach within a framework and allows the experience of others to extend its scope. He does not have to rediscover everything for himself as he goes along but can tap into existing experience and methods. GPs at behavioural workshops have often remarked that much of what they are learning is applied common sense, and which they do anyway instinctively. We do not see this as a criticism but believe rather that the nearer a behavioural intervention can be made to common sense and everyday life the more likely it is to be successful.

In order to modify problems, however, change must be achieved. If the required change were completely obvious and easy the sufferer would probably have made it himself anyway and would not be seeking professional advice. Some additional knowledge and skill are required and the behavioural approach can provide these.

Behaviour therapy can operate at three levels in primary care. With the most complex problems an understanding of what is possible enables the GP or health visitor confidently to refer a patient with a difficult problem, which they feel is beyond their personal resources, to the appropriate professional agency. This in most cases will be a clinical psychologist, or possibly psychiatrist, based in the community or in a local hospital department. At the second level the GP or other primary care worker decides to undertake an intervention himself. This will often involve more time in the early stages than the six-minute consultation allows. It is important that as accurate and complete analysis of the problem as possible is carried out. It need not, however, require a *great deal* more time and the later supervision sessions can be fitted back into normal surgery hours. At the third level it will be found that a knowledge of the behavioural approach is constantly useful when giving advice on everyday problems. For example conditions are clarified by the use of a diary record and to be able to fit a problem such as childhood tantrums in to an operant conditioning framework clears the thinking and improves the quality of the advice given.

Suitable Problems

Behaviour therapy has many possible applications and more are being developed every day. If the therapist thinks that there is a behavioural approach to a problem then it is reasonable to try it, with the proviso that proper monitoring and evaluation are carried out.

Suitable problems may, however, be fitted into three main groups:

Specific Psychological Disorders

(a) Anxiety states, phobic conditions and obsessive compulsive disorders.

(b) Depression — often combined in the primary care setting with antidepressant drug therapy.

Problems of Living

(a) Family, marital and sexual relationships.

(b) Self-damaging habits, such as smoking or excessive eating or drinking.

(c) Problems in childhood, such as enuresis, encopresis, eating problems, sleep disorders and tantrums.

(d) Failure to cope at school or work.

(e) Difficulties in adjusting to handicap or disability.

Problems Associated with Physical Illness

(a) Adherence to treatment.

(b) Preparation for surgery and recovery from illness and surgery.

(c) Chronic pain, hypertension, asthma and migraine.

(d) Illness and disability in old age including dementia.

This is by no means an exclusive list but is included simply to give some idea of the field covered. More information is given in the second part of the book where individual problem groups are considered.

Misconceptions

Before going further a number of common misconceptions about behaviour therapy should be discussed.

(a) 'You only treat the symptoms and unless you get to the underlying problem a second symptom soon replaces the first'. Although behavioural treatments are now available for a wide range of disorders, there is no evidence that symptom substitution takes place. There are strong suggestions, in fact, that by achieving success in one area a patient may be able to use the same approach to cope with other difficulties (generalisation).

(b) 'Positive reinforcement is only bribery disguised as pseudoscience'. Bribery implies a reward for doing something underhand or disreputable whereas reinforcement is normal in many areas of life — for example the pay packet or saying 'thank you'. A further difference is that bribery usually occurs before, and reinforcement after, the task.

(c) 'There is too much reliance on mechanical aversion'. This may have had some truth in it in the early days but now aversive therapy is little used. When it is, there is always emphasis on building positive behaviours at the same time.

References

Balint, M. (1974) *The Doctor, his Patient and the Illness*, London, Pitman

Beck, A. T. (1976) *Cognitive Therapy and Emotional Disorders*, New York, International Universities Press

Berne, E. (1966) *Games People Play: The Psychology of Human Relationships*, London, Andre Deutsch

Gelder, M. G., Marks, I. M. and Wolff, H. H. (1967) 'Desensitisation and psychotherapy in the treatment of phobic states: A controlled enquiry', *British Journal of Psychiatry, 113*, 53–73

Jones, M. C. (1924) 'Elimination of children's fears', *Journal of Experimental Psychology, 7*, 382

Mahoney, M. J. (1974) *Cognition and Behaviour Modification*, Cambridge, Ballinger

Marks, I. M. (1969) *Fears and Phobias*, London, Heinemann Medical

Meichenbaum, D. (1977) *Cognitive Behavior Modification*, New York, Plenum

Mowrer, O. H. and Mowrer, W. M. (1938) 'Enuresis: A method for its study and treatment', *American Journal of Orthopsychiatry, 8*, 436–59

Pavlov, I. P. (1927) *Conditioned Reflexes: An investigation of the physiological activity of the cerebral cortex* (trans. by G. V. Anrep) London and New York, Oxford University Press

Rachman, S. (1966) 'Studies in desensitisation: II Flooding', *Behaviour Research and*

Therapy, 4, 1–15

Rogers, C. R. (1951) *Client-centred Therapy: Its current practice, implications and theory,* Boston, Houghton Mifflin

Seligman, M. E. P. (1975) *Helplessness: On Depression, Development and Death,* San Francisco, Freeman

Skinner, B. F. (1953) *Science and Human Behaviour,* New York, Macmillan

Skinner, B. F. (1976) *Walden Two,* New York, Macmillan (New edition)

Thorndike, E. L. (1913) *The Psychology of Learning* (Educational Psychology II) New York, Teachers' College

Watson, J. B. and Rayner, P. (1920) 'Conditioned emotional reactions', *Journal of Experimental Psychology, 3,* 1

Wolpe, J. (1954) 'Reciprocal inhibition as the main basis of psychotherapeutic effects', *Archives of Neurology and Psychiatry, 72,* 205

Useful Addresses

Association for the Advancement of Behavior Therapy, Membership Chairperson, 15 West 36th Street, New York, NY10018. The AABT publishes *Behaviour Therapy* five times per year. It also holds an annual convention, has an active committee structure and provides discounts on journal subscriptions.

British Association for Behavioural Psychotherapy, Membership Secretary, Social Services Department, Craig House, Bank Street, Bury, Lancashire BL9 0BA. Journal: *Behavioural Psychotherapy* (Academic Press). The association holds an annual conference and workshop conventions. It also has active regional branches and provides discounts on journals.

Other Journals

Behaviour Research and Therapy, Pergamon Press, Oxford and New York.

Journal of Behaviour Therapy and Experimental Psychiatry, Pergamon Press, Oxford and New York.

Journal of Behavioral Medicine, Plenum Press, New York.

PART ONE: METHODS

2 BEHAVIOURAL ASSESSMENT

We now come to consider the order and content of the assessment interview. There is no need to carry out the scheme presented here in its entirety on every occasion. Often time will not permit this in primary care and sometimes much more detail will be required about certain parts of the scheme at the expense of others. There is of course no need to complete the interview assessment at one sitting — frequently the information contained in it can be built up over several shorter interviews. This system is particularly suitable if the work is to be contained in normal surgery hours. A checklist of the various assessment stages is included at the end of this chapter for easy reference.

Presenting Problem(s)

Some statement of the presenting problem will have been made before the decision to adopt the behavioural approach has been taken. A much more detailed description is likely to be necessary as most patients present their problems in vague general terms such as 'I feel awful' or 'I'm always so tense'. Sometimes problems are described from the outset in terms of possible solutions, e.g. 'I think I need a tonic' or even 'I must have something for my nerves'. None of these descriptions really tells us very much and the first job is a gentle but searching clarification of the problem. It may turn out that feeling awful or needing tranquillisers is related to a recent episode of shouting at a child who has repeatedly asked a question. This is followed by guilty thoughts related to 'having lost control as a mother' which has in turn produced a depressed feeling 'because mothers shouldn't behave like that therefore I am an inadequate mother'.

The Problem

The patient must describe precisely the frequency and intensity of the problem and give an idea of why they have come for treatment at

11

this time. The history and development of the condition and previous episodes of difficulty are helpful in as much as they clarify the surrounding circumstances. Those circumstances which lead to the problem behaviour are the antecedents and those which occur as a result of the behaviour are the consequences. It is generally the consequences that reinforce the behaviour, maintain it and thus make it difficult for the patient to overcome the problem themselves.

This detailed description of the facts and how they have affected the patient's thinking allows the clinician to get to grips with the problem. Once a clear description has been obtained it is worth summarising this with the patient who will thus be able to confirm that it is correct and will probably also be reassured that his or her difficulty has been understood. Patients frequently agonise for a long time before seeking professional services on personal and psychological matters. Upmost in their minds during this time is the fear that their problems may be misunderstood and inappropriately treated. Some reassurance, therefore, that the clinician is on the right track is extremely welcome at this early stage.

None of this should imply that a problem or problem list cannot be revised later. Often patients are themselves only dimly aware of the real nature of a problem at a first interview and the picture may change radically later.

Other Problems or Problem Areas

A balance has to be struck between allowing the interview to drift off into irrelevant topics and missing some other essential ingredient of the patient's distress. Usually a few open questions will uncover other important problems and these may then be clarified by limited direct questioning. Suitable questions might be 'If this problem were put right would anything else be bothering you?' or quite simply 'Do you have any troubles in other parts of life?' The patient may not always see these as relevant to the chief reason for his seeking help. They may none the less be important in their own right, substantially affect the persistence of the presenting problems or alter the possible channels of intervention. A patient suffering from panic attacks in shops is not likely to get much help from her spouse as co-therapist if there is a pre-existing marital problem. A mother of five small children living at the top of a tower block with a broken lift is unlikely to do homework tasks outside the home.

Positive Characteristics of the Patient (Client Assets)

The patient's strengths and skills can usefully be discussed at this point for three reasons. First, it is useful to note how aware he is of his good points and how ready he is to talk about them. Second, a short time spent on the things he does well may relieve the gloom of the discussion of difficulties. Third, the discovered assets will often be used in a subsequent treatment plan. As well as the things he currently does well and enjoys doing, it is useful to enquire about past activities which have now been discontinued, as the re-introduction of these will often be a goal in treatment of certain types of disorder.

Functional Analysis of the Problem(s)

This is the core of the whole interview. It is essential that it is adequately carried out before any sort of treatment plan is formed. The object is to discover the factors currently maintaining the problem, in what way it is interfering with the patient's life and also whether its persistence is serving any useful purpose for him or for others.

The maintaining factors may be considered either as *antecedents* to the *behaviour* or as its *consequences*, conveniently remembered as the A-B-C model. Under B, the behaviour itself, should be considered background environmental factors which coincide with the behaviour. Each of these factors may *increase* or *decrease* the behaviour, making it more or less likely and they may occur either *externally* (overtly) in the outside world or *internally* (covertly) in the internal thoughts and feelings of the patient.

Antecedents or cues are typified by Pavlov's bell (see Chapter 1) (the continued stimulus) producing salivation in the dogs (the conditioned response). In a current clinical situation the end-of-meal cup of coffee serving as a stimulus for lighting a cigarette would be a typical example. Certain therapy programmes, particularly those designed to cope with habit disorders, rely on interrupting the link between cue and response. Cues often do not operate in isolation but lead from one to the other in a chain before finally producing a response. Each cue produces its own intermediate response which in turn acts as a cue for the next response and so on. The length of this chain materially affects the ease with which the terminal response can be obtained. Let us consider the man who wants to smoke with his after-lunch coffee. He may simply be offered a cigarette and a light by a fellow diner. This constitutes a very short chain and the links are easily forged. If however, he needs to fetch his cheque book from his locked car, go to the bank, stand in a queue, cash a cheque, go to the tobacconist, buy cigarettes and lighter fuel, refill his lighter and finally light the cigarette, the chain is long and the final response only reached after considerable effort. The differences can be used advantageously when designing a programme to modify an unwanted response.

The background and general environment in which a problem occurs also have importance. Technically these factors may also be cues of a sort but if important elements are not to be overlooked it is wise to consider them separately. For example, panic attacks may occur in a tube train but not in an overground train and sexual difficulties may present themselves in a bedroom but not on a rug in the living room.

The third element of the A-B-C model, the consequences, in most cases is most important of all. The effects that the patient's problem are having on himself and those around him must be considered. These may be either good or bad, positive or negative, and by a feedback mechanism may have a strong effect on the frequency or severity of the problem. The effect that consequences have upon an event producing them is the result of *operant conditioning* which, although first described in detail by Skinner (1953 — see Chapter 1), has probably been a feature of human behaviour since the beginning of the race. Put very simply, we do those things more intensely and more often which we know from experience are likely to be rewarded, e.g. a worker does a week's work in the reasonable expectation of getting a pay packet on Friday. Actions may however have other results; a reward may follow the stopping of a particular behaviour, the behaviour may be punished or it may achieve no results at all.

Behaviour can therefore be changed by altering the consequences, as removal of the reinforcers will cause extinction of the behaviour. Punishment will tend to reduce the frequency of a behaviour unless the punishment holds reward value itself, such as providing attention for a person being punished who might otherwise be ignored.

When referring to and analysing the problem there are three aspects which require consideration each in terms of the antecedents, behaviour and consequences of the problem (the ABC)

(1) the overt external behaviour itself (always observable)
(2) the physical or bodily reactions (either observable, measurable or reported)
(3) the associated internal factors, the thoughts and feelings (always reported).

The use of operant techniques in therapy will be discussed in Chapter 4 but supporting factors must be understood in the assessment before they can be modified in treatment.

Most of the discussion so far has involved the externally observable (overt) first and second aspects of the ABC model. The internal information processing systems, however, can be involved at any point producing *cognitive* (covert) cues, background factors and consequences. It is important to note that negative thoughts can be powerful in initiating and maintaining maladaptive behaviour. Thus statements such as 'I wonder if I'm going to panic', 'I'll never get a girlfriend again', 'I know I won't get to sleep', 'I've failed again' all help to feed fear and anticipatory anxiety, or reinforce the feelings of failure and inability to cope. The meaning of the problem to the patient should also be considered at this point. For example, he is unlikely to respond well to biofeedback treatment of his tension headaches if he believes these to be due to hypertension and this possibility has not been discussed nor his blood pressure measured.

Finally under this section an enquiry should be made about any incompatible behaviours which could be of use in management. It is virtually impossible to eat a doughnut while playing the piano, thus if doughnut eating is a part of the problem, piano playing may help to modify it. Patients generate their own incompatible behaviours with a little guidance and it is well to let them do so without the prejudices and values of the therapist intruding. As a cautionary tale one of the authors remembers well telling a patient that in his opinion smoking was incompatible with wet shaving, only to receive the serious reply that this was quite untrue as the patient did it every morning. He was a pipe smoker and there was no problem as long as the pipe was well alight before he began to lather around it! Incompatible behaviours also have their cognitive aspect in certain distraction techniques which will be discussed later under their appropriate sections.

Development of the Problem

The origins and development of the problem are not of prime importance as they are held to be in general medicine or psychoanalysis. Some information on this aspect may reveal important additional facts and can be used to test the data obtained from the functional analysis. A problem may have occurred for the first time in connection with job change, marriage, childbirth or some other significant transition. A significant life event in a parent, spouse or friend may give rise to a problem. All GPs will be familiar with the man who develops chest pain following sudden death from a heart attack of a colleague at work. The mediating mechanism in this case might well include (i) an overestimate of the risk of coronary heart disease in his age group, (ii) selective attention to otherwise unimportant chest sensations, and (iii) a gloomy estimate of the stress produced by the job. These three together combine to initiate worrying thoughts about heart attacks with a subsequent increase of the bodily symptoms.

Some enquiry about changed circumstances can also be made at this point. A wife's returning to work may have quite profound effects on both partners as may a change from employed to self-employed status with its additional responsibilities. It is worth finding out if previously valued activities have been abandoned. It is common to find rewarding activities becoming more and more infrequent with depression and other problems. If this is the case, is it because of lack of time, interest, money or because they are no longer eagerly anticipated? What would need to happen for them to be reinstated?

Previous Coping Attempts

There have almost always been some previous attempts to cope with the problem. The ones that the patient has thought it worthwhile to use himself are particularly important. Any intervention based on these has more chance of success and will also serve to boost his, probably flagging, sense of self esteem. Some self-management attempts will however have been clearly inappropriate. For example, progressively avoiding places where anxiety occurs until even leaving the house is a problem or reliance on alcohol for the relief of tension. His wife or friends may have made some attempt to help and he may have received outside amateur or professional help from a number of sources. The results — good or bad — of all these efforts are important. Lastly, if it is not already available, the nature and effect of any medication which has been prescribed for the problem should be considered. Benzodiazepines interfere with learning and by altering a person's response to anxiety-provoking situations do not allow the patient to use anxiety reactions as cues for anxiety management procedures. Anxiolytics or beta blocking drugs can be useful if a patient is required to enter a one-off situation while still early in treatment and where a severe panic would be a risk. For example: an agoraphobic having to attend a wedding reception while still struggling to get to the corner shop or a business man or woman needing to give a presentation at a client's firm while still finding it difficult to speak at meetings.

Expectations of Outcome

The importance of the patient's own interpretation of his own problem has been mentioned earlier. It follows therefore that it is also necessary to discover what sort of management the patient is expecting and whether he believes that it can help. He may have come expecting a prescription for benzodiazepines and some preparation, perhaps with the help of a booklet, may be necessary before he is prepared to accept another approach. In this situation the short consultation can prove useful, as the seeds of an idea can be sown at one visit and time for consideration and perhaps home reading allowed before the next. This is particularly valuable when the clinician is thinking of using an approach which may be unfamiliar to and unexpected by the patient. Previous attempts at treatment should be described and possible reasons for failure discussed. When the current treatment and rationale are explained, differences from previous attempts may be highlighted. For example, the current treatment may offer more regular appointments, partner cooperation, consideration of cognitive factors or a complete change of approach such as from drug treatment to a behavioural approach.

Effects of Change

Assessment also requires an investigation of the limits that have been placed on a person's life as a result of the problem. Situations which directly provoke or exacerbate a problem may gradually be avoided and this avoidance often spreads at an alarming rate until the patient's life is very restricted. These facts can be elicited from a discussion of how life used to be and how this pattern has changed. Some patients have always avoided certain situations because they feel incapable of handling them. The assessment should discover what they want life to be like. As well as considering whether the patient thinks change is possible, it is important to consider the effect of change, for better or worse, upon the patient, his family and the environment. Some will have unrealistic expectations of the effect of a desired change. The fat girl who loses weight will not necessarily find the world a Utopia — rather she may have difficulties with her female friends who now perceive in her a threat which was not present previously. The agoraphobic who achieves a life's ambition to go to Oxford Street sales has obviously benefited but what about her husband who has devoted his life to doing the shopping so that she does not have to go out? Is he going to be able to adjust to her increased competence and, by extension, to his changed role?

Forming an Hypothesis

From the information gathered in the interview it should now be possible for patient and therapist in cooperation to form an hypothesis of the rationale and maintenance of the problem. In one sense this takes the place of a diagnosis but it should always be provisional, flexible and subject to modification in the light of further information. A medical diagnosis usually leads to a standard form of treatment. A behavioural hypothesis, on the other hand, is first further tested by means of baseline measurements followed by the setting of goals and the formation of a mutually agreed individual treatment plan.

Interview Assessment Behavioural Checklist

(1) Exact description of the *presenting problem(s)*.

(2) Outline of *other problem areas*.

(3) Obtain information about skills, pleasures and positive characteristics of the patient (*client assets*).

(4) *Functional analysis of the problem(s)*, with regard to both behaviour and cognitions.

    (i)   *Antecedents* producing increase or decrease.

    (ii) *Background* environment producing increase or decrease.

    (iii) *Consequences* of behaviour either positive or negative on patient/spouse/others.

    (iv) *Incompatible behaviours* — physical or functional.

(5) Obtain a short description of the *development* of the problem.

(6) Obtain information about the *previous coping attempts* of the patient/spouse/others.

(7) Discuss the patient's *expectations of treatment* and whether change is possible.

(8) Obtain information about the likely *effect of change* on patient/spouse/others.

Recommended for Further Reading

Hersen, M. and Bellack, A. S. (1976) *Behavioural Assessment: A practical handbook*, Oxford and New York, Pergamon Press.

3 DATA COLLECTION AND MONITORING

It is sometimes difficult to obtain precise antecedents and consequences but these can often be disentangled with the help of charts, questionnaires and diaries. The problem itself may be ill-defined and it is useful to ask the patient to keep a record of a typical occurrence or a typical day or week after the initial appointment. For example patients may complain that they 'never sleep a wink' or are 'never without a headache.' It is often informative and therapeutic to discover, by keeping a precise record, that their problem is not quite as severe as they describe. The fact that they do sleep an hour or two or have the odd moment without a headache provides a glimmer of hope. It also helps motivation to search for the pertinent factors controlling the problem before embarking on a regime of therapy.

All stages of a programme require the collection of data for the purposes of monitoring. It is necessary to arrive at baseline measurements, to show change during a programme and to assess outcome. The data collected during the baseline period serve to clarify and confirm the initial hypothesis which in its turn has indicated what sort of data may be required. At this stage a preliminary contract may be agreed with the patient. This should include:

(i)   Tentative goals of treatment
(ii) Agreement on methods to be used
(iii) Responsibilities of both parties
(iv) Time limit.

Once agreement on the methods to be used has been reached the details of baseline recording can be decided. Theoretically this recording may be of three kinds:

(i)   Mechanical recording of physiological variables such as heart rate, blood pressure, electro-myographic studies and galvanic skin response.
(ii) Measurement of a permanent product such as pages of work written or numbers of wet beds.
(iii) Observational recording.

Observational Recording

In the primary care setting this is likely to be overwhelmingly the most frequently used. Before any piece of observational recording is attempted a number of questions must be considered. These are:

(i) What precisely is to be observed and recorded?
(ii) Who is to do it?
(iii) When is it to be done?
(iv) For how long is it to be done?
(v) What is to happen if problems are encountered?

All of these require some further consideration.

What Precisely Is to be Observed and Recorded?

Many problems are initially expressed in terms far too vague to permit accurate measurement. 'Bad behaviour' in a child and 'failing to help in the house' by a husband are subject to far too many differing interpretations to be amenable to proper measurement. The number of times Jason punches Tracy would be an exact and measurable refinement of 'bad behaviour.' Even so, problems of definition may occur. For example, does a nudge during tea-time count as a punch? It does not matter greatly what the decision is as long as it is clearly understood by all involved and the same definition is consistently applied.

When considering what is to be measured it should be borne in mind that only a few specified behaviours can be recorded at any one time without inaccuracies creeping into the results.

Who Is to Do It?

Most commonly it will be the patient himself and there will be no problem. If a child is the subject and the parents are to do the recording it must be decided how the task is to be shared or else confusion will result.

When Is It to be Done?

This often requires the most judgement and must be decided according to the expected nature and frequency of the problem. If Jason punches Tracy only intermittently then a simple count of punches, similar to a boxing referee's score sheet, may suffice, noting the time of each punch. This is called *event frequency recording.* If however the rate of punching is increased then this type of recording may be too time-consuming and we may have to be satisfied with counting the punches in the first ten minutes of each hour — a technique called *time sampling.* An alternative way of limiting the number of observations to be made is *interval recording* where the day is divided into a number of equal periods and a record made of whether any punches occur during each interval. More continuous behaviour such as dribbling or studying may require a *duration record* to yield adequate information. Where the incidents to be studied are more complex, such as panic attacks or depressive episodes, a diary record of several aspects of the same event may be necessary.

For How Long Is It to be Done?

This must be decided in advance and will be determined by such factors as the expected frequency of the problem and the timing of the next appointment. Too long a baseline recording period may alienate the patient whereas too short a one may not yield adequate information.

What Is to Happen if Difficulties Arise?

It is wise to foresee the unforeseen and include an agreed mechanism for dealing with difficulties. This will usually involve some mechanism for contacting the therapist before the next planned appointment. If a breakdown entails a long wait before the next appointment time is lost and morale inevitably suffers.

The Behavioural Diary

The 'diary' is the most universal assessment tool for behavioural difficulties. It can be made simple or complicated and adapted to changing requirements as therapy progresses and different information is required.

Many patients are at first unable to specify when a problem occurs or to describe the events surrounding the problem. Similarly they may have lost awareness of avoidance behaviour and can use the diary to pinpoint what they are *not* doing as well as what they *are* doing.

The diary can also serve to put the problem in perspective and allow the patient to see a trend of progress over time even though there may be setbacks or plateau phases in the course of treatment. Some crude overall rating over time also highlights any cyclical nature of problems. Detailed counts of specific behaviours or behavioural deficits can be made and these can be rated and related to changes in mood.

The diary can be expanded to monitor thoughts (see Chapter 8 for an example of a record). Like avoidance, thoughts can be so automatic that this type of recording is essential to make the patient aware of them. They then see the association between certain behaviours and moods and the thoughts which provoke or accompany them.

Physiological reactions, if recorded in a consistent way, can then be used to link to coping strategies like muscle relaxation for the early stages of panic.

It is useful to design an outline of what you require and add more if the patient feels this can be managed. It is possible to design charts (especially useful for children) where only a tick, cross or star is needed to complete the chart.

The diary is flexible and can be appropriately modified to self-monitor in any type of adult problem. Sometimes practice is required to get over the embarrassment of recording personal details on paper or, at the other extreme, the tendency of some patients to write a full scale autobiography each week must be gently but firmly curbed. Diaries are not uncommonly 'forgotten' when coming to the next appointment and this should always remind the clinician to explore possible blocks. It should also be remembered that even today illiteracy is still common and the possibility that the patient may be educationally rather than psychologically incapable of writing must be borne in mind.

When the concern is with cognitions rather than external events, the diary is used both to identify thoughts and feelings and to record alternatives generated in the course of therapy. Figures 3.1–3.3 show examples of typical diaries.

Rating Scales

These can be considered in two groups, homemade scales tailored for individual problems and used in conjunction with diaries, and formal questionnaires and schedules usually addressed to a particular type of problem or problem group.

Figure 3.1: Urgency and Frequency of Micturition

Date	Time	Where	Anxiety (0–10)	Urgency (0–10)	Amount (0–10)	Drinks
Wed. 14	7.15	Home	4	7	8/10	1 cup hot water 2 cups coffee
	7.50	Home	4	4	4	
	8.10	Leaving	6	4	1	
	11.45	Office	3	8	10	2 cups coffee
	1.00	Office	3	4	6	1 cup coffee
	5.00	Office	3	6	10	1 glass sherry
	10.30	Home	2	4	10	1 cup coffee
Thurs. 15	6.35	Home	2	2	8	1 cup water
	7.15	Home	2	3	4	2 cups coffee
	7.55	Home	2	7	1	
	8.10	Home	4	6	1	
	11.35	Office before dictation	5	8	5	2 cups coffee
	2.00	Office	3	5	6	1 cup coffee
	7.00	Theatre	7	9	5	1 glass wine
	9.00	Theatre	7	9	2	1 cup coffee
	11.30	Home	2	6	8	1 mug milk

Note: The aim of the diary is to discriminate cues for urgency with and without need to urinate.

The former can be infinitely adapted to suit individual situations. They are used to impose a measurement system on something such as a symptom which is not usually subjected to measurement. This in turn has several uses:

(i)   It serves to clarify the pattern of the problem in the patient's own mind.

(ii) It enables him to describe that pattern more easily to the therapist.

(iii) It enables change and outcome to be measured and recorded.

Such scales, however, may seem contrived and unfamiliar to some patients and thus the reason for their use requires careful explanation and sometimes preliminary practice. Once they are familiar with the idea few problems usually arise, as patients seem to sense that rating their problem gives them some additional control over it.

Figure 3.2: Record of Sleep

Date	Time to bed	Approx. time to sleeping	Number times awake	Action	Feelings next day (Rate 0–10)
18.	11.00	1.30–2	3–4	Moved to spare room	6–7
19.	11.00	11.30ish	3–4	Husband to other room	6
20.	11.45	12.30	2	No probs.	7–8
21.	11.30	3.30	many	Went to spare room	6–7
22.	11.30	3.00	3–4	Ditto	5–6
23.	10.30	11.00	2 (one long)	Got up made drink	6
24.	9.30–11.00	1.00	many (noise outside)	(1) to spare room (2) ear plugs	7–8
25.	11.00	3.00	3–4	To spare room with drink and snack	5
26.	11.15	11.30	2–3	Husband in other bed	6–7
27.	12.00	12.30	3	Ditto	7–8
28.	11.00	11.20 12.45	several	took sleep pill because bladder over-sensitive	7

Figure 3.3: Baseline Diary Relating Relevance of Cigars to Beer Consumption

Day	No. Cigars before 17.30	No. Cigars after 17.30	Pints of Beer	Total Cigars
Tues.	2	9	7	11
Wed.	3	5	3	8
Thurs.	2	7	7	9
Fri.	2	4	5	6
Sat.	1	8	6	5
Sun.	2	0	0	0

Whilst any system can be used, two in particular seem to fit into the pattern of a number of diverse situations. The first is the use of a *visual analogue scale* (VAS) with verbal tags at certain points as shown below:

0	1	2	3	4	5	6	7	8
Calm		Slightly anxious		Definitely anxious		Markedly anxious		The most anxious you could be

As will be discussed later, this type of scale is used in a number of formal assessment instruments but it can easily be adapted for individual use in other situations. There can be any number of points on the scale but there is evidence that nine points is, in most cases, optimal as fewer do not allow sufficient discrimination and more do not increase sensitivity.

The second method is simply to rate the symptom out of 100 and express the result as a percentage. The term *subjective units of disturbance* or SUDs (Wolpe 1973 p. 120) is also used to express this type of rating, mainly in the context of anxiety, whereas Beck (Beck *et al.* 1979) simply uses percentages to express degrees of emotion and belief in thoughts.

It should not be forgotten that artificial scales should be used only where no direct method of measurement exists or to supplement direct measures. It is more important to find out how far an agoraphobic can go from home and what situations she avoids than to determine the subjective degree of anxiety, although the latter may be of subsidiary value.

The use of formal questionnaires and schedules is likely to be less important in the context of primary care as they have a number of disadvantages.

(i)   They are not designed for the individual problem.

(ii) The clinician using them must fully understand the usefulness and limitations of each instrument and in many cases this requires special training.

(iii) A stock of forms and in some cases score sheets must be readily available.

(iv) Many originate in the USA and there may be some cross-cultural wording difficulties in their use in other countries.

(v)   There is a tendency to rely too much on a score which may be misleading, or accurate only for a limited time (state-dependent).

(vi) They may be seen as mechanistic, and may adversely affect the clinician-patient relationship if used insensitively.

There are a number of compensatory advantages:

(i) They provide additional information about severity and progress.
(ii) This information is in a form in which comparison is possible with that of other workers for research purposes.
(iii) For the most part they have been designed by authorities with a great deal of care and thus may be better expressed and balanced than homemade alternatives.
(iv) They are usually comprehensive in their subject and may pick up important points which can be missed at interview.

Vast numbers of questionnaires exist covering every conceivable topic and problem area. Even full-time professionals cannot know more than a limited number selected for appropriateness for their field of work. The best advice for the primary care worker is to get to know reasonably well a few that are appropriate for problems which frequently occur in that setting.

Details of several questionnaires which have been found useful are:

Beck Depression Inventory (Reproduced in full in Chapter 8)
Beck Anxiety Checklist (Reproduced in full in Chapter 5)
Marks and Mathews Fear Questionnaire (Reproduced in full in Chapter 5)

Other more specialised ones are included in their appropriate chapters.

Assignments and Homework Tasks

For a number of reasons these feature strongly in behaviour therapy. First, the behaviour is observed first-hand by the patient himself which increases the clarity with which he sees and under-stands the factors maintaining the problem. Second, controlling the recording may increase the sense of control over the problem itself thus alleviating feelings of helplessness. Third, this part of the work is done by the patient himself thus confirming the self-management philosophy of this form of treatment. Fourth, it reduces the requirement for expensive therapist time. It is strange that GPs have always been aware of time pressures in their job but have been largely reluctant to allow the patient to take control of at least part of his treatment himself. Specifically homework assignments may be used:

(i)   To observe and record a live situation and thus test a hypothesis formed previously. For example, if it appears that panic attacks in the supermarket only occur when there is a long check-out queue the patient may be asked to attend the supermarket when crowded and when empty. She makes recordings, comparing her reactions under both conditions.

(ii)   To practise a new technique between sessions in order to acquire a skill. For example, learning deep muscular relaxation from taped instruction.

(iii) To try out a new technique and test its effect in a particular situation. For example, starting a conversation with a member of the opposite sex in a pub.

(iv)   To test the validity of some belief or opinion (behavioural experiments). For example, if it is believed that other children do not wake up at night, an enquiry is made from other mothers as to how their children do in fact behave.

Clarification of Goals

After the collection of baseline data the treatment goals are clarified, modified if necessary and re-stated and the treatment contract adjusted in any other way indicated by the new information.

Goal Setting

In the initial stages of assessment when the patients are considerably distressed by their problem, it may be difficult to concentrate on long term goals and they may decide on fairly modest changes. Other patients suffer considerable anticipatory anxiety if too much emphasis is put on defining goals high on their hierarchy of difficulty. It may be better to concentrate on more immediate tasks and renegotiate further goals as treatment progresses.

Some patients 'aim high' and may need to be encouraged to set modest goals where prospects of achieving 'ideal lives' or 'miracles' are bleak. Alternatively there are people who seem unable to concentrate their minds on any long term aims. One useful technique is to ask them to project themselves in time to think what they would like to see themselves doing in one month, one year or even five years' time. It may then be possible to find some ideal goals and use a problem solving approach to find a hierarchical pathway to achieve these ends. At least this will allow the patient to feel that his efforts are heading in the right direction, however long the path.

Goals should always be described in terms of overt, observable behaviours. For example, in the case of a person who is socially anxious:

(a) to enter a pub and buy a drink
(b) to have lunch in the canteen at work with colleagues.

not as vague statements, such as 'feeling better', 'better able to cope,' 'being more sociable' etc.

Allied to the agreement on goals is the need for discussion and agreement on the type and method of treatment. Where a choice of treatment methods exists, a brief outline of the main features of each can be given to help the patient decide. For example, whether desensitisation or a flooding approach would be preferred in the treatment of a phobia.

The Contract

It is very easy to embark on therapy without a formal contract. Treatment may then drift on through the year, lose direction and be very difficult to terminate. This situation is perhaps more likely to occur in general practice where a patient can obtain access through an open surgery. The idea of a contract may seem rigid and inflexible, but it is useful, and keeps the patient and therapist clear about what is expected of them. It is always open to renegotiation. It also ensures that an adequate explanation of the treatment plan is presented to the patient. If time is specially set aside out of surgery hours, it is important to fix the number of sessions from the start. An agreement is often made to review progress after the fixed number of sessions and for both parties to decide if further work will be beneficial.

Scheme of Intervention. The type of treatment programme is the joint decision of the patient and therapist. This decision depends on the preferences of the patient, which factors can be modified and the relative strengths of the available treatment resources. Early success is important, so simpler problems may be tackled first. There is no point in working at targets, however desirable, that are beyond the scope of the available resources. Early monitoring will indicate the progress of the programme and a change of approach should be considered quickly if progress is lacking. If possible, follow-up data should be obtained to check the permanence of effects once these have been achieved.

Reference

Wolpe, J. (1973) *The Practice of Behavior Therapy*, New York and Oxford, Pergamon

Recommended for Further Reading

Gambrill, E. D. (1977) *Behavior Modification*, San Francisco, Jossey-Bass

THE BASIC CONCEPTS OF INTERVENTION

The purpose of this chapter is to give an idea of the range of techniques used in behavioural treatments. The main concepts are covered in outline, leaving the practical applications and more specialised techniques to be considered in the second part of the book under individual problems.

It is convenient to consider two classes of measures, those designed to increase and those designed to decrease particular behaviours. This distinction is, however, by no means clear-cut, as certain techniques can be used in different ways to obtain change in either direction. The first part of each section will deal with basic techniques leading to a description of more complex compound methods later.

Measures to Increase Behaviour

Reinforcement

This is probably the most important behavioural tool with large numbers of applications over many problem areas. It derives from the basic operant principle that behaviour is maintained by its consequences. The reinforcer is defined as that consequence (or the C part of the A-B-C model mentioned in Chapter 2) which, when following a behaviour, increases the likelihood or frequency of that behaviour occurring in the future. It is thus almost identical to a reward in ordinary language but the latter has rather more limited, less universal, connotations. It is a truism that reinforcers are not the prerogative of behaviour therapy. Everyone who passes an exam, gets a smile or collects a pay packet has received a reinforcer. A reinforcer may be supplied directly such as food or a toy for a child or indirectly by means of a star on a chart or a smile of approval. Money is really an indirect reinforcer but has come to occupy an inter-mediate position because its value is universally apparent and acknowledged. Many indirect reinforcers have widely differing values from person to person — a smile from a particular person may have a powerful reinforcing value to one recipient but none at all to another. As with other behavioural concepts, reinforcement may be from outside (overt) or from within the person himself (covert) and methods of covert reinforcement will be considered later. The effects of a particular reinforcer will depend upon how it is applied and this applies equally to negative or unpleasant consequences — see Table 4.1.

These will be considered individually in their appropriate sections. Positive reinforcement may be applied continuously or intermittently. If intermittently the ratio may be fixed or variable. The type of schedule selected will vary the effect on the behaviour. A reward after every performance results in a behaviour pattern being acquired quickly but if the reinforcer is withdrawn the behaviour ceases (extinguishes) equally quickly.

Fixed intermittent ratio schedules can be learned so that the response pattern increases when the reinforcer is expected as is shown by the increased queue for the fruit machine when the next jackpot is thought to be due. The punters assume that the machine operates on a fixed schedule and a certain amount of time or number of pulls must elapse between one jackpot and the next. They may, however, be wrong and the machine may operate on a variable schedule with no fixed interval between reinforcers.

Variable schedules promote the slowest but most permanent learning. Many unrewarded trials have to take place before the respondent becomes sure that no reinforcer is forthcoming and the response is extinguished. There are many examples of different reinforcement schedules in everyday life. Investing in the stock market, doing piece work, waiting for buses or doing scientific research may be quoted as just a few. The behaviour therapist looks at the schedules of reinforcement operating in his subject's life and sees if they can be changed or modified to produce improvement in the target problem.

In order to promote reinforcement of changed behaviour certain rules have to be observed for maximum effectiveness. Reinforcement must be *immediate* — delayed reinforcement is greatly

Table 4.1: Application of Reinforcers

Consequence	Administered	Withdrawn
Positive (Reward)	Behaviour increases (Positive rein.)	Behaviour decreases (Response cost)
Negative (Punishment)	Behaviour decreases (Punishment)	Behaviour increases (Negative rein.)

weakened (few will wait an extra month for their pay).

It must be *consistent* — great damage is done if the expected reinforcer doesn't materialise. This of course only applies to continuous and fixed ratio schedules.

It must be *significant* to the subject. Ice creams are not reinforcers if you don't like ice creams even if your parents and therapist do.

It must be *appropriate* — too small a reinforcer is ineffective, too large a one unmanageable. We know that Richard III offered his kingdom for a horse but his value system was modified by extreme circumstances. Some parents involved in behavioural programmes are a little like Richard III. They suggest reinforcers out of proportion to the task such as a bicycle if Kevin takes his tablets for a week. If too valuable a reinforcer is used it distorts the value of the behaviour being reinforced and makes it difficult to design a continuing programme. There is a danger that the supply of reinforcers will become quickly exhausted. It is often possible to work towards a valuable terminal material reinforcer by using a points system as token reinforcement. For example, if Kevin takes his tablets he gets one point per day recorded on a chart towards the 100 points needed for a bicycle. Small tangible intermediate reinforcers e.g. marbles or toys may be used in addition to points.

It must be *frequent* — whether a continuous or intermittent schedule is used the reinforcer has to be available often enough to have some effect.

It must be *specific* — 'some money', 'a treat' or 'be nice to you' are not specific. They might be replaced by 'give you 5p', 'allow you to watch TV half an hour longer' or 'take you out to dinner at the Chinese restaurant'.

It must be *unmixed with criticisms* — 'thank you very much for doing the washing up but why didn't you start doing it 10 years ago' will not serve as a positive reinforcement. If possible reinforcers of *variable kinds* should be used rather than a single system. This applies particularly in families where praise from mother, father, granny and older sister will be more effective than just mother alone. It is also important to be specific about the action that has earned the reward and this can, with advantage, be repeated to others. For example Kirk, a diabetic aged 10, is told 'You earned your points for preparing your syringe, cleaning the skin, filling the syringe with the right dose of insulin and giving your injection correctly!' When father appears for breakfast, mother repeats the same statement in front of father and son in the hope of gaining some back-up of approval from father thus increasing the reinforcement. It also makes clear exactly what has to be done to earn the reinforcement.

The examples quoted have concerned children and adolescents but the same principles apply to adults being reinforced by themselves or others. In the main, such programmes are somewhat easier for children as it is simpler to gain control over the potential reinforcers.

Under certain circumstances it may be difficult to find sufficient desirable behaviour to reinforce. With, for example, a disruptive child, it may be necessary to engineer a situation where the child does something that can be reinforced and start the process of shaping (p. 36) from there.

From Table 4.1 it will be noted that negative reinforcement also acts as a reward and thus increases behaviour. It works in the same way as the old saying about banging your head against a brick wall — it's nice when it stops. A classic clinical example of both positive and negative reinforcement is the child that cries at night and is taken into bed with his mother to get him to stop. The child receives positive reinforcement from the mother's warm bed. The mother gets negative reinforcement as the crying stops and she can get back to sleep. The result of this sequence is that both the crying and the taking into bed are likely to be repeated. The short term negative reinforcement of mother may become a long term punishment for her (and father) when the child in bed becomes a nuisance.

Prompting, modelling and shaping are all used to create new behavioural patterns.

Prompting or Cueing

These belong to the A or antecedent end of the A-B-C model (Chapter 2) and occur in a number of different forms. A prompt may be a set of verbal instructions to cope with a particular social or business situation such as initiating a conversation or asking for a rise or it may also be a therapy manual or instructions for a set of homework tasks. With children, prompting will often take the form of physical guidance through a task, by holding the child's hand. Once this has been done a number of times the therapist gradually *fades* his involvement by allowing the child to undertake progressively more steps by himself. Quite complicated chains of behaviour can be taught even to retarded children if these are first broken down into a series of smaller and simpler steps. The final steps in the chain, e.g. actually putting the food in the mouth or pulling up the pants and flushing the toilet, are usually taught first by vigorous reinforcement. In this way the achieving of the final target can also be used as an additional reinforcer (backward chaining).

Many adult programmes also involve the use of cues in the form of prompt cards with positive statements like 'I did it last time so I can do it again now' or 'It won't be easy but I'm sure I can make it' written on them. Cues for relaxation sequences may be provided by the patient saying a key word such as 'calm' to himself or looking at a red spot or the date on a watch. Cue discrimination is taught by teaching the patient to spot the earliest physical sensations produced by hyperventilation or those leading to panic so that an appropriate alternative, more helpful, response can be put into operation. In the cognitive treatment of depression the identification of worrying thoughts serves as a cue to generate more rational alternatives which will be discussed in more detail in Chapter 8.

Modelling

The presentation of an appropriate model is a useful way of forming new behaviour patterns. The model may either be the therapist or a competent performer observed in real life. A member of a peer group, if feasible, is likely to be a more effective model than someone who appears remote or authoritarian. Someone who performs the task with a struggle (the coping model) will be more effective than a perfectly accomplished performer (the mastery model) (Meichenbaum 1971). A suitable setting may be found in role play, films or videos, or in real life. A short role play of situations like interviews or asking for a date is perfectly feasible in the consulting room and the rehearsal may prove invaluable for the real life attempt. For modelling to be successful a system of small individual steps may have to be used so that the eventual goal is reached gradually. Judgement, experience and negotiation are required to assess how much is achievable at each step. The power of modelling in changing behaviour is seen in populations at war or in a crisis when panic or courage can be transmitted by the behaviour of a few prominent individuals (Rachman 1980).

A problematic form of modelling is frequently seen in the consulting room when children of headache sufferers themselves complain of the same symptom or express other forms of distress in terms which they have learnt from common family usage. More useful is the apprenticeship type of craft training used in many professions and trades including medicine. The medical student is expected to develop his diagnostic skills by emulating the eminent consultant on his teaching round. Later the GP trainee is provided with a model in the form of his trainer. A traditional but effective form of modelling is the examination of the doll or the teddy bear's chest so that the young patient can learn what to expect before his turn comes and at the same time be persuaded that 'Teddy didn't mind so he won't either'.

There are many further practical uses of this technique. Demonstrations to the newly diagnosed diabetic of a competent performer giving his own injections are helpful. Films of similar children coping with an operation are shown to children about to undergo surgery to accustom them to the sights, sounds and stages of the procedures they will experience.

Shaping

This is the third and most complex method of developing new behaviour. Essentially the steps followed are:

(i) Deciding the eventual goal.

(ii) Breaking down the change required to achieve the goal into small steps.

(iii) Either finding or engineering something in the subject's current repertory which is in the direction of the first step. This is then reinforced so that its frequency increases.

(iv) Choosing the next approximate step in the right direction from the new range of behaviour. This is then reinforced, at the same time extinguishing those variations not in the direction of the goal. This process is continued until the goal is reached.

In practice, shaping is often carried out by starting near the goal and working backwards through the behaviour chain, as with prompting. For example, if the goal is to get Julian to put all the clothes away in his bedroom, he may initially be rewarded for putting the final sock away in a bedroom which has been tidied by his mother. This has the advantage that not only does he get praise and points (or whatever reinforcer has previously been arranged) but also the neat tidy bedroom may have reinforcing value of its own.

Shaping is therefore a system of successive approximation towards a new pattern by differential reinforcement of selected behaviour. Inevitably it often requires patience and a lot of time. Parents, however, will often be prepared to spend time if the problems are severe and support and supervision are forthcoming from a doctor or health visitor. Shaping programmes fail if (i) the steps are too great or (ii) the next step is tackled before the previous one has been properly learned. In the first case an attempt must be made to find smaller steps and in the second a return must be made to relearn an earlier step.

Measures to Decrease Behaviour

Extinction

Any action which produces no reward of any kind, either internal or external, is likely to cease in time. If the monthly pay cheque stops arriving you will not continue doing that job for long. When the cheque first fails to arrive the natural reaction is to inquire from the pay office, grumble to the boss and make a fuss. When it is clear that there really is no more pay you stop doing the job and look for some other way of earning your living. In exactly the same way, extinction schedules work in behaviour therapy. Kevin may be getting a great deal of attention by throwing the teacups at the cat and screaming. It is decided to extinguish this behaviour whilst reinforcing the drawing of cats and teacups in his drawing book. Initially when he stops getting attention, he will try hard to find teacups and cat in order to continue the behaviour pattern which he knows has gained him the centre of the stage in the past. Once he realises that this is futile he will give up and seek alternatives, at which point picture drawing can more easily be shaped and reinforced. This example introduces two important points about reducing behaviour by means of extinction. The first is that the unwanted behaviour will always increase in a desperate attempt to gain the withdrawn reinforcement before it finally begins to lessen (extinction burst). The second is that extinction should wherever possible be used in such a fashion that there is a positive as well as a negative dimension to the programme. Both these points can lead to difficulties in practice as spouses, care-givers for the elderly and parents often get discouraged at the point of upsurge in an unwanted behaviour and despondently abandon the programme. The professional can help by warning that this problem will occur and giving support when it does.

Parents sometimes launch themselves into extinction programmes with punitive vigour but without thought of anything positive to replace the behaviour being extinguished. Extinction, of course, should never be punitive — the goal being withdrawing of attention of any sort either favourable or unfavourable. Parents often need to be reminded that *attention*, not praise or pleasure, is the reward the child is seeking. A parent 'blowing his or her top' may be highly reinforcing to a child who has previously noted that quiet constructive play results in being ignored while mother gets on with the ironing.

It should be noted that the rapidity with which extinction is effective depends on the previous schedule of reinforcement. If the behaviour has been continuously reinforced it will be extinguished the more rapidly. Equally, inconsistent extinction with occasional 'giving in' is in fact identical to a variable reinforcement schedule. This will prove ineffective in reducing behaviour — rather, the latter will slowly but strongly increase. The child that gets its request for sweets refused ten times but granted on the eleventh has not been taught that sweets cannot be obtained by pestering, rather that sweets are only obtained by pestering *persistently*. From the practical point of view, therefore, it is very important that extinction schedules are not used unless the user has the resources to use them consistently. It is perfectly true that night-time waking and crying in a young child can be extinguished if the mother possesses the resolution and perhaps lack of normal maternal feelings to be able to carry it through but few mothers can do this.

Punishment

Early and much publicised behavioural work made considerable use of punishment in the form of aversion therapy. In this, an attempt was made to reduce undesirable behaviours by pairing them with an unpleasant event such as an electric shock. Such attempts met with only limited success and a number of theoretical and practical snags became apparent. Aversion therapy is often found to be specific to the treatment situation and does not generalise into outside life. Even when successful, it does nothing to replace the suppressed behaviour with desirable behaviour — the negative may be removed leaving an awkward vacuum rather than anything positive. The exhibitionist may cease to flash but is no nearer achieving an appropriate sexual performance. The model may be an unfortunate one in that the child that is slapped by its parents may be taught that violence is needed to control others. He then tries out this lesson in his dealings with smaller children at school or in the family.

The subject, whether child or adult, may try to escape the punishment in unforeseen and undesirable ways by cheating, lying or avoiding being caught. Lastly, there is the temptation for the punisher to use the technique inappropriately through the sequence behaviour/punishment/forgiveness in which, for example, pulling the cat's tail is followed by a modest slap and then a kiss and a cuddle from mother. It may happen that kisses and cuddles are only available when 'naughtiness' is to be forgiven. The pattern of 'making it up' after punishment is particularly seductive as the child receives strong terminal positive reinforcement and the mother is negatively reinforced by the calming of her feelings of guilt at having been unkind to her child. In spite of its superficial attraction, as a way of changing behaviour it is useless, as there are no clear signals as to what is expected next time. Parallel examples exist in adult life — it is not uncommon to come across couples who have sexual intercourse only at the end of a major row.

When all these factors have been taken into account, punishment has been and is likely to continue to be frequently used in everyday life. It has occasional applications in behavioural management and it is worth listing the rules for its effective use which are:

(i)   It should be decisive and not subject to negotiation.
(ii) It should be of appropriate intensity, neither too severe, producing anxiety or too mild, having no effect.
(iii) It should be immediate.
(iv) It should be consistent. Intermittent punishment lacks effect and may induce anxiety more rapidly.
(v)   The reason for it should be made clear.
(vi) An appropriate alternative behaviour should be available and achievable.

Response Cost

This involves the loss of positive reinforcement under certain contract conditions. In the case of a teenager an agreement might be reached that making his bed in the morning permits going out in the evening after supper. Failure to make his bed in the morning entails the response cost of loss of the evening reinforcer. Natural contracts may replace artificial ones. For example the response of smoking 40 cigarettes a day for many years may entail the cost of loss of the reward of normal pulmonary function. This cost is, sadly, irreversible but the principle is used when giving medical advice about smoking. The technique is also used in a variety of points token programmes where certain actions entail a loss of points. It has been extensively employed as part of programmes for the management of obesity or smoking in the form of money deposits which are forfeited if goals are not met. Attempts are sometimes made to strengthen the cost involved in these programmes by stipulating that the money, if lost, goes to some agency strongly disliked by the subject. For example a churchman might agree to his forfeit going to a left-wing atheist organisation or vice versa. One of the problems with response cost programmes is that they may unwittingly contribute to a belief by the subject that once the reinforcer has been lost he has failed totally and there is no point in trying any more. This abstinence violation effect can be avoided by careful programme design and will be discussed in more detail in Chapter 7.

Time-out

(See also Chapter 12.) This can for practical purposes be regarded as a special form of response cost. There is, however, an important theoretical difference as the latter is removal of reinforcers already earned whereas time-out (short for 'time out from positive reinforcement') involves the use of an environment in which no reinforcement is available. The common practice of sending a child to his bedroom without his supper is an attempt to use time-out in everyday family life. Used in this way it is often ineffective as there is no consistent planning in its use, and sources of reinforcement such as toys, books and household plumbing may still be available. This technique is probably most effectively used in institutions where it is possible to provide a special setting, i.e. a small, bare, dull room and staff trained in its use. Paradoxically it is in these settings that it has come in for criticisms from the media where it is easily and frequently misrepresented. Correctly used, however, whether in home or school, it is an effective and humane way of reducing unwanted behaviour and to be preferred to conventional punishment in almost every way.

   The object of the technique is that following unwanted behaviour the child is temporarily removed from all reinforcers that are currently available to him. In order to do this several decisions have to be taken. (McAuley and McAuley 1977)

(i) Where? Bedrooms and bathrooms are not recommended as they are too vulnerable and cannot be observed. Equally, dark cupboards are frightening and should not be used. The corner of a hall, kitchen or living room is probably to be preferred.

(ii) How long? Two to three minutes after becoming quiet is enough for a very young child. Five to six minutes may be used for an older child and ten minutes for an eleven-year-old.

(iii) How? It is important that the whole procedure is explained to the child in advance. The sequence is then as follows:

    (a) Parent commands. If child complies reward is given. If child does not comply:

    (b) Parent repeats command with the threat of time out. If child complies reward is given. If child does not comply:

    (c) Child is sent to time-out for the predetermined time. The whole sequence is repeated as required and a later opportunity is taken to explain again when and why time out is used.

Differential Reinforcement of Other Behaviour (DRO)

From the above sections it will be apparent that if an alternative is reinforced the original behaviour is likely to reduce. This principle, therefore must be considered amongst the ways of reducing unwanted behaviour. In practice the use of physically or functionally incompatible behaviours is frequently included in both purely behavioural and cognitive treatment plans. The smoker may be encouraged to fight his craving by going for a run or a swim and the anxious patient to visualise scenes or make self statements about coping competently with the situation which makes him anxious. This will be discussed in more detail in the sections dealing with strategies for individual problems.

Stimulus Control

With this technique we return to the A end of the A-B-C model. Certain behaviours are classically conditioned and occur in response to a recurrent stimulus. For example a smoker may always want a cigarette at the end of a meal. A panicky patient may have an attack in a supermarket queue as she knows by past experience that this is 'when it will start'. Particularly in the case of the former it may be appropriate to try and change the circumstances surrounding the end of the meal by having it in a different place or getting up and going for a walk straight after the last mouthful. In this way the expected conditioned response of wanting a cigarette may be avoided. Many everyday actions occur as a result of a response chain which can potentially be interrupted at several different points. It has been observed that the terminal response is less likely to occur if the chain is lengthened. Let us take our smoker mentioned in Chapter 2. In order to have his cigarette he needs normally to pull out the packet and his lighter, operate the lighter and take the first puff. Supposing, however, he needs to buy cigarettes and in order to do that he needs to go to the bank and get money, and his cheque book is locked in the boot of the car in a car park ten minutes' walk away. The whole chain is now considerably longer. The likelihood of his resisting the urge to smoke is in itself greater and there are more links in the chain which might be modified by alternative behaviour. Various methods of controlling stimuli and lengthening response chains can be built into a number of treatment programmes.

Compound and Complex Techniques

A number of commonly used behavioural techniques include several of the elements described under the appropriate problem sections; some occur often enough to be worth considering here.

Exposure

Fears are reduced by repeated or continuous exposure to the stimulus producing the fear. This is a commonplace incorporated in such everyday remarks as 'it's always worse at first' and 'it will be better when you get used to it'. Anybody who doubts the truth of this should try to remember their first day at a new school. In spite of this, many patients respond to fearful situations by avoiding them, thus making the problem worse. Various techniques for encouraging exposure have thus been devised in behaviour therapy to overcome this problem. These will be described in detail in the section devoted to anxiety related problems. Theoretically, exposure may be considered a mixed technique as, consequent upon it, fear is extinguished. This diminution of fear, however, acts as negative reinforcement of the previously avoided behaviour which now increases in frequency and extent.

Massed Practice

This is a technique used to reduce or eliminate minor problems such as tics and habit spasms. The patient is encouraged to perform the tic for a certain length of time each day deliberately which contrasts strongly with the usual reaction of 'Do stop doing that, William'! This may be regarded as a method of reducing unwanted behaviour but it probably depends for its effectiveness on several different elements. First, the practising of the habit produces fatigue and boredom. Second, it teaches control over the elements making up the tic. Third, relief occurs when the practice is stopped and, finally, the reaction of the family, which although probably unfavourable may reinforce through providing attention, is removed. Massed practice can be used very simply in primary care as these kinds of problems are relatively simple to define, supervision is not time-consuming and the results are often extremely worthwhile.

Contingency Contracts

These are agreements, ideally in written form, made between two or more people specifying relationships between behaviour and its consequences. They provide a framework for mutual reinforcement and fulfil much the same function as commercial contracts, i.e. the job to be performed is clearly stated and is to be rewarded in a specified way. A personal contract may also be used. For example, a smoker who gives up may contract with himself that after six months abstinence he will treat himself to a week's holiday in Spain. The intermediate reinforcer might be watching the saved money accumulate in a Dimple Haig bottle on the mantleshelf.

Interpersonal contracts are of use with family and marital problems where both the task and the reward may be broken down into intermediate stages. For example if a bicycle is to be the terminal reward for making the bed and tidying the bedroom each morning for six months, a points system could be arranged in which Bicycle = 1,000 points. Early points may be awarded against a sub-contract which states that, for the first two weeks, one point may be earned for having no clothes on the floor at morning inspection. This is introduced in order to *shape* the required room tidying in small steps.

There are a number of rules which are helpful in arranging any contract (Stuart 1971):

(i)   Contract reinforcement should be earned, not given, as a right and when earned it should be granted immediately.

(ii) The arrangement should be reciprocal so that reinforcing others earns reinforcement from them.

(iii) The value of the reinforcers exchanged must be seen to be equal from the point of view of value and frequency in the estimation of the contracting parties *not* just in the estimation of the therapist or contract manager. Scales of values amongst individuals are very different. For example, going to a party may be a reinforcer for one person but a punishment for another. Ideally the reinforcers exchanged should be small enough to be earned frequently.

(iv) Reinforcers should always follow, never precede, the task. 'If I give you a cuddle now, will you go to bed at once afterwards?' is the wrong way round and doomed to failure.

(v)   The terms of the contract must be clear and carried out systematically. In this way freedom of decision and action is actually increased as each party knows where they are. They know what the choices are and what the consequent rewards or costs will be.

When suggesting a contract to parents some attitude change is frequently necessary on their part. They must abandon the 'because I say so' approach in favour of a much more equal relationship. Marriage partners, also, frequently feel that they have a right to expect the other party to change in response to a criticism without the criticiser conceding anything in return. These attitudes must be explored and modified before a contract will be successful.

Assertion and Social Skills

These topics will be discussed in Chapter 6. Some aspects of them, however, form an integral part of many behavioural programmes so it is not out of place to make some mention here of the general principles involved. Without adequate assertive behaviour many of the normal reinforcers of everyday life are simply out of reach. No man will arrive at a sexually fulfilled relationship unless he is able to hold a conversation with a girl. Social skill may be described as an ability to behave in a way that is likely to be rewarded by others around you and is unlikely to be punished, ignored or met with disapproval. Social behaviour may be divided into three types. The *aggressive* which is hostile and criticises and attempts to coerce the other person. The *submissive* where the person is unable to express his rights and aspirations and allows himself to be trampled over, often with hidden resentment. The *assertive* where the subject, without attacking or attempting to coerce the other, expresses clearly what he thinks, wants and has a right to receive. Establishing the differences among the three is often central to management in parenthood, education, working life and marriage. It is also important in dealing with the medical profession either as a colleague or a patient.

Cognitive Techniques

Many of the methods described above for external behaviour have internal parallels which can be used for work with thoughts, feelings and information processing aspects of problems. For example, exposure techniques can be used either *in vivo* or in imagination. Undesirable activities such as overeating can be subjected to *covert sensitisation*. In this technique the patient is asked, for example, to imagine consuming his favourite food and then feeling sick and eventually vomiting in front of some important person in his life, such as the boss or an admired friend. This technique attempts to link undesirable behaviour to undesired consequences and thus reduce its frequency.

Thought Stopping

This was the earliest cognitive technique to be widely used and is applied very simply. A patient is asked to concentrate on the thoughts that worry him. The therapist then shouts 'Stop' and the patient, often to his surprise notices that the thoughts do actually cease, at least for a time. The second and third stages of the technique involve the patient's saying 'Stop' to himself, first out loud and then to himself. A variation is to get the patient to visualise the word 'Stop' on a TV screen in front of him gradually moving like a programme credit. The technique, although it has its uses, can be a rather transient and crude one. It is more effective if the unwanted thought is immediately replaced by a prepared pleasant or relaxing image (see Chapter 5).

Distraction

This may be regarded as a development of thought stopping, as the attention is switched off the worrying thoughts but this time onto another activity. This may involve focusing the attention on some aspect of the surroundings such as birds singing, counting bald men in the train or focusing for 30 seconds on a red spot stuck on a watch. Alternatively one can engage in some distracting physical activity like doing a crossword or mental activity like reciting poetry or doing mental arithmetic.

Challenging Worrying Thoughts and Thinking Patterns

Recently a great deal of attention has been focused on the way that worrying thoughts can produce anxiety, and gloomy thoughts depression. Ellis, (1974) Beck and Meichenbaum (see References, Chapter 1) have developed a number of approaches to identifying these faulty thinking patterns and generating more rational and helpful alternatives. Beck (Beck *et al.* 1979) sees the problem of depression and anxiety in terms of the way the patient looks at himself, the world and the future. This in turn creates thinking patterns, and thoughts which automatically pop up in the patient's mind, affecting his mood and emotions. Although a relatively complex system of therapy, many of the ideas are easily adapted to the primary care setting and form a useful adjunct or alternative to other forms of treatment. These will be discussed in more detail in later sections, particularly those devoted to anxiety and depression.

References

Beck A. T., Rush, A. J., Shaw, B. F. and Emery, G. (1979) *Cognitive Therapy of Depression*, New York, Guilford Press and Chichester, John Wiley

Ellis, A. (1974) *Humanistic Psychotherapy: The Rational Motive Approach*, New York, McGraw Hill

McAuley, R., and McAuley, P. (1977) *Child Behaviour Problems*, London, Macmillan

Meichenbaum, D. (1971) 'Examination of model characteristics in reducing avoidance behavior', *Journal of Personality and Social Psychology, 17*, 298–307

Rachman, S. J. (1980) *Fear and Courage*, San Francisco, W. H. Freeman

Stuart, R. B. (1971) 'Behavioral contracting with the families of delinquents', *Journal of Behavior Therapy and Experimental Psychiatry, 2*, 11

PART TWO: PROBLEMS

5 ANXIETY AND RELATED DISORDERS

The Nature of Anxiety

Fear and anxiety are more easily recognised than defined and training the sufferer to recognise and correctly attribute his symptoms is an important part of management. A working definition is that anxiety is a state of body and mind produced by the perception of threat or danger — real or imagined. This state includes three main components.

Apprehensive Thoughts and Feelings

These are subjective and are therefore the most easily described, recognised and correctly attributed to anxiety.

Bodily Changes

Muscle tension, palpitations, headaches and related physical symptoms may all be produced by anxiety. The sensations may be correctly recognised but their cause misattributed to some physical mishap such as a heart attack or brain tumour.

Behaviour Changes

Anxiety will cause the sufferer to escape from disturbing situations and to learn to avoid those which he fears. Both escape and avoidance make it more difficult to face the situation next time round.

Fears and phobias refer to situations where the cause of the feeling can be easily identified, whereas anxiety is used to describe a situation where the cause of the problem is not readily apparent. The terms targetted and non-targetted anxiety are also used which are, perhaps, as explicit as any. Table 5.1 outlines the channels through which anxiety is expressed.

The Origins and Maintenance of Anxiety

Anxiety and fear are both frequently adaptive and protective. Fear crossing a road or climbing a mountain may be essential to preserve

Table 5.1: The Three Channels of Anxiety (often not synchronous)

Disturbing Thoughts and Feelings	Bodily Changes	Behaviour Changes
Fearful thoughts or terror feelings associated with a definite cause. *Anxiety* producing similar thoughts and feelings where the cause is not obvious. *Memory defects* associated with learning storage or retrieval. *Attention deficits* from loss of concentration, intrusive thoughts or catastrophic images. *Performance deterioration*, loss of adequate problem-solving, detachment and spectatoring.	*Sympathetic nervous system arousal:* Dry mouth, rapid over-breathing, fast pulse, raised blood pressure, giddiness, tingling hands, carpo-pedal spasm. *Related secondary problems:* Tension headaches, tiredness, difficulty in falling asleep, asthma, changes in bowel habit.	*Tension* of voluntary muscles. *Distraction* away from the task. *Speed/accuracy deterioration.* *Restricted repertory* due to rigidity or compulsive rituals. *Avoidance or escape.*

life. The bodily responses of anxiety assist in preparing the muscles and circulation for the physical effort involved in running a race or playing in a match. A feeling of tension may aid concentration of attention when making decisions or taking examinations. All is well if anxiety and fear remain proportional to the needs of the situation but problems arise once symptoms become disproportionate, resulting in diminishing self-confidence and performance. In particular these may take the form of anxiety: (i) in the absence of real danger; (ii) in excess of the amount of danger; or (iii) lasting long after the danger has passed.

Distress also occurs when physical symptoms develop in a situation where a physical response is inappropriate. Letters from the bank manager cannot be dealt with by punching the writer on the nose, and physical escape from mid-flight anxiety is hardly possible.

Anxiety may be maintained by a set of factors entirely different from its original cause. The child who has received an injection from a doctor wearing a white coat may become anxious the next time he sees a white coat. This is an example of classical conditioning in which the pairing of two cues produces the same response when either is presented separately and parallels Pavlov's experiment with the bell and the salivating dogs (see Chapter 1).

Many other factors may contribute to the maintenance of anxiety after its initial occurrence — most notably:

Upsetting Thoughts

These usually occur in connection with attempts to find an explanation for the symptoms — 'Am I going mad?' 'Am I going to have a heart attack?' 'If I fail my driving test it will be the end of everything'. Such thinking errors fall into four classes:

(a) Overestimate the probability of a disaster e.g. a plane crash.
(b) Overestimate the severity of a feared event e.g. taking an examination
(c) Underestimate of the subject's own coping resources e.g. ability to speak clearly when feeling anxious
(d) Underestimate of outside rescue factors e.g. husband's support during childbirth

Once such thoughts occur a feedback spiral is established. For example your heart misses a beat, you think 'Help! I'll never manage this' and your heart starts thumping in earnest. The bodily feelings feed the thoughts which are thus in turn confirmed by the increase in feelings.

Avoidance or Escape

Avoidance of difficult, anxiety-producing situations or *escape* if once caught in them is perfectly reasonable in the face of real danger but may become a severe handicap when it is greater than normal and interferes with functioning. The list of avoided situations may increase and involve more and more of everyday life. Temporary relief is gained by escape but on the next occasion the situation occurs it is even more difficult to face. Eventually, as in the severe agoraphobic, the life style may become so restricted that they never leave the house for years on end.

Loss of Confidence

Confidence is built upon recurrent experience of success, thus avoidance and escape sap confidence as they provide only experience of failure. One failure inevitably leads to fear of another and tasks that were once easy now seem difficult — 'I was once the bloke they always came to for advice. Now they know that I am always in such a state that they don't dare ask'.

Vulnerability and the Role of Life Events

These may feature both in the original cause and in the maintenance of anxiety. Every GP will recognise that certain particularly important life events produce a clinically disabling degree of anxiety in some people. Typical examples would be moving house, taking a driving test or awaiting an operation. Such anxiety may be transient but is disabling and frequently requires help. A more serious situation occurs when two or more of these stressful events come together or when a particularly timid or socially vulnerable person is involved. Under these circumstances the severity of the resultant anxiety often seems multiplied rather than simply cumulative.

The Size of the Problem

Most authorities agree that anxiety-based problems are the most common psychological conditions to be found in primary care although such assertions are fraught with difficulties of definition and classification. It has been calculated that about 10 per cent of the population consults a doctor about tension at some time and an Oxford GP survey in 1977 (Skegg *et al.* 1977) found that amongst registered patients more than 20 per cent of women and about 10 per cent of men received at least one prescription for a psychotropic drug during a year. This figure rose to 30 percent amongst 45-year-old women. Another survey found that 50 per cent of patients found suitable for psychological intervention in general practice suffered from anxiety-based problems (Robson *et al.* 1984).

The Assessment of Anxiety Problems

We are aware that there is some repetition from previous chapters in this section but we feel that the importance of assessment in anxiety for both patient and therapist makes it necessary to include everything at this point in its correct order.

Interview

A clear and exact statement of the *nature of the problem* and the *disability* resulting from it is obtained. Enquiries are made about *other significant problem areas*.

As much time as possible is spent seeking out:

(i)   *Triggers* that precede anxiety.
(ii) *Situations* in which anxiety is likely to occur.
(iii) The immediate and long standing *consequences* of the problem.
(iv) The factors which are associated with its *increase* or *decrease*.

It is valuable to know how the *patient interprets his problem*. Classically the physical effects of panic are attributed to evidence of catastrophic events such as heart attacks and brain tumours. No intervention is likely to succeed unless this self-interpretation is uncovered and discussed.

How has he tried to *cope* with the problem previously? What methods has he tried? What outside help — from professionals, friends or relatives — has he obtained and did it make any difference? Information about *what sort of help* he wants and expects and how improvement in the problem would affect him and his family is also useful.

It is important to know what the patient enjoys, does well or used to do well. Did he used to take part in sport or other exercise which he has now discontinued? Using these *assets* may be important when planning treatment.

The development of the problem is often of much more interest to the patient than to the therapist. The former may wonder repeatedly what caused his difficulties in the first place whereas the latter will be more concerned with what is maintaining them currently. Nevertheless some information on development may be important and help to confirm or modify the significance of other data.

Baseline Measurements

The most usual and valuable baseline assessment instrument is a diary recording the situations in which anxiety occurs, its associated thoughts and feelings and a rating of severity (see also Chapter 3). Its exact form will depend on the individual problem and the information which is thought to be important in the particular case. Figure 5.1 is an example of such a diary.

It is noticeable how often the severity of a problem alters once a prospective record is being kept. A symptom which is said to be constantly present may in fact only occur at specific and relatively infrequent times of day. It is commonly found that certain problems disappear altogether once a diary is being kept. It is probable that diary-keeping may be as effective an anxiolytic as benzodiazepines in certain cases although no formal research has been carried out to demonstrate this. The mechanisms involved probably include an increased sense of control, and a reduced tendency to remember only the worse moments once the patient is observing and recording.

A number of self-administered inventories and questionnaires are available to measure anxiety. Amongst the most common used are:

Figure 5.1: Anxiety Diary

Date/Time	Situation	Feelings (0–100%)	Thoughts	Outcome
1/7 5 p.m.	Husband late: Bad day with kids	Tense 60 Anger 30	Has he had a crash? He's ruined my meal	Arrived 9 p.m. Had row
2/7 10 a.m.	Outside shop	Fear 70 Palpitations 50	Will I have an attack like last time?	Rushed home. Felt ashamed

The State Trait Anxiety Inventory (Spielberger). This is an American instrument with two scales of 20 questions each. The first scale measures anxiety 'at this moment' (state anxiety) and the second scale 'how you generally feel' (trait anxiety).

The Marks and Mathews (1979) Fear Questionnaire. This is an English set of scales that measure Main phobia/Agoraphobia/ Blood-injury phobia/Social phobia/General anxiety and depression/ Overall disturbance and disability. This is an extremely comprehensive instrument based on vast experience but is aimed more at the phobic than the generally anxious patient — see Figure 5.2.

The Anxiety Checklist (Beck *et al.*). This is a two scale American list measuring a series of commonly occurring symptoms with four possible degrees of severity and frequency.

The insensitive use of questionnaires may damage the therapeutic relationship in a distressed patient and instruments should be properly introduced and carefully explained. They are, however, useful measures of severity and change. They may also serve to pick up important symptoms that may have been missed in a short assessment interview. With tact most patients will accept them readily enough.

Psychophysiological Measurements. Direct measurement of changes in pulse rate, blood pressure and skin conductance in real or imagined fearful situations can be made with polygraphs which are similar to the now notorious lie detector used in other settings. Although these can provide an accurate record of the bodily changes of fear, it is likely that they will remain a feature of the research laboratory and large clinic rather than finding their way into primary care. Some simplified instruments do have their use in simple biofeedback treatments which will be described later. (See details at the end of chapter.)

Behavioural Tests. Typical is the Behavioural Approach Test which is used in single object phobias. The patient is simply asked to approach the feared object or a photograph of it and the proximity achieved measured. As the phobia improves the object can be approached more and more closely and perhaps eventually picked

Figure 5.2: Marks and Mathews Fear Questionnaire

FEAR QUESTIONNAIRE.   Name .... Age .... Sex .... Date ....

Choose a number from the scale below to show how much you avoid each of the situations listed, because of fear or other unpleasant feelings. Then write the number you chose in the box opposite each situation.

0	1	2	3	4	5	6	7	8
Would not avoid it		Slightly avoid it		Definitely avoid it		Markedly avoid it		Always avoid it

1.   Main phobia you want treated (describe in your own words)
. . . .
2.   Injections or minor surgery . . . .   —
3.   Eating and drinking with other people . . . .   —
4.   Hospitals . . . .   —
5.   Travelling alone by bus or coach . . . .   —
6.   Walking alone in busy streets . . . .   —
7.   Being watched or stared at . . . .   —
8.   Going into crowded shops . . . .   —
9.   Talking to people in authority . . . .   —
10.   Sight of blood . . . .   —
11.   Being criticised . . . .   —
12.   Going alone far from home . . . .   —
13.   Thought of injury or illness . . . .   —
14.   Speaking or acting to an audience . . . .   —
15.   Large open spaces . . . .   —
16.   Going to the dentist . . . .   —
17.   Other situations (describe) . . . .   —

Leave blank   — — —   — —

Ag Bl Soc TOTAL
(Omit 1&17)

Now choose a number from the scale below to show how much you are troubled by each problem listed, and write the number in the box opposite.

0	1	2	3	4	5	6	7	8
Hardly at all		Slightly troublesome		Definitely troublesome		Markedly troublesome		Very severely troublesome

18.   Feeling miserable or depressed . . . .   —
19.   Feeling irritable or angry . . . .   —
20.   Feeling tense or panicky . . . .   —
21.   Upsetting thoughts coming into your mind . . . .   —
22.   Feeling you or your surroundings are strange or unreal . . . .   —
23.   Other feelings (please describe) . . . .
. . . . TOTAL

— —

How would you state the present state of your phobic sysmptoms on the scale below?

0	1	2	3	4	5	6	7	8
No phobias present		slightly disturbing not really disabling		definitely disturbing/ disabling		markedly disturbing/ disabling		very severely disturbing/ disabling

Please circle one number between 0 and 8.

Acknowledgement: This scale is reproduced by kind permission of the authors, Professor Isaac Marks and Professor Andrew Mathews. Further information and permission to use and reproduce the scale may be obtained from the authors at The Institute of Psychiatry, De Crespigny Park, London SE5 8AF.

Figure 5.3: The Anxiety Checklist

NAME: DATE:

Instructions: Please read the following descriptive phrases carefully. Indicate in each column after the phrase the number choice from the top of the column that best applies to you. The time period to be covered is the past week. Under "severity" indicate the worst you felt. Under frequency indicate how much of the time you experienced the symptom to any degree.

SEVERITY	FREQUENCY
(0) Not at all (1) Mildly — it did not bother me much (2) Moderately — it was very unpleasant, but I could stand it (3) Severely — I could barely stand it	(0) Not at all (1) Sometimes (2) Most of the time (3) All the time or almost all the time

During the past week I have felt		During the last week I have felt
nervous	—	—
jittery	—	—
dizzy, lightheaded or faint	—	—
like I'm smothering	—	—
frightened	—	—
my heart is pounding or racing	—	—
rapid breathing	—	—
sweating (not due to heat)	—	—
strange feelings of unreality	—	—
nausea or vomiting	—	—
a lump in the throat	—	—
difficulty holding my urine	—	—
anxious	—	—
scared	—	—
wobbliness in my legs	—	—
numbness or tingling	—	—
jumpy	—	—
numbness or tingling in my hands, feet, or face	—	—
difficulty breathing	—	—
shaky	—	—
alarmed	—	—

up and handled. The same principle is used with situational fears but in this case the patient is asked to go into the feared setting, e.g. a supermarket, and remain there as long as possible, rating the amount of discomfort on a previously agreed scale — for example, 0–100 (where 0 = not at all anxious and 100 = the most anxious you could ever be).

Planning Treatment

At this stage it should be possible to form a hypothesis about the type of anxiety and the factors maintaining it. The interpretation of the problem factors is agreed in discussion with the patient. If agreement cannot be reached the outlook for cooperation and success is not good and perhaps the hypothesis needs modification or more time should be spent on explanation. At this time too, treatment goals should be settled, and the patient needs to understand that the object of most behavioural programmes is to give him control over anxiety, *not* to abolish it altogether. The plan most often successful will be a 'package' involving a mixture of techniques; for the sake of convenience, however, the main types of anxiety-based problems will be described in turn, together with the treatment approaches most commonly used for each.

Types of Anxiety-based Problems

General Anxiety

By this is meant anxiety arising when there is no obvious object or situation responsible. It is also described as free-floating or non-targetted anxiety. General anxiety has only recently received attention from behaviour therapists, probably because the symptoms are the most diffuse and because the recent recognition of the major role of cognitive factors has focused attention on a condition where thoughts and feelings are of first importance. It is the most common type of anxiety seen in primary care and its treatment encompasses many of the techniques that are also of use in the treatment of the other varieties.

It has already been pointed out that anxiety is both necessary and universal. Fearlessness is only found in mythical Greek and Teutonic heroes and almost all of these came to sticky ends. It is only when distress exceeds the danger that a clinical problem arises. Although by definition in general anxiety there is no specific fear, there may be a number of stress factors present which need to be considered. These can arise from marital or child-rearing difficulties, money problems, work relationships, exams, moving house and many other situations which may require a practical problem-solving approach to go hand in hand with management of the anxiety symptoms.

Anxiety Management Training. This consists of three groups of elements: (i) explanation of the nature of anxiety and the rationale of treatment to the patient; (ii) control of symptoms using relaxation, distraction, exercise, restructuring of thoughts and panic management; (iii) avoidance control by exposure and confidence rebuilding by encouraging positive activities.

If much of the treatment is to be done by the patient himself at home the programme must be set out in a manual (see p. 63) which can be studied by the patient at all times. The therapist's task is to assist the clear definition of the problem(s), oversee record keeping and symptom monitoring, help to produce suitable homework assignments and assist in overcoming blocks and difficulties. At all times the manual serves as a guide. Although the original versions of these manuals were designed for use by psychologists they require little modification for use in primary care by a GP or other primary care worker who is prepared to become familiar with the principles involved.

Rationale. This is the first section of the programme and is designed to explain how thoughts and feelings interact producing anxiety through the autonomic nervous system — particularly the sympathetic division. Table 5.2 gives some idea of how this works.

Fear or anxiety becomes a problem when it occurs in the wrong situation, wrong amount or goes on for too long. This often happens as a result of a double feedback system increasing the fear to an unreasonable extent (see Figure 5.4). This results from worry that there is real danger, something physically wrong or just anticipation that the unpleasant symptoms are going to start all over again (fear of fear).

It is explained that relief from anxiety is often sought by avoiding the situations that produce it like crowded places, shops or meeting

Table 5.2: Autonomic Nervous System

Sympathetic	Parasympathetic
Provides physical response to stress (Fight or Flight)	Provides physical response to calm
Pulse rate and BP raised	Pulse rate and BP lowered
Respiratory rate raised	Respiratory rate lowered
Digestion stops	Digestion promoted
In the male promotes ejaculation not erection (Premature ejaculation)	Promotes sustained erection

Figure 5.4: The Feedback Cycle of Anxiety and Points of Possible Intervention

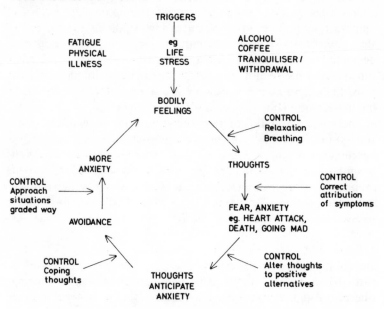

particular people. This may produce temporary relief. This avoidance is, however, not always possible every time something is avoided it is more difficult to face the next time it crops up. In this way more and more things are gradually avoided and life becomes more and more restricted.

Loss of confidence occurs because anxiety makes it harder to do things which were once easy. Confidence is a pleasurable feeling that comes from succeeding and is increased by repeatedly experiencing success. Failure at things which were once possible leads to the abandoning of further attempts and the avoidance of similar tasks because they might prove too difficult. Lost confidence can be regained by learning how to cope with small things before building up to progressively bigger challenges.

Symptom Control. Any previous successful attempts at coping should be developed and encouraged. *Deep muscle relaxation* is introduced as a way of (1) reducing muscular tension, which can be worrying in itself, (2) inducing a relaxed mood and sense of physical well-being and (3) providing an alternative distracting response which the patient can use as soon as he senses the beginning of anxiety symptoms. All of these assist slowing down which counteracts the hurry usually associated with anxiety. Relaxation is taught with taped instructions along the lines that follow on page 82. Relaxation is most effective when taught 'live' but this is unlikely to be possible in primary care unless someone is enthusiastic enough to run groups. Instructions recorded in the voice of the therapist provide the next best option and this has the added advantage that the therapist must learn how to do it himself!

The taped sequence is first practised in full, then a shortened version of the exercises is introduced for quick relaxation. Lastly, instructions are given to recognise the cues of tension and use them to initiate the short sequence. A series of relaxing scenes may be prepared by the patient to aid mental relaxation after the physical sequence is finished. Relaxed posture and slow breathing may be stressed separately.

Exercise. Under certain circumstances exercise will provide a more appropriate means of symptom control than relaxation. This is particularly true with those people who find relaxation difficult or where anger is associated with anxiety. The use of exercise in treatment is one way of resolving the paradox that modern non-physical stress frequently produces a primitive somatic response. A businessman developing his own firm found that he was much better able to deal with the problems of the day after a brisk morning swim in the neighbouring pool. A woman with children, although always feeling tired, found a short structured jogging programme and weekly yoga class improved her sense of well-being and energy.

Timetable restructuring to avoid rushing, may be introduced at this point. A useful technique is to suggest that the patient plans hour by hour what can reasonably be done in a morning, whilst sitting down with a cup of coffee and a pencil and paper after he gets up. A similar procedure after lunch plans the afternoon. The time-tables are adjusted after the first day in the light of the previous day's experience. Often to the patient's surprise they find that they are in fact doing more than when they were rushing at it 'hell-for-leather'.

On similar lines more long term plans can be made by deciding in advance what activities are essential in the next week or month and how they can be best arranged. This may involve leaving out some of the less essential items or making a decision that a particular evening or weekend will be kept free regardless of how many invitations have to be refused. This system may be extended by drawing up a programme where each area of activity has a separate column. The tasks connected with each activity are then listed in the appropriate column and a time allotted for each according to priority. If insufficient time is available the less urgent items are postponed or left out. As each item is completed it is ticked in the relevant column thereby increasing the patient's sense of control over his activities (see Figure 5.5).

Distraction is used to counteract tension in three ways:

(1) Concentrating on the surroundings e.g. conversations, items of clothing of others present or concentrating on a pre-arranged object like a spot on a watch dial. The latter can also be used as a cue for relaxation.
(2) Mental activity e.g. reciting a poem, doing calculations or remembering a list or classification.
(3) Physical activities e.g. jogging, doing exercises or just keeping busy in any way.

Control of upsetting thoughts and images. These occur in the presence of tension and anxiety, making matters worse as described in Figure 5.4. They have the following characteristics:

(1) They are *automatic* — they occur fleetingly without effort.
(2) They are *distorted* — they do not fit the facts.
(3) They are *unhelpful* — making change difficult.
(4) They are *plausible* — they go unquestioned.
(5) They are *involuntary* — very difficult to switch off.

Figure 5.5: A Task Programme

Husband	Builders	Children	Work
Wine bar with husband (1)	Phone Surveyor (2) Clear room (1)	Dentist (1) Library (1) Shoes (2) Presents for party (1)	Finish report (2) Arrange meeting (1)

Note: Priority 1 = Urgent; priority 2 = can be postponed

A routine can be followed to identify these thoughts. A recent occasion when the anxiety symptoms were troublesome is identified and recalled. The situation is described in terms of time, place, activity and companions. The onset of anxious feelings is remembered and these feelings rated out of 100. The associated thoughts are then recalled in terms of words, images and meaning. Once the thoughts have been identified their role in the provocation or increase in anxiety can be examined, followed by an attempt to challenge them in terms of unreasonableness, unreality and exaggeration. Alternative ways of thinking about the problem can then be explored.

Avoidance and loss of confidence. A description is obtained of any situations which are being avoided. These are then arranged in an hierarchical list, starting with the least difficult situations and progressing to the most difficult ones. A graded approach is adopted in which the easiest situations or tasks are tackled first and repeated until they can be managed without undue anxiety or difficulty. As confidence in this item is built up the next most difficult item is attempted until a satisfactory point or the top of the hierarchy is reached. Practice must be regular and frequent, and if a block occurs because one step is too hard it must be broken down into smaller components so that success is achieved. The patient instruction leaflet we use is as follows:

SELF HELP FOR ANXIETY

Anxiety is necessary to help cope with danger or difficulty such as driving in fog or working with dangerous tools. Problems with excess anxiety are, however, very common and about one person in ten consults a doctor about them at some time. Tablets such as tranquillisers are one answer and they do help for a while but gradually they lose effect as you go on taking them. They also may give rise to side effects when you try to stop them.

What is Anxiety?

It affects both body and mind producing worrying feelings of fear and apprehension together with physical feelings of tension, trembling, churning stomach, nausea, diarrhoea, backache and palpitations. These physical symptoms can easily be put down to other worrying causes like cancer or heart attacks — thus increasing fear.

When is Anxiety a Real Problem?

When it interferes with life in the absence of real danger or goes on too long after the danger is past.

Why Does This Happen?

All of us come under stress at some time or another. Some of us feel the effects more than others but even those who become anxious rather easily can learn to cope with it.

What are the Consequences of Persistent Anxiety?

(1) Upsetting Thoughts that you may have a serious physical illness or be in real danger increase the feelings:

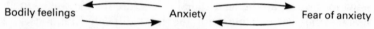

Bodily feelings   Anxiety   Fear of anxiety

(2) Avoiding Things or Places that Make You Anxious. It is normal to avoid real danger but anxiety may lead you to avoid things like shops, crowded places and trains which are not really dangerous. At first avoidance makes you feel better but:

  (i)   Relief is only temporary — you may worry what will happen next time;
  (ii) Every time you avoid something it *is* harder next time you try to face it;
  (iii) Gradually you want to avoid more and more things.

(3) Loss of Confidence. Confidence is built up by doing things successfully. If you find that you can no longer do things that you used to do successfully, confidence is lost and can only be regained by building gradually from tackling the easiest tasks first.

REMEMBER (i) Anxiety does produce physical symptoms like rapid heart rate but it does not produce physical harm like heart attacks.
(ii) It makes you tired by using energy uselessly but does not cause nervous breakdowns.

Controlling Symptoms

Many people already know some ways of making their symptoms better and some things which make them worse. Write these down and see if you can use this information to help in other circumstances.

Relaxation

Relaxation can help in relieving uncomfortable muscular tension, tiredness and worry. It also helps to slow down the speeding up and mental wheelspin which occur with anxiety.

Tape recorded instructions show you first how to relax your whole body, then how you can do it quickly in a number of different situations and finally how to use it to cope with the onset of feelings and anxiety or tension. The exercises teach you what it feels like to be totally relaxed and where your particular centres of tension are.

Regular practice is essential and should be at a settled time of day which is reserved for it. When you have completed the relaxation exercises try to imagine yourself in a situation where you have felt perfectly calm and contented. Re-create the sights and sounds of that situation in your mind. A list of relaxing situations such as good days in the country or on holiday is useful for this purpose.

Start to use relaxation in circumstances when you are beginning to feel anxious — good exercises for this purpose are relaxing the brows and neck, dropping the shoulders and practising slow, regular shallow breathing. A key word like 'calm' or 'relax' can be used to start the sequence. Physical exercise like jogging, cycling, swimming or playing a ball game may also help to relieve symptoms.

Rapid Anxious Breathing

Such breathing can make you tremble, feel dizzy, produce a thumping heart and give you a tingling sensation in your hands and feet. This can be very worrying and give you the idea that you may be having a serious illness like a stroke or heart attack. These symptoms can be quickly controlled by slow, shallow breathing at the rate of 8–12 breaths per minute.

Rushing and Posture

Plan your timetable in advance in order to avoid rushing. You will probably find that you get just as much done. When you have finished or are having a planned break, sit in a comfortable relaxed posture — not hunched on the edge of your chair.

Distraction

Tense, worrying thoughts tend to produce a vicious circle. Try to turn your attention off these thoughts and fill your mind with something else — for example:

(i)   Concentrating on what is going on around you. According to where you are you can try counting the branches on a tree, the cars in the street or the soup tins in a stack. There are many possible variations on this theme.
(ii) Mental activity such as remembering a list, or a poem or doing mental arithmetic.
(iii) Physical activity such as walking, gardening or ironing.

Controlling Upsetting Thoughts

Half-formed upsetting thoughts and images can make you feel anxious or keep anxiety going. The thought that the sharp pain in your chest may be due to a heart attack makes the pain more sinister and threatening. It is important first to study your thinking and find out exactly what your upsetting thoughts are. This is quite difficult because they are automatic and come and go very quickly so that initially you may not be aware of them and need to practise hard in order to identify them. Try to write them down exactly as they occur when you feel tense. They may be quite simple like 'Here we go again' or 'This is the way it started last time'. Once you know what you are thinking you can examine the thoughts carefully and identify those that are exaggerated or unrealistic. 'I didn't get the job so perhaps nobody will employ me', 'I feel tense about talking at the meeting which shows I shall make a hash of it' or 'I punished William unfairly so I am a lousy mother'. There are positive and more reasonable alternatives to all these thoughts. Try to write them down and then look at some of your own thoughts and try to find more reasonable alternatives. This is quite difficult at first but with practice, and sometimes a bit of help, it gets easier.

Dealing with Avoidance and Loss of Confidence

Avoidance easily builds up with anxiety and makes things harder. It is countered by gradually getting back into the habit of doing things which build up confidence. The steps are as follows:

(1) Make a list of the situations that you avoid or that make you anxious.
(2) Arrange these in order according to how difficult it would be for you to face each one.
(3) Select the easiest item on the list as the first target when you start to practise.
(4) Make yourself repeat this item many times until you can do it without difficulty.
(5) Then move on to the next item on the list and so on until you are able to tackle the whole list.

Remember that to be helpful, practice must be regular, frequent and prolonged.

Our thanks are due to Ms Gillian Butler and the Dept of Psychiatry, Oxford University for their permission to use much of the material on this advice sheet.

Phobias

Phobias are anxieties occurring in response to a particular situation. They may be very specific, for example fear of spiders, rats, thunder or flying, or more general and related to social situations or anxiety about illness. The latter are obviously of particular importance to the GP.

Agoraphobia. This is the most important and diffuse member of the phobic family. Originally it derived from the Greek for fear of the market place. This meaning has acquired new force with the advent of the modern supermarket. It is now extended to cover a wide range of patterns of fear related to the central theme of being in public, away from home and in some sense trapped, with escape socially or physically difficult. Common examples found in many case histories are as in Table 5.3.

The fear produced in these situations has a number of physical features. Some of these are produced by direct stimulation of the sympathetic nervous system and adrenal medulla such as high pulse rate, sweaty hands and rapid breathing. Some are mediated by

Table 5.3: Percentage of Agoraphobic People reporting Certain Situations that Provoke Anxiety

Situation	%
Joining a line in a store	96
A definite appointment	91
Feeling trapped in a hairdresser etc.	89
Increasing distance from home	87
Particular places in the neighbourhood	66
Thinking about my problem	82
Domestic arguments and stress	87

Source: Burns and Thorpe 1977

hyperventilation such as tingling fingers, dizziness and carpo-pedal spasm. Experience of such unexplained sensations increases fear and apprehension which in turn leads to an increase of the symptoms. Fear of the distressing symptoms occurring in the future is also important. Such 'fear of fear' may lead to increasing avoidance of a wider and wider range of activities, eventually producing the classic long-standing agoraphobic who has not gone out alone for many years. This in turn may lead to a number of secondary problems. For example, one of us dealt with a problem of truancy which was eventually tracked down to an agoraphobic mother who was able to leave the house only in the company of her school-age daughter. Shopping and visiting were thus only possible if the girl remained at home.

The fearful thoughts described by agoraphobics often involve death, becoming insane, losing control, making a fool of oneself or collapsing. Various factors are described as improving the problem. Chief amongst these is the presence of a reliable, 'safe' person such as the child described above but more often a spouse or close friend.

Treatment The full range of possibilities described under General Anxiety may be involved but the main drive is towards

(i)   explanation of the nature of the condition
(ii) a programme of exposure to the feared situation(s) which may be either
   (a) rapid (flooding or implosion), or
   (b) gradual (desensitisation in vivo or in imagination).

Rapid exposure is a straightforward and effective way of treating phobic anxiety. After a suitable explanation of the rationale of exposure in reducing fear the patient is accompanied by the therapist into the feared environment, e.g. a shopping centre or a train. With the support and encouragement of the therapist she remains in this environment until her symptoms begin to subside. After the early accompanied sessions she is encouraged to spend time by herself in the feared situation thus demonstrating that, with time, anxiety subsides even in the absence of the therapist. Although this is an effective method of treatment, it will often require the services of a trained professional capable of helping the patient through the very high levels of anxiety frequently generated for several hours at a time during the early stages of treatment. For obvious reasons this may be difficult to arrange in primary care.

Graded Exposure The most suitable approach for a home-based programme initiated in the community is real-life graded exposure (Mathews *et al.* 1977). This is based on the principle that fear becomes less with familiarity and even daunting tasks can be tackled if broken down into small steps. There are many commonplace examples of this approach. The rider is advised to get straight back on his horse after a fall; the new swimmer takes a few strokes, then swims a width and finally a length of the pool.

Often a relative or friend can be enrolled as a co-therapist. The rationale of exposure treatment is explained to both the patient and anyone else who is helping with the programme. The patient, with help, then draws up a list of all the situations that he finds in any way a problem and these are then arranged as a hierarchy in order of difficulty — see Table. 5.4.

The hierarchy is then used to draw up a comparable list of clearly defined goals starting from the least worrying and rising to the most

Table 5.4: Agoraphobia Hierarchy (unmixed)

Neutral Situation: At home in front of TV
 1. Preparing to post a letter
 2. Going to the letter box (50m) with husband
 3. Going to small corner shop with husband
 4. Letter box without husband
 5. Supermarket with husband on Monday
 6. Supermarket alone on a Monday
 7. At supermarket check-out with husband, three people waiting
 8. At supermarket check-out with husband on busy night with queue
 9. At supermarket on a quiet day alone
10. Taking the bus to shop in big supermarket in a nearby town

threatening. These items are then tackled in order, by means of regular daily practice with the help of a relative if possible. Anxiety is measured by means of a fear diary in which the patient records the degree of disturbance each item causes on a rating scale from 0 = absent to 100 = the most anxious you could ever be. Each item may have to be repeated many times before symptoms decrease sufficiently to move on to the next item. Eventually in this way the top of the hierarchy is reached.

If an item proves too difficult there can be either a return to re-practise the previous item or, often more profitably, the step between the two lines is sub-divided so that smaller intermediate grades can be tackled. It will be evident that, on the hierarchy example given, there are a number of potential intermediate steps should these be required. As soon as reasonable progress has been made the patient is encouraged to practise freely experiencing a range of situations of comparable difficulty to those already mastered. In this way her whole repertory of behaviour is increased and the gains made are thus consolidated. Daily practice of both current and mastered items is important in order to avoid regression and discouragement. This is a very suitable approach for the general practitioner whose main task is to plan the extensive between-session tasks, help with setbacks and motivate and encourage the patient.

Social Phobias. These demonstrate some of the features of agoraphobia and a clear distinction may not always be possible. By and large the social phobic's problems revolve round fears such as 'people are looking at me' or 'I shall make a fool of myself' rather than the overwhelming fear of crowds or public situations in themselves. When the fear is explored in more detail, often worry about vomiting, trembling or spilling food or drink is prominent. An example of a hierarchy of a social phobic is shown in Table 5.5.

The fear(s) may have originated in a single embarrassing or disturbing incident. Often, however, the sufferer has avoided social situations for so long that he has no idea if in reality problems would occur or not. Social phobias may occur at any age but most commonly develop in young adults and, unlike agoraphobia which for reasons of traditional gender roles is a mainly female problem, both sexes are equally represented. Extreme shyness or phobia of social contact may remain hidden until a change of circumstances brings it to the fore. An example was the insurance executive of 32

Table 5.5: Social Phobia Hierarchy

1. Getting a sandwich to take away from a snack-bar
2. Having a drink in a quiet pub
3. Having a drink in a busy pub
4. A pub meal
5. Going out motor racing, meeting with friends
6. A sit-down Chinese meal
7. A meal in a London restaurant
8. A formal business dinner with speeches (by others)
9. A formal business dinner with patient giving a vote of thanks

with a love of cricket who coped fairly well until his promotion within the firm meant that he had to attend boardroom lunches. He began to avoid these, to his professional disadvantage, but only sought advice when an important client, knowing his love of cricket, invited him to lunch at Lord's Cricket Ground. It is apparent that many sufferers are bewildered by their symptoms and do not know where to turn for advice. Many will, however, present to their GP eventually, often having first rearranged their symptoms into a form which they think will provide a more acceptable 'ticket of entry'.

As with other phobias, treatment depends largely on rebuilding confidence by exposure to a series of graded situations derived from the hierarchy. In addition, it is essential to see that the patient actually possesses the resources required to cope with the various social situations. If these are lacking, social skills training (see Chapter 6) may be needed before graded exposure can succeed. Equally, if the patient feels that he is socially unacceptable because of his physical appearance this will have to be considered separately.

In addition some time can be spent on helping the patient to cope with the situation in spite of anxiety. Various techniques are employed including cued relaxation of the head and neck or part of the body where he feels tension, and controlling breathing. Imagery training, in which he sees himself coping or having coped successfully with the situation, and distraction by concentrating on an aspect of his surroundings are also useful. Many of these techniques have been described when general anxiety was considered.

Hypochondriacal Fears. Phobias of vomiting or being unable to swallow may constitute part of a social phobia or may exist in isolation. The principles of management are the same and menu control, photographs, audio or video tapes or role play of vomiting will be used to create a step-by-step approach to overcome the problem. It may also be helpful to use specifically adapted techniques such as the scheduling of quantities of food, timing of eating and biofeedback-aided relaxation of throat muscles.

General practitioners will need no introduction to the patient with phobic fears of cancer or venereal disease. Michael Balint (1974) introduced us to the concept of the drug 'doctor' and these are the addicts. Avoidance is impossible as the problem is felt to lie within the patient himself and perpetual reassurance from relatives, GPs, specialists and a variety of alternative practitioners produces only very temporary improvement. The GP is in a unique position to deal with this problem to his own relief as well as the patient's. Specialists will often inadvertently reinforce the problem by expressing apparent surprise and concern that they find nothing wrong *within their speciality* thereby implying, at least to a phobic patient, that there may be some grave defect elsewhere.

A proper understanding of the patient's own perception of his problem and an agreed realistic assessment of the chances of the feared medical condition actually occurring are essential. The management then revolves round getting the patient to understand as much as possible about the feared illness by reading articles, looking at pictures and in some cases reading medical textbooks. Once he has a clear and boring understanding of the real, as opposed to the fantasy, illness the importance of living with realistic uncertainty is encouraged and reassurance from all sources is withdrawn. A useful device is to draw up a schedule of increasingly infrequent visits to the surgery. When scheduled visits are made the doctor is warm and welcoming and congratulates the patient warmly on his progress. Unscheduled visits are treated much more coolly with attention devoted to doing the minimum to insure that no unrelated clinical condition has arisen. It is usually fairly easy to detect a problem which requires treatment aside from the phobia and, surprisingly, patients seldom have difficulty in understanding the 'rules of the game'. This is another of the many problems where an early understanding of the real nature of the condition can prevent an ingrained, long-standing chronic situation from developing. (See also section on obsessions.)

Specific Phobias. Fear of blood, wounds, injections and dental treatment are amongst the single object phobias which have particular medical relevance. Single animal, object or situation fears are extremely common and indeed it is probable, at least in childhood, that all of us are affected to some degree. Many of these are not a problem, as avoidance causes no disability, or such a minor problem as not to warrant behavioural treatment beyond brief explanatory counselling. It seems more sensible to treat a postman who experiences anxiety once a year when he gets on the plane for his annual holiday with a small dose of diazepam rather than a behavioural programme. If, however, the flying phobic is an oil company worker who must take the helicopter to an offshore rig twice a week, then desensitisation is fully worthwhile. In this latter case it is probable that an element of desensitisation in imagination would have to be used as it is difficult to manipulate real-life exposure to graded flying situations. It is important to incorporate as much real-life practice as is feasible and tapes and slides (some of which are available commercially — see note at end of chapter) can be used to fill some of the gaps.

Other single phobias are managed by exposure using such materials as are available and the design of these programmes can be a fascinating exercise in resourcefulness. The more frequent and the longer the exposure trials, the better and quicker are the results. Finally it should be emphasised that much of these programmes can be undertaken as homework assignments with very limited person-to-person contact, thus improving the patient's own sense of control over his problem and increasing the programme's suitability for primary care use. More time than the standard consultation may be needed at assessment but after that the therapist has only to monitor progress and help surmount difficulties and set-backs.

Sleep Disorders in Adults

Disordered sleep is so often a feature of anxiety-based conditions that it seems logical to deal with it at this point although it may equally reasonably be classified as a habit problem. Sleeping difficulties of children present a number of different features and are considered in Chapter 12.

Assessment. Medically, insomnia has frequently been regarded in the past as a single disorder with a single treatment — hypnotics. In recent years it has been realised that there are many different elements to insomnia and many associated problems, and that hypnotics often create more problems than they solve.

An important step in assessment is to discover whether the lack of sleep is a relatively isolated problem, possibly learnt by the gradual adoption of faulty habits, or whether it is a symptom of an underlying disorder such as anxiety, which may have to be treated first and to some extent separately. Once associated difficulties have been adequately considered an assessment is made of the sleep pattern itself. This should reveal:

(1) The time of going to bed, the time of going to sleep and how the latent period between the two is occupied.
(2) The number, time and length of middle-night waking periods and how these are occupied.
(3) The time of final waking in the morning.

It is also important to find out the patient's idea of what constitutes a 'good night's sleep' and what ill-effects he expects if he is deprived of it. All of this information can be obtained at interview and may be confirmed by a baseline record chart recording these details from night to night over a week or a fortnight. This method of recording may present some practical difficulties — it is, for example, sometimes a problem to record the exact moment you fall asleep — but worthwhile records are usually obtained and the information they contain often surprises the sufferer. A patient who believes quite genuinely that he doesn't sleep a wink is often astonished when his record shows relatively minor periods of night waking. This sort of information may in itself promote change by relieving anxiety attached to the problem and increasing the patient's sense of control over it.

Management. This is tailored to the type of problem revealed by the assessment, but a number of techniques are frequently used. These can be incorporated in a short patient information sheet (q.v.). The elements of this sheet are:

(1) Information — that sleep requirements often diminish (sometimes dramatically) with age and that four hours per night may be quite sufficient for the older person
(2) Reassurance — that lack of sleep in itself, unless enforced, seldom causes ill effects
(3) Adjustment of sleeping goals — going to bed later and being prepared to get up early and start other activities

(4) Stimulus control — ensuring that bed is only a place for sleeping (and, if appropriate, sex which of course itself aids relaxation and sleep) and not for eating, watching TV or coping with tomorrow's problems

(5) Preparing for periods of insomnia — making sure there is a warm, comfortable place with perhaps a kettle, teapot and paperback book to get up to during the night.

One patient found that watching a horror video promoted sleep and although this would appear to be somewhat unusual, it does emphasise the point that individual variations have to be considered and that the programme cannot be slavishly applied to everyone. Commonly, reading in bed will promote somnolence in some people but wakefulness in others.

The leaflet we use for patients is as follows:

HELP WITH SLEEPING PROBLEMS

Many people come to their doctor complaining of being unable to sleep. They assume that they may become ill if they do not get enough sleep. In fact this is unlikely to happen as the body will take all the sleep it needs unless this is forcibly prevented. The amount of sleep people require varies enormously and usually gets less as they get older. A person who had ten hours a night at 20 may require five or less at 60. Some people fear that they will not be able to perform as well if they do not get a certain amount of sleep. This fear also is usually groundless.

It is possible to compare the amount of sleep you have had with your performance and the way you feel the following day by keeping a record as below:

Date	Hours of sleep	Activities	Competence	Alertness
		(day after)	0–10	0–10

From this you can draw your own conclusions as to whether your present pattern is harmful.

If you decide to try and increase the amount of sleep that you are getting, it is important to make sure that you are prepared for sleeping and that being in bed is linked in your mind only with sleeping not with other preoccupations. Usually excitement or hectic activity will prevent sleep and calm and relaxation help in getting off but this also varies a lot from person to person — for example, reading keeps some awake and sends others to sleep. It is important therefore to study and get to know your own pattern. The following suggestions may be helpful.

If you have Difficulty in Getting to Sleep:

(1) Go to bed only when sleepy and do not try to get more sleep by going to bed early.
(2) Do not read, watch TV or eat in bed unless you are sure, from past experience, that these activities help you to get to sleep.
(3) When in bed try to get all your muscles as relaxed as you can. Taped or written instructions may help this.
(4) Do not think about getting to sleep or worry about the day's activities. Try instead to think about pleasant events or places.
(5) If you cannot find some pleasant thoughts at that moment listen to any relaxing sound from outside the house — birds, people or distant traffic.
(6) If you are unable to get to sleep after 10 minutes, get up immediately and do something different such as reading or going into a different room. Return to bed only when sleepy.
(7) Set your alarm and get up at the same time each morning regardless of how much sleep you received during the night.
(8) Do not take a nap during the day.

If you wake During the Night

(1) Once you are fully awake do not lie in bed worrying about daily problems and not sleeping but get up.
(2) Go to a different room, make a drink if you feel like it, and sit comfortably in a chair reading a book or a magazine. (It is often worthwhile to prepare a chair with a reading lamp, rug if necessary or heater and a suitable paperback the night before.)
(3) Only return to sleep when you feel sleepy. When in bed relax and think of pleasant events or places.
(4) If sleep does not come in ten minutes, return to the chair and repeat the cycle.

REMEMBER THAT WORRYING ABOUT NOT SLEEPING IS MUCH MORE TIRING THAT JUST BEING AWAKE

Tranquilliser Withdrawal

Associated with anxiety and sleep difficulties, one major problem which presents regularly is that of dependence on tranquillisers and sleeping pills. Current adverse publicity has made many people aware of the dangers of regular consumption of these drugs. Often, however, awareness has come too late when dependency has already developed, sometimes after relatively short-term use for acute difficulties.

Self-help groups in the community such as Tranx, where they exist, are excellent in providing group support. In other cases withdrawal may be attempted by gradual dose reduction week-by-week over a predetermined number of weeks. It is usual to change short-acting benzodiazepines to equivalent dosage of the longer half-life varieties before beginning to cut down. Some reports suggest the use of beta blockers to aid symptom control during withdrawal but this is not as yet clearly supported by research.

The type and duration of withdrawal symptoms vary enormously from patient to patient but they can undoubtedly be extremely persistent and severe over several months (Lister and File 1984). Treatment is aimed at reducing anxiety. This may stem both from the original problem or personality trait and from fear of the extent and intensity of the withdrawal symptoms. The latter often mimic other anxiety symptoms quite closely and may be minimised by a range of the techniques described previously under anxiety management. In some cases however patients may also need help just to 'live with' the symptoms for a time and find ways to adjust their lives to make them easier during the period of withdrawal. Commonly, advice will also be required to help with insomnia, panic attacks, perceptual disturbances and a number of other particular problems which may occur at this time.

Cognitive methods may be helpful in enabling the patient to re-attribute symptoms to withdrawal rather than impending breakdown or death. Symptoms are monitored for frequency and intensity and as far as possible positive coping strategies are advised which can be applied to each symptom as soon as it occurs.

Several other points are important. It has been suggested that alcohol, even in small amounts, may exacerbate symptoms and that sudden falls in blood sugar may prove a problem at this time so that the importance of regular eating should be stressed. A careful balance needs to be struck between the suggesting of too many symptoms and failing generally to prepare the patient so that he may again resort to medication when caught unawares by an unexpected event such as perceptual disturbance.

Obsessive Ruminations and Compulsive Rituals

Elements of obsessionality and the occasional compulsive ritual are common in daily life — most people can remember avoiding the cracks in the paving stones when out walking as small children. Ruminations and obsessions can however become extremely disabling. Recurring ideas of a distressing kind can prevent logical thought and most of the day can be taken up with rituals involving washing and checking. Relatives and friends, whilst complaining of the disabling nature of the rituals, often cooperate in making them possible. The parents of a patient obsessed with ideas of contamination were prepared to see the furniture removed wholesale from their sitting room whilst the patient sat in splendid isolation on a metal-framed deck chair placed on a carpet of old newspapers. One can only speculate that a more spirited defence of their domestic rights by the parents in the early stages might have materially altered this unfortunate young man's intractable clinical course.

Obsessions and compulsions are not commonly seen in primary care and if fully developed will require more resources than are usually available. Early referral to a unit specialising in this work is often indicated. Excellent results are obtainable using response prevention programmes (Marks 1975). The ritual situations are sought out by the patient in the company of a therapist who assists him in resisting the urge and at the same time models appropriate behaviour. Milder cases can be treated in primary care simply by instructing the patient to resist his ritualising. The rationale of all response prevention approaches is that intrusive thoughts produce anxiety which is then relieved temporarily by the ritual. If the urge to ritualise is resisted the anxiety eventually diminishes (cf. flooding treatment for phobias described earlier).

The hypochondriacal patient who consults frequently in general practice may be a particular type of obsessive-compulsive. His compulsion is to seek and obtain reassurance but this of course produces only temporary relief and he is soon back. The treatment plan is to identify the real problem (i.e. the obsession rather than the symptoms) and then apply response prevention by withholding reassurance. This is discussed with the patient and if his cooperation is obtained a series of appointments are made at fixed intervals to discuss his progress in managing his disturbing thought, *not* to discuss his symptoms. Casual attendances contingent on symptoms are treated with the minimum attention compatible with safety. Referral to diverse specialists must also be resisted by both doctor and patient as this will only reinforce the compulsive behaviour. (See also Hypochondriacal Fears).

Where ruminations occur without compulsive behaviour treatment may be by either:

(1) Thought stopping. The patient interrupts the circular thought pattern by shouting 'stop' and substituting a pleasant scene or thought. This is first done with therapist help, then out loud by the patient and finally by the patient silently to himself.

(2) Habituation Training. The patient tries repeatedly to imagine the disturbing image or thought for as long as possible until it fades. Measurement is taken of the duration and intensity of the thoughts within the session and the frequency, intensity and duration of thoughts between sessions. With satisfactory progress the thoughts become less intense and less troublesome.

First Aid in Anxiety

First aid advice for the anxious patient is a frequent requirement in general practice. Often the patient's attempt at coping with anxiety symptoms consists of trying to pretend that they don't exist, pushing them out of their mind and increasing the often already frantic pace of their daily life. Such a course is doomed to disaster as, of course, the symptoms do exist and hurry is often already part of the problem. At the first interview simple advice to accept symptoms at face value, try consciously to slow down, make an effort to look at natural surroundings and plan the day ahead with a timetable may give immediate relief and be all that is necessary in the mild, transient case. As anxiety increases, once a certain point is reached efficiency decreases. The sufferer may counter this effect by even more effort and his alarm at his lack of success may initiate an anxiety cycle. A simple simile such as that of mental wheelspin may serve to explain this process and enable the sufferer to gain sufficient confidence to cope with this problem from his own resources after a few minutes' discussion.

Biofeedback in Anxiety

It is unlikely that many primary care teams will be able or wish to afford extensive biofeedback equipment. There are, however, a number of relatively inexpensive machines on the market which can aid relaxation training by measuring the galvanic skin response (GSR). Typically they provide an auditory (sometimes also visual) signal which gets lower in frequency and pitch as the patient relaxes and the GSR falls. For many patients simply teaching relaxation provides as good results but these instruments do have a place for those who are unconvinced of the value of relaxation, find it difficult to achieve or are simply impressed by high-tech machinery. The current cost starts from under £100 and a good range can be supplied by Aleph-One Ltd, Cambridge. (See end of chapter.)

Electro-myographic feedback is useful where a feature of the problem is contraction or pain in one muscle or muscle group. Some of the evidence from research is conflicting but promising clinical results have been obtained from this equipment, treating several conditions. These include stress-related recurrent sore throats, tension headaches and backache where muscle tension is a contributory cause. Equipment is also obtainable from a number of suppliers including Aleph-One (see end of chapter) but is more expensive than GSR instruments.

Management of Panic Attacks

By their very nature panic attacks occur suddenly and often unexpectedly and the GP will usually be the first on the scene. His explanation and emergency management of the attack, particularly if it is the first of its kind, may have a lasting and important effect on the subsequent course of the problem. If he grunts and gives intramuscular diazepam the patient cannot be blamed for thinking that he has an inexplicable and probably serious condition which will only respond to potent medication. Whatever the hour of the night it is essential to get an exact description of the symptoms, details of any recent stressful circumstances and the patient's own ideas about the cause of his problems. Fears of suffocation, heart attacks and strokes often figure largely and any management is likely to prove ineffective unless such fears are discovered and discussed. An adequate physical examination is also necessary as much as an anxiolytic as to exclude any physical cause for the problem. The attack commonly consists of an intense feeling of fright or impending doom which is associated with a wide range of physical sensations mostly mediated by the autonomic nervous system. These physical feelings can be misinterpreted so that the patient may fear he is going to die in an unspecified way, go mad or make a fool of himself. The physical symptoms most frequently found are, dizziness, giddiness, palpitations, numbness, paraesthesia of the hands, feet and round the mouth, nausea, breathlessness or a sensation of a band round the chest.

In panic attacks the patients invariably misinterpret their sensations and regard them as being much more serious than they are. The aim of treatment is to help the patient re-attribute their sensations to innocuous causes.

The sensations closely resemble the list of effects of hyperventilation. There is now considerable evidence (Clark *et al.* 1985) that in many cases hyperventilation plays a key role in panic attacks. A careful description of the type and frequency of the attacks will often confirm that this is likely to be the case and in the recurrent problem this information is supplemented by a Panic Attack Diary which records the frequency and type of attack.

Treatment. This is directed (i) towards explaining the nature of hyperventilation and panic attacks and seeing that the symptoms are correctly attributed and (ii) to teaching controlled respiration as a method of managing attacks. The management takes place in four phases:

(1) Interview and baseline diary record;
(2) Experimental voluntary hyperventilation. The patient is asked to overbreathe for about two minutes. He is then asked to concentrate on and describe his physical symptoms. (A symptom rating scale is available in Clark and Hemsley 1982). It is important that during the introspection period the patient is asked to stand up as some symptoms e.g. 'jelly legs' may occur only on standing. The symptoms may then be terminated by re-breathing into a paper bag. The patient is then asked to rate the similarity of his symptoms during the experiment to those that he experiences during an attack, where 100 = identical and 0 = no similarity, so that the extent to which overbreathing is involved can be gauged.
(3) An explanation is then given, with an information sheet, of how hyperventilation causes panic.
(4) Training in slow, smooth controlled breathing which is incompatible with hyperventilation is then given. Initial training is done with a tape on which 'in-out' breathing instructions are recorded at the rate of eight and twelve breaths per minute (7.5 and 5 seconds per cycle respectively). This is incompatible with hyperventilation. Practice is then continued without the tape. Finally the patient hyperventilates and terminates it by switching to controlled breathing. When he feels confident that he can start to control the panic sensations by using the technique he is encouraged to go into a situation that he has previously avoided, and practise.

The instruction leaflet below is reproduced by kind permission of P. M. Salkovskis and D. M. Clark.

COPING WITH A PANIC ATTACK

During a panic attack you are extremely likely to breathe very fast and/or deeply. This will have the effect of reducing the amount of carbon dioxide you will have in your lungs which will create a lot of unpleasant body sensations which are likely to make you afraid. A vicious circle of fear leading to overbreathing which leads to unpleasant body sensations (faintness, dizziness, tingling, headaches, racing heart, flushes, nausea, chest pain, shakiness, etc.) which cause more fear which leads again to overbreathing and so on, gets established.

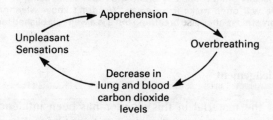

To stop this very nasty process you have to raise the amount of carbon dioxide in your lungs. You can do this in two ways:

(a) If you have a paper bag handy hold it tightly over your nose and mouth so that no air can get to your lungs from outside the bag and breathe the air in the bag for several minutes until you calm down.

(b) If a bag is not handy or it would be embarrassing to use one (say in a supermarket) then you should change your breathing so that you breathe in less air in a given period of time. You can probably do this most easily by slowing down your breathing in small steps. Attempt to breathe in smoothly and slowly and to let your breath out just as slowly. As you slow your breathing down you are bound to increase the depth of each breath somewhat. However try to avoid a very big increase in depth because that would undo the good you have done by slowing down. The ideal you are aiming for is smooth, slow, regular and fairly shallow breathing. If you have managed to slow down for a few seconds but feel out of breath* and a strong urge to take a quick gulp, *don't*. Resist it by swallowing a couple of times, that should get rid of the urge; if it doesn't then go ahead, take a gulp BUT once you've let the air in HOLD IT for about five seconds and then let it out SLOWLY. If you can hold a gulp for a few seconds you prevent it from lowering your carbon dioxide levels.

To sum up, breathe in and out as slowly and evenly as you can and avoid any big increase in depth as you do so.

To help yourself slow down you could:

(a) remember how you breathed with the tape and try to do that;

(b) count to yourself while breathing. To start off with you might say 'one thousand' to yourself while breathing in and 'two thousand' while breathing out so your breathing would be

in	out	in	out
one thousand	two thousand	one thousand	two thousand

and soon you might be able to say more to yourself while breathing in and out and so take longer doing it. For example:

in	out
one thousand, two thousand	three thousand, four thousand
in	out
one thousand, two thousand	three thousand, four thousand

---

* The feeling of being out of breath that people sometimes get when anxious is paradoxically often caused by breathing too much. Taking in *less* air for a little while will often make it go away. We don't know why some people become breathless after overbreathing but it is a well established fact that they do.

Acknowledgement

Much of the material in this chapter has been influenced by or derived from the work of The University of Oxford Psychological Treatment Research Unit, the Warneford Hospital, whose help has been invaluable. We are particularly grateful to Gillian Butler, David Clark and Paul Salkovskis who not only allowed many of their ideas to be adapted and used but who made many helpful comments on the draft and to Professor Michael Gelder for his permission to make use of the material.

Appendix 5.1: Deep Muscle Relaxation

The technique described here is adapted from the Jacobson method. It is the one most commonly used by behaviour therapists and depends on the alternative tensing and relaxing of various muscle groups with emphasis on learning to discriminate between the two. With practice, progressively deeper relaxation of any or all muscle groups can be produced at will.

The technique is most effective when taught by an instructor in person either to individuals or groups, followed by practice using a tape recording made at the live session. Under many circumstances, however, this will prove too time-consuming and commercial or previously prepared tapes or written instructions have to be used.

(See 'Books for Patients', at the end of this chapter.)

The subject may use a couch, bed or even the floor but is probably best seated in a comfortable reclining chair. Uninterrupted quiet is essential. Most instructors develop their own routine and there are small variations in order and wording. The following is given as an example:

Anxiety and stress are often associated with physically tense muscles although you do not always realise that your muscles are tense. The series of exercises that we are going to do will help you to distinguish between tension and relaxation in the muscles and teach you how to relax the tension away at will. We will work through the various groups, first tensing them then relaxing them at the key word 'Relax'. We will start with the right hand and arm. Make a tight fist and, bending the elbow, coil the forearm up to the shoulder. Get the muscles of the forearm and upper arm as tight as you can and notice the feeling of tension in them. When they are as tight as possible begin to uncoil the arm from the shoulder allowing the forearm to rest beside you with the fist open, fingers and palms downwards and, to the key word 'Relax', allow the last little bit of tension to run out of the fingertips. (Pause 15 seconds) I now want you to make a fist again and coil the forearm and arm up to the shoulder trying to get all the muscles a little firmer and a little more tense than last time. When you have got everything as tight as you possibly can, let the arm uncoil again noticing how different the relaxed muscles feel from the tension of a moment before. Try to relax the arms, (Pause 5 seconds) forearms, (Pause 5 seconds) and fingers a little more than the last time. Try to find that last little bit of tension and release it.

A similar double sequence of tension and relaxation is then used with the following muscle groups in turn:

Left Arm. This is really just a repeat of the right arm. It is included for the sake of symmetry and to provide further practice of the general principles with another easy muscle group.

Shoulders and Back of Neck. The tension phase is achieved by pulling the neck back into extension and pulling the shoulders up so that they press firmly into the neck on either side. Relaxation allows the neck to come forward and the shoulders to fall, releasing the tension. This latter part of the sequence can be taught as a single manoeuvre to be used at the cue of anxious sensations in public as it is invisible to other people present. The instruction 'When you begin to feel tense just concentrate on letting your shoulders drop' is often found to be helpful. Neck tension is a specific problem in a number of painful conditions and here also the technique is of use.

Forehead and Eyes. This is the most important group for the control of tension headaches. The eyebrows are pulled down into a deep frown and the eyes screwed tightly shut. The forehead is then allowed to smooth out and the eyes relax and open. Attention is drawn to the tingling 'leathery' feeling of the frontalis areas as the muscle relaxes.

Jaw and tongue. The big masseter muscles at the side of the jaw are clamped tightly and the tongue firmly pressed against the roof of the mouth. Relaxation consists of unclenching the jaw and letting it fall slightly open whilst at the same time the tongue falls loosely down from the roof of the mouth.

Muscles at the Front of the Neck. The strap muscles are tensed to bring the chin down pressing tightly into the sternal notch. As the muscles relax the chin comes forward and up.

Chest and Breathing. This is of great importance in the control of hyperventilation and the emergency management of panic attacks. A deep breath is taken which is then forced out against a fixed diaphragm and closed throat producing a feeling of pressure in the ribs and intercostal muscles. The patient is asked to note how the muscles feel and then gradually let the breath go allowing the chest muscles to relax and a pattern of slow, shallow, rhythmic, even breathing to take over. (See Instruction Sheet for panic attacks, p. 81). These four descriptive words can be used as key words that the patient remembers when using the sequence in future. It should be added that some instructions ask the subject to take deep breaths but except at the beginning of the sequence this has no value and may make the physical consequence of hyperventilation worse by increasing respiratory alkalosis.

Back and Buttocks. The tension phase consists of pulling together the shoulders and the buttocks and arching the back. The simile of a bridge between two pillars is useful to give the patient the idea. After relaxation the whole body rests completely heavy on the chair or couch 'like a lump of lead' whilst the muscles of the shoulders and back are checked to release the last bit of tension.

Stomach. The stomach muscles are pulled tight producing a great feeling of tautness round the umbilicus 'as if somebody heavy was about to step on your stomach'. As the muscles are relaxed the sensation of slow, shallow, rhythmic, even breathing takes over again but this time concentration is on how the stomach muscles move in response to this.

Thighs, Legs and Feet. Unless there are special reasons such as local cramps, these are generally taken together. In tension the knees are pushed hard down in extension and the ankles and toes pushed out in full plantar flexion 'like trying to reach a point just out of reach beyond the toes'. The sensation of tightness in the thighs, calves and toes is noted. With relaxation the joints ease slightly into flexion and the knees fall slightly apart. Once more attention is drawn to the difference in the physical feeling of the two phases.

After the completion of the sequence of muscle groups, the patient is asked to check each in turn to make sure it is completely relaxed. This is followed by a pause of about one minute to enable the full feeling of complete relaxation to be appreciated and savoured. In order to allow normal activities to be resumed without a sudden jar a backward count from five is usually incorporated to end the programme. The complete sequence takes just over 30 minutes and can be recorded on one side of a C90 cassette tape.

The phrases 'let it go a little bit further' and 'let the last little bit of tension flow out of the muscles' are usually used frequently during the sequence as they can be recalled more easily later when the patient is practising by himself. In the same way it is important to incorporate a key word such as 'relax' or 'calm' which can be remembered as a cue.

Normally the complete programme is taught initially but subsequently this is modified, when applied in practice, by omitting the tension phase and selecting parts which are most practical and useful in real life situations. For example, whereas the whole programme could not be used in a check-out queue, the breathing exercises and the relaxation phase of the head and neck exercises are perfectly feasible.

Often some form of relaxing imagery, a pleasant scene or idea, is included in the beginning or end of the programme. This is useful but the image should be selected according to the patient's own individual requirements so no suggestion has been included here.

References

Balint, M. (1974) *The Doctor, his Patient and the Illness*, London, Pitman

Beck, A. T. and Emery, G. (1985) *Anxiety Disorders and Phobias*, New York, Basic Books.

Burns, L. E. and Thorpe, G. L. (1977) 'The epidemiology of fears and phobias with particular reference to the national survey of agoraphobics', *Journal of International Medical Research, 5*, 1–7

Clark, D. M. and Hemsley, D. R. (1982) 'Effects of hyperventilation: individual variability and its relation to personality', *Journal of Behaviour Therapy and Experimental Psychiatry, 13*, 41–7

Clark, D. M., Salkovskis, P. M. and Chalkley, A. J. (1985) 'Respiratory control as a treatment for panic attacks', *Journal of Behavior Therapy and Experimental Psychiatry, 16*, 23–30

Lister, R. G. and File, S. E. (1984) 'The nature of lorazepam-induced amnesia, *Psychopharmacology, 83*, 183–7

Marks, I. M. (1975) 'Behavioural treatments of phobic and obsessive compulsive disorders: A critical appraisal' in R. Hersen *et al.* (eds), *Progress in Behavior Therapy*, New York, Academic Press

Mathews, A. M., Teasdale, J., Munby, J., Johnston, D. and Shaw, P. (1977) 'A home-based treatment programme for agoraphobia', *Behavior Therapy, 8*, 915–24

Robson, M. H., France, R. and Bland, M. (1984) 'Clinical psychologist in primary care: controlled clinical and economic evaluation', *British Medical Journal, 288*, 1805–8

Skegg, D. C. G., Doll, R. and Perry, J. (1977) 'Use of medicines in general practice', *British Medical Journal, 1*, 1561–3

Recommended for Further Reading

Beck, A. T. and Emery, G. (1985) *Anxiety Disorders and Phobias*, New York, Basic Books

Rachman, S. J. (1980) *Fear and Courage*, San Francisco, W. H. Freeman

Mathews, A. M., Gelder, M. H. and Johnston, D. W. (1981) *Agoraphobia — Nature and Treatment*, London and New York, Tavistock Publications

Books for Patients

Coleman, V. *Life Without Tranquillisers*, Judy Piatkins (Publishers) Ltd

Madders, J. *Stress and Relaxation* (with cassette *Self Help Relaxation*) obtainable from Aleph One Ltd., The Old Court House, Cambridge, CB5 9BA, UK

Marks, I. M. (1978) *Living with Fear*, New York, McGraw Hill
The Flier's Handbook (with cassettes *Fly without Fear* and *Relax and Enjoy It*) also
    obtainable from Aleph One (see above)
Melville, J. (1984) *The Tranquilliser Trap and How to Get Out of It*, London, Fontana
Mills, J. W. (1982) *Coping with Stress*, New York, John Wiley
Weeks, C. (1962) *Self-help for Your Nerves*, London, Angus and Robertson

Relaxation and stress control tapes together with Relaxometers, EMG equipment
and other biofeedback apparatus can be obtained from: Aleph One, The Old Court
House, High Street, Bottisham, Cambridge, CB5 9BA, UK

6 INTERPERSONAL PROBLEMS

This category covers the more intimate and social sides of interpersonal skills. Problems related to work will be dealt with later, although there will be some overlap. Social, marital and psychosexual problems will be considered in turn.

Social Skills

Social skills are the component techniques of everyday behaviour between people in society (Argyle 1967). In the ordinary way these are acquired by gradual learning involving trial and error within family, school or leisure activities. Equally if there are any problems most of these areas of life may be affected, leading to a reduction in social reinforcement and thus loss of confidence. Failure to use effective social skills may be because there has never been an opportunity to learn them or because some other factor such as shyness or depression gets in the way. In other words there may be a *skills deficit* or a *performance deficit*.

The behavioural interview has to estimate the type and proportion of these deficits in any individual problems. Detailed information is obtained about the current situations being avoided or causing problems, the skills lacking and the factors such as illness or isolation which may account for that lack. There are a huge number of cultural, social and personal variables which must be taken into account. There are considerable cultural differences. Assertive behaviour in one country may seem aggressive or submissive in another.

Performance Deficits

A wide variety of co-existing problems may hinder social performance. Depression, obsessionality and most forms of anxiety are obvious examples. Wider problems like physical and mental handicap and illness will play a part. The most frequent difficulty is, however, anxiety about the social situation itself which is based on the fear of making a fool of oneself in front of other people (negative social evaluation). This has been discussed earlier, in Chapter 5. In the social skills context, a useful component of treatment is to help the patient divide the feared tasks into manageable components which are then tackled in a graded approach. For example, a patient is afraid to ask a friend for coffee as she thinks she may not be able to end the visit if she becomes too panicky. It may be helpful first to invite the visitor when there is a quick natural end to the time available such as having to fetch a child from playgroup in half an hour's time.

When setting goals for homework practice it is important to make tasks as easy as possible in order to ensure success. Patients may need reassuring that this is not 'cheating'. For example, someone who becomes anxious when eating with other people in public might first try going into the canteen and buying a sandwich and a carton of drink so that he can walk out at any time. Once he becomes more confident he can order a full meal, first perhaps by himself and then with friends.

Skills Deficits

The appropriate behaviours in various situations may never have been learnt perhaps because of illness or a particularly isolated upbringing. Training can be provided in both an individual and a group setting. Group settings have the advantage that they provide a ready-made social situation for role-play and modelling. Although they have sometimes been used successfully, they are rather cumbersome to set up in primary care and require an enthusiastic leader with the necessary skill and time. The involvement of GPs and others in this field may be limited to items of individual advice and to referral for more detailed training to local Departments of Clinical Psychology who often organise groups and workshops. In order to do either of these it is necessary to have a knowledge of the content of social skills training to see where it fits into the management of problems presented in the surgery. The outline given below is insufficient to enable someone to lead a group and those interested in doing so are advised to read further (Falloon *et al.* 1974; Trower *et al.* 1978) and attend practical training sessions or workshops.

Outline of Social Skills Training Group

Before accepting a patient as a group member an assessment interview should be carried out on an individual basis in order to estimate his or her needs and suitability for membership. It is the responsibility of leaders to remember individual needs once the group gets going and to fit these as far as possible into the working framework. A typical group programme might include:

(1) *Early Sessions.* The rationale is explained by demonstrating that *assertive* behaviour includes:

(i)   the ability to express one's own wishes and to strive to achieve them (more use of 'I');
(ii) respect for one's own rights and at the same time the rights of others;
(iii) by this means getting positive responses from others and avoiding being punished and ignored (positive and negative reinforcement).

Aggressive and *servile* behaviours on the other hand invite punishment or extinction. These points are clarified by modelling and role-play in the session and home work practice and recording between sessions. Work on *dressing, grooming, presentation* and *posture* is also included as appropriate.

The influence of age, sex, status, the type of occasion (e.g. diplomatic ball vs teenage disco), number of people present, and nature of the transaction (e.g. complaint about shoddy goods or asking for a date) and the way that they influence appropriateness are discussed.

The same format of modelling, role-play and homework is then applied.

(2) *Non-verbal communication* including the influence of personal space (i.e. the comfortable distance to engage in any activity with another person), facial expression, smiling, eye contact and gestures.

(3) *Vocal characteristics* ('How to say it') involving tone of voice, volume, emphasis, clarity, pace, fluency and pitch and the information these give us about the state of the communicator (e.g. anxiety or diffidence) and the importance of the communication.

(4) *Initiating, continuing and terminating conversations* including suitable opening and closure phrases and also the importance of listening, relaxing, turn-taking and allowing silences.

(5) *Accepting, refusing and asking* in such a manner as to get the desired response, e.g. explaining that you can't go out that evening but you would still like to see the person again, etc.

(6) *Losing arguments and accepting other people's point of view* without being aggressive or losing one's dignity as a person.

(7) *Intimate situations*, including how to give and accept compliments graciously; the importance of touching and closeness, tone of voice and remembering things (e.g. birthdays) that are important to the other person; how to give and accept presents and services.

(8) *Complaints* both in the home and in the world outside involve the same rules. These include being clear, not allowing the conversation to generalise onto other irrelevant issues, not getting angry and making it possible for an agreed solution to evolve.

The *format of the group session* may be as follows:

(1) Introductions if necessary and general report of the week including any positive events
(2) Report on homework
(3) General theoretical points raised from homework and in preparation for the exercises
(4) Modelling and role-play exercises
(5) Setting of homework

After four to six sessions less time is spent on general exercises and more may be devoted to role-playing individual members' problems. At this time blocks to treatment may be uncovered in the form of individual negative self-statements and thoughts which were not apparent at the initial interview. These can then be discussed and solutions sought.

Without elaborate group work some of these points can be discussed or role-played in the surgery. One patient was greeted by his almost estranged wife with the unexpected suggestion that they went out for a drink together. He replied 'What's come over you all of a sudden?' and a row ensued. At a brief consultation he was able to find positive alternative responses. The use of these, to his delight, later greatly improved the relationship.

Marital Therapy

Marital problems are usually presented in the surgery by one partner often in connection with other, ostensibly more acceptable 'medical' symptoms. Ideally it is best to see the other partner alone in a second consultation in order to maintain the balance and attempt to assess 'secret factors' such as sexual affairs. It may be a necessary part of therapy to encourage honesty between partners and it is, of course, important to discover if either partner is so involved elsewhere that they have no intention of continuing with the marriage. Other typical 'secrets' may include jealousy, dislike of stepchildren, venereal disease, incest and other 'skeletons in the cupboard'.

Once these initial interviews are complete a decision can be taken with both partners about further treatment. It can be explained to the couple that a relationship such as a marriage may develop problems in itself which are almost independent of the individual people involved. Most of us can recall marriages where both partners are charming agreeable people with everybody, except their husband or wife. In such cases it is the relationship that needs the attention and there is no such thing as a sick or guilty party. The state of a relationship is dependent on what is said and done in it. Thus actions and words will receive a major part of the attention although additional factors such as thinking and attitude blocks may also be important and need help.

If the couple accept this model, two further questions are helpful. First, are both prepared to commit themselves to trying to make the relationship work? Second, are both prepared to change in order to achieve this? It may seem rather unfair to ask questions at this early stage but even if the patients' own awareness of the factors maintaining the problem is incomplete, it is helpful to get some sort of commitment in each other's presence.

After the decision to continue has been taken, the assessment should include a detailed description in behavioural terms of the incidents which lead to conflict and the partners' expectations of each other. It should also stress the (often forgotten) positive factors in each other and the relationship. Time should be spent on deciding on goals of treatment that are clear and acceptable to both. Once detailed information is obtained about precipitating factors, it may become clear that only one or two aspects of life such as sex or money difficulties are leading to problems. It is useful to find out about what a couple used to do together and trace the development of the problem which is now engulfing both of them.

Often at least one partner is ambivalent about asking for help and a low-key early session may be helpful in making both sides aware of the difficulties. Any changes suggested at the assessment stage should be designed to be non-threatening and to give positive results, to encourage confidence on both sides.

Both partners can be asked to keep independent weekly records of behaviour which they feel has led to unhappiness and rows. They may also note positive behaviours and give a daily satisfaction rating.

A checklist of commonly occurring problem areas in marriage may be of help in making sure that nothing has been left out. This might include:

Sex
Communication
Alcohol, smoking and food
Religion
Free time and holidays
Money
Housing
Friends
Children
Relatives

Intervention Strategies

These are a selection of commonly helpful techniques all or some of which can be applied as appropriate:

Disengagement. Partners are asked to aim to treat each other as friendly flatmates. They may greet each other on arrival and departure, enquire about each other's day, give an idea of when they might expect each other home and whether they might eat together.

Love Days or Evenings. Each partner in turn makes an effort to try and please the other unconditionally. This is useful before dealing with areas of conflict.

Going Out. Planning a night out together — just a walk, drink or local cinema rather than an expensive treat where too much is invested or expected — can be used. Other companionship exercises include planning a perfect week-end or holiday and seeing what each other would like to do. Some of these activities, once discovered, can then perhaps be incorporated in the normal week's timetable.

Using 'I'. This makes needs and wants clear without resorting to hints, double meanings or unfair questions i.e. those with only one permitted answer, e.g. 'Do you mind if we don't go out on Friday — I've got to work late at the office.'

Timetabling. The idea of this is to change the couple's routine at certain times when there is a high probability of conflict. Suggestions should be the result of a discussion of ideas put forward by the couple. The therapist only has to make sure that the ideas are realistic and are expressed in terms that can be clearly translated into precise actions. Some examples might be:

(1) 'Change Sunday lunch' to the evening so that all members of the family can go out in the morning.
(2) Decide to get up 15 minutes earlier in the morning and alter some of the responsibilities. In this way frayed tempers are avoided and duties shared more evenly, possibly getting the children to help.
(3) Have separate bank accounts so each partner can feel in control of their finances, clarifying who pays what.

Role-playing. It can be illuminating for couples to role-play their reception of one another when they meet in the evening. Areas of modification usually become apparent. This technique can also be used to teach or improve basic skills such as asking a favour, making a protest or appreciating something the other has done.

Reverse role-playing, if used with care, can make a partner see how it feels to be in the other's shoes and increase their awareness of which aspects of behaviour to change.

Contracting. Behavioural contracts are like commercial ones in that they express clearly, usually in writing, the duties and rewards of both parties. They can aid clarity, recall and compliance in changing behaviour but, more important, if used properly they are seen to be fair and equitable. The first step is for a grid to be drawn up as follows:

	Increase Desired	*Decrease Desired*
Wife's behaviour	Serving fish	Nagging about leak
(according to husband)	Coming to pub	Going to bed at 9 p.m.
	Wearing low cut dress	

	Increase Desired	*Decrease Desired*
Husband's behaviour	Flowers brought	Socks on floor
(according to wife)	Help with Kevin's bath	Late without 'phoning
	Kiss when arrives home	

Once the grid is complete the actual contract can be agreed. These are of two types:

(1) A quid pro quo contract. This is a straightforward exchange of behaviour. In the example given above serving fish twice weekly might be exchanged for 15 minutes' help at Kevin's bath time. The behaviours are equal and interdependent.

(2) A parallel contract. Each behaviour is treated independently and has its own reward, and sometimes punishment for breach. e.g. Husband phones before being late. Reward: a kiss on arrival. Punishment: supper removed at 7 p.m. on ensuing nights.

Problem-solving Techniques. These are often clearly lacking in troubled marriages. There are three stages: (i) *defining the problem* — this should be clear, specific, unemotional and brief; (ii) *generating solutions* — only one problem is taken at a time but no solution is too ridiculous or way-out to be mentioned; (iii) *selecting a solution* — again it is important to be clear and specific. Who is going to do what, when, where and how often? Some provision for follow-up and monitoring change can also be made.

A useful technique which provides a framework for problem solving is *executive sessions*. The rules are as follows: (i) either partner who has a problem may approach the other and ask for a session; (ii) the second partner fixes a time and place for the session, which must not be unreasonably delayed — a suitable example would be 'in the kitchen at 7 p.m. after the children are in bed'; (iii) at the session the first, convening, partner has ten minutes to put the problem, during which time the responding second partner must listen but not speak; (iv) the second ten minutes gives the responding partner the right to reply, during which time the convenor must listen but may not speak; (v) the final ten minutes is spent generating solutions along problem-solving lines, which are then tested. If success is not achieved either partner may call another session.

The highly structured nature of this system allows reasoned

communication between partners who normally cannot speak without fighting.

New Behaviours. These may be suggested to increase or decrease interdependence such as joining clubs or evening classes either together or apart.

Cognitive Factors. Thinking errors and dysfunctional schemata and assumptions play an extremely important part in marital problems (Bagarozzi & Winter Giddings 1983). They come to light in the initial assessment and as blocks to progress later in treatment. Attempts to deal with these should follow the lines described in Chapter 8.

Sexual Problems

Sexual problems present fairly frequently in day-to-day general practice. If a family planning service is offered and health visitors look for problems occurring after childbirth or in families with young children, the numbers may be even greater. When problems are recognised early, brief counselling may often be enough to sort things out but in other cases a more intense and lengthy treatment programme may be needed. This can be provided by the primary care worker or by referral to a special sex-problems clinic. Success rates are reasonably high and this type of treatment is rewarding for both patient and therapist.

The most common problems seen are:

In men:

(1) Impotence
(2) Premature ejaculation
(3) Non-ejaculation

In women:

(1) Vaginismus or non-consummation
(2) Loss of sexual interest
(3) Orgasmic dysfunction

In men and women

(1) Problems with frequency of intercourse
(2) Lack of education or information
(3) Sexual difficulties related to illness, surgery or handicap

The commonest causes for sexual problems are:

(1) anxiety-based, either following a traumatic conditioning experience or due to stress;
(2) anger or resentment in the relationship leading to inability to share pleasure with the partner;
(3) related to moral or religious commitments;
(4) related to physical illness or handicap;
(5) related to alcohol, drugs, circulatory or endocrine problems, ageing or disorders such as diabetes.

An outline of the main categories of problems and types of treatment is given. Before embarking on more complex problems, the reader is recommended to consult one of the texts (e.g. Hawton 1985; Jehu 1979) listed under 'Further Reading'.

It is important to have time available for regular, not necessarily long, appointments. If treatment is too hurried or misdirected, couples may become disheartened and a later, second round of therapy is difficult to initiate.

Assessment

A sexual history should be obtained from each partner, together or separately. Joint interviews help mutual understanding of the problems. Seeing couples separately, however, allows a partner to disclose secrets. If these are relevant, they can then be brought into therapy as soon as the couple are seen together, once the anxiety surrounding them has been dispersed. Some secrets from the past such as certain venereal infections or previous relationships may have no importance for the present problem and disclosure of these need not be pressed.

A precise description should be taken of the problem and the circumstances leading up to the initial and current difficulties. Other aspects which should be considered are:

(1) Thoughts and feelings related to sexual activity, as negative feelings can lead to lack of interest and eventually to dread of physical contact. Often such feelings are not accessible at the first interview and emerge later in therapy during the monitoring of some sexual task.
(2) Stress, either for one partner alone or within the relationship.
(3) Any current medication or physical problem.
(4) Details of past and current methods of contraception.

Precise details are important even if these are difficult to obtain immediately. When considering impotence, for example, it is important to find out whether there is an erection which is lost or no erection at all. In such cases it is important to discover whether there is an erection, in the morning, with masturbation or under other circumstances. This will provide valuable information as to the exact nature of the problem.

An illustration of the importance of accurate assessment is the case of a man who suffered from non-ejaculation after 18 months in hospital on heavy medication. It was discovered that until recently he had used withdrawal as his normal method of contraception and it was this, not the drugs, that was in fact responsible for his loss of ability to ejaculate.

Treatment

Behavioural Assessment. This in itself is sometimes therapeutic in clarifying problems for the couple concerned and can be a chance to remove blame from one partner in particular and allow therapy to start from equal positions.

Education. Questions in the assessment can serve to highlight areas of ignorance of sexual information. This allows physiological details to be explained, old wives' myths to be explored and a rationale for treatment to be given. Certain books e.g. Delvin's *Book of Love* (see 'Books for Patients') can be strongly recommended for physiological information and contraceptive advice.

Permission Giving. Suggestions for homework assignments may allow couples to consider sexual behaviours that they had previously thought improper or deviant, perhaps from attitudes instilled in childhood. A brief discussion may assure a patient that there is nothing wrong in masturbation or oral sex and relieve years of misery. If problems are related to strong religious convictions which are in conflict with current wishes, a session with a sympathetic and liberal clergyman may be helpful in overcoming a block to progress.

At the same time, care should obviously be taken not to inflict unwanted behaviours or values onto patients or suggest that they break strongly-held convictions or taboos.

The Modified Masters and Johnson (Masters and Johnson 1970) Approach to Therapy. After assessing and defining the problem, patients are given a brief explanation of treatment. Sexual intercourse or mutual masturbation is banned in the early stages in order to prevent performance anxiety (masturbation alone is still permissible).

Stage One. At this stage the aim is to increase pleasurable non-sexual contact between the couple. They are instructed to caress each other over all parts of the body except the genital areas and the breasts(sensate focus). This should be done in turn with one partner touching and giving pleasure. The other is allowed to do nothing except concentrate on the thoughts and feelings aroused and give some feedback on how, where and in what way they enjoy being touched. Each partner should take it in turns to initiate these sessions. At least half an hour three times per week should be put aside for practice. Where one partner has felt under pressure to have intercourse frequently, it may be easier to give that partner the responsibility to start or get them to make a commitment to practise, say, twice a week at set times. The same pre-set technique may be used separately from Masters and Johnson programmes to regulate intercourse under those circumstances where the demands of one partner for sex have overwhelmed the other, resulting in the latter avoiding all kinds of physical contact.

Initially couples may find that these instructions are too false or embarrassing and the use of a lubricant such as baby lotion may help to get them started. Couples with sex problems often lead extremely hectic lives and fill every spare moment of the day. Whether this is the cause or an effect of the problem should be clarified and the timetable re-structured in order to make time for sessions. This may have other unexpected benefits in improving their lifestyle.

Some couples genuinely find these exercises too threatening. They may need to spend time trying to initiate some more ritualised physical contact such as kissing 'Hello' and 'Goodbye', holding hands when out walking and doing some touching when clothed. Such extreme cases are not common and may suggest the possibility of a phobic reaction calling for desensitisation before further therapy.

Stage Two. Once the initial difficulties are overcome, another week of sensate focus exercises without any attempt at intercourse or genital touching is required. The aim now is to increase the pleasure of being touched by being more directive to the partner. Each in turn describes the sensations felt in different areas and guides their partner's hand to increase the pleasurable ones. They should be reminded that sensations will probably not be the same every day so that continuing feedback is important. The importance of the intercourse ban and the hazards of cheating should be stressed. Even if they have intercourse satisfactorily at this time they may increase anxiety about future failure. If it goes badly they may undo the progress made so far and tension and frustration return. If, however, the problem has only been a minor short-term one, it may have resolved completely at this stage allowing intercourse to be resumed. This calls for clinical judgement.

Stage Three. When both partners feel ready and can enjoy Stages One and Two with no anxiety, they can begin to include the genital areas in the session. They should continue as before with light touching all over the body but gradually increase the time devoted to the genitals and breasts as well. It should be stressed that the aim is not sexual arousal but to explore different ways of giving pleasure. Lotion can still be used to prevent soreness and increase sensitivity. Guidance and feedback from the partner should be encouraged. When the man is being given pleasure by the woman, the aim is not to achieve an erection but one may occur. If he has a partial erection, she should carry on caressing, but if a full erection is obtained she should stop the touching, allow it to diminish and then continue as before. The idea is to enjoy genital pleasuring with no goals of arousal or fears about sexual performance.

Stage Four. This is reached when the woman can be relaxed and aroused and the man can obtain a full erection. The penis can now be inserted into the vagina. The woman should be in control of this in the female superior position astride the man on her knees at about the level of his chest. She can then place the penis in her vagina and move slowly back until it is fully inserted. They should both remain motionless and enjoy the sensation of the penis inside the woman. They should not go on to intercourse or worry about how long the erection lasts. If the erection goes down they can change positions, return to pleasuring and repeat the cycle if a full erection returns. This exercise increases confidence by allowing time to concentrate on feelings and communication without being worried about performance.

After several sessions have been spent doing this exercise, it can be prolonged and include some movement. The man should attempt to thrust gently — just enough to maintain the erection — alternating with the woman moving gently for as long as they both find it pleasurable. This may be followed by more rapid movements proceeding to climax. As in earlier stages they may stop, withdraw for a while and lie quietly before resuming the exercise. They should not aim to reach a climax every time but to continue to enjoy sexual feelings without the pressure to perform.

The rate of moving from one stage to another depends on mutual agreement of the partners. Even if they remain at a particular stage for some time a commitment to regular practice and review is very important.

Some couples find it therapeutic to practise their homework at a different time or in a different situation or room from that associated in the past with distressing experiences. As an example, a female patient with loss of libido found it hard to initiate the sensate focus stage of therapy in bed. This created negative thoughts related to her husband's former demands and also fear that any contact or cuddle was bound to lead to intercourse. She felt much safer on the sofa which had not previously been associated with sexual activity.

Cognitive Aspects. Couples should be asked to keep a diary of their homework and record in it any emotions and thoughts evoked by the exercises. The assumption of the 'spectator' role is a particularly common block to progress that may be discovered in this way. One or other partner feels that they cannot lose themselves in the pleasurable sensations but rather that they remain as an onlooker seeing everything which takes place from outside. Other negative thoughts unearthed in this way may help to identify attitudes to sex and relationships which are hindering progress. Some of the techniques of marital and cognitive therapy may be used to relieve these problems. For example, a patient felt angry and resentful during sensate focus. Closer examination of her thoughts showed that her anger was due to her partner being so relaxed, when she was aware of all the jobs which needed doing in the flat and of her unfinished thesis lying on the desk. Some re-dividing of the chores and adjustment of her work timetable made her think of the relationship as more equitable. She was then able to relax and enjoy sexual activity.

Another patient felt that sex was stupid. She felt angry that physical contact only occurred during sex and adopted a 'spectator' role. Increasing day-to-day non-sexual physical contact helped her to begin to enjoy sex.

Techniques for Specific Problems

The Masturbatory Programme for Anorgasmic Women (Lo Piccolo and Lobitz 1972). This is another multi-stage programme:

Stage One. Self-exploration is a useful exercise for those women who suffer from anorgasmia, vaginismus or whose sex life is affected by a negative body image. Time needs to be set aside so that a relaxed and private situation can be found. The woman should then just examine and explore her naked body, being aware of the thoughts and feelings produced by different areas. A mirror can be used to examine the genital areas and a book with diagrams of the female genitalia can be used to identify the specific parts. Patients should be reassured that everyone differs slightly in case minor variation make them worry that they are anatomically abnormal.

Stage Two. The patient touches herself on the breasts and genital areas but without attempting arousal. This graded approach helps any phobic fears or points of avoidance to be identified.

Stage Three. The woman is asked to continue visual exploration and try to identify any sensitive areas by touch.

Stage Four. The sensitive areas are now stimulated to try and increase pleasurable feelings. A lubricant such as baby cream may be used to increase sensation or avoid soreness.

Stage Five. The length of the session should be increased to allow time to try and vary the intensity of stimulation, with occasional pauses. Encouragement is given to concentrate on erotic fantasies to increase arousal and reach orgasm.

Stage Six. If orgasm has not been achieved by this stage a vibrator may be used. These can be obtained from mail order or specialist shops. The patient may also be encouraged to role play orgasm with movement, moaning and crying aloud. This helps to release inhibitions about voluntary movements and overcome fears of losing self-control. If the idea of using a vibrator is unacceptable, it may be helpful to stress that it only needs to be used temporarily to obtain orgasm although it can be used in loveplay later if so wished.

Stage Seven. The partner should now be involved and orgasm attempted in his presence. This helps to overcome feelings of inhibition and shows him how to stimulate his partner to produce orgasm.

Stage Eight. The partner may try and stimulate the woman to orgasm using the vibrator as necessary. She gently guides his endeavours.

Stage Nine. The couple may have intercourse, using the vibrator and manual stimulation of the woman. Once she gains more confidence in her ability to achieve orgasm the vibrator may be dispensed with on occasions if preferred.

Premature Ejaculation. When Stage Four of the sensate focus (p. 100) is reached (or earlier if ejaculation occurs during Stages One, Two or Three), the woman should be asked to stimulate her partner until he reaches the point of orgasm. When he indicates to her that he has reached this point, she immediately stops until the urge has decreased when stimulation can be restarted. When this cycle has been repeated three or four times they may continue to orgasm. At Stage Four the same stop-start technique is used with the penis inside the woman eventually proceeding to ejaculation. (Semans 1956.)

An alternative technique, now less used, is for the woman to squeeze the penis just below the glans to abolish her partner's urge to ejaculate. After the urge subsides stimulation is restarted. This technique can create anxiety in both parties about damage to the penis and the other seems equally effective.

Men who have a regular masturbation habit or who have no

current partner can also learn to control premature ejaculation by using the stop-start techniques when masturbating. At the same time it may be useful to learn to increase the awareness of the point at which ejaculation becomes inevitable. It is possible for uncontrolled rapid masturbation to reinforce premature ejaculation when intercourse is resumed with a partner.

Impotence. Temporary impotence is a common, although extremely worrying, condition. Exploration and explanation of the problem may be all that is necessary. The attitude of the patient's partner is important, as it is very helpful if she is understanding and relaxed. Some women, however, see their partner's erectile failure as a result of their own loss of attractiveness or even of his excessive sexual activities elsewhere. These attitudes should be explored and corrected. If further therapy is needed, for most men the ban on intercourse and the first two stages of sensate focus provide a lot of confidence. Sometimes it is helpful to instruct the man to try to get an erection at this stage, using the technique known as paradoxical intention to lessen performance anxiety. Genital touching is introduced in Stage Three. The woman should stroke and fondle the man's penis and then stop so that the exciting sensations are lost and the contrast of feelings recognised without anxiety. She then stimulates him again so that the sensations return. This teasing technique should be continued for some time whether he gains an erection or not. When his confidence has increased she may try to stimulate him to orgasm without penetration.

The next stage is to attempt the teasing technique with the penis inside the vagina using the female superior position. First there is no movement and later a gradually increasing amount of thrusting is allowed.

Failure of an erection at any point in this programme can be dealt with by going back a couple of stages. This restores confidence and may shed more light on any particular difficulty which has been encountered.

Vaginismus. This can be treated successfully but sometimes more time and resources may be needed if there are complicated or deep-seated psychological problems.

It is important to discover the woman's thoughts and feelings about genitalia (of both partners) and sexual intercourse. The problem is often revealed at vaginal examination and it may be possible after discussion of anxieties to pursue the examination sympathetically.

After assessment consultation, the woman is asked to find a relaxed opportunity to examine and touch her genital areas. Considerable avoidance may be encountered and it may be necessary to help and encourage her to do this first in the surgery. Pelvic floor exercises will help her to obtain some feeling of control over the vaginal muscles and will also be useful later. As the vagina is approached, there is often extreme tension in the feet, legs and thighs and practising general relaxation exercises (see Chapter 5) will help to alleviate this.

The next stage is to ask the woman to insert her finger a short way into the vagina, gradually progressing to complete insertion followed by the insertion of two fingers. A lubricant may help. If difficulty is encountered at this stage, an examination by a female therapist may facilitate progress and the patient can then try to insert her own finger under supervision. Graded dilators may be preferable at this stage as they sometimes permit a more relaxed position to be adopted allowing introspection on any anxieties or negative feelings caused by having something in the vagina. Use of dilators may be continued for a time before an attempt is made to insert a finger. The use of tampons is a major breakthrough and helps to consolidate progress.

Practice is then transferred to pleasuring sessions with first the woman and then her partner placing a finger near, then just inside the vagina. The woman should feel relatively relaxed and comfortable with the finger or dilator in her vagina before any attempt is made towards movement or penetration with her partner's penis. Penetration with a finger or penis should always be under the woman's guidance and control so that at no stage does she feel frightened or forced.

In cases of vaginismus, perhaps more than in other sexual difficulties, blocks may occur in treatment. Negative attitudes may be revealed and resolved but if this is impossible referral may be the best course of action. For example, a woman of 28 had never had intercourse, although she was able to enjoy mutual masturbation with her boyfriend. Using graded dilators considerable progress was made, until halted by her being unable to face her feelings, related to an incestuous relationship in her childhood. Brief psychotherapy helped her resolve some of these feelings and she was able to return to sex therapy and achieve intercourse some weeks later. Another patient was so tense that, after relaxation failed, graded dilatation was eventually achieved under intravenous diazepam which has led to successful consummation of the marriage.

Brief Interventions

As a result of causes such as stress, illness or getting back together after childbirth many people find their sex lives have simply got into a muddle. In such cases sex problems develop rapidly from minor upsets and well-timed brief counselling in primary care can prevent more intractable difficulties and the need for long term therapy. Such cases still require a thorough assessment of the complaint although a shorter treatment programme will often be enough. Such treatment should concentrate on information and permission giving and usually some form of sensate focus. Acknowledgement of the problem in attending the surgery may in itself often relieve anxiety and improve communication between the couple. An example was a woman of 60 who attended the surgery because she had lost interest in sex for some months. Her husband had been threatened with redundancy six months before and as a result of this stress the couple did not have sex for three months. When the employment problem was resolved the wife was unable to regain her interest. Brief discussion about possible causes of the problem, a lot of reassurance and specific instructions to ban intercourse and do some sensate focus resulted in a return to their former activity level in three weeks.

Transcultural Differences Affecting Interpersonal Problems (by Patricia d'Ardenne)

The health service has belatedly undertaken the task of making itself more responsive to the needs of a multiracial society. This is particularly true in the case of primary and community based care, including psychological and psychiatric treatments. Barriers of language and culture between patients and their doctors are probably most difficult to overcome here. Ethnic minority patients may be understandably reluctant to go for treatment to people who do not share their values, culture or language. At the same time they experience all the cumulative stresses of racism, alienation and poverty.

Behaviour modification offers a symptom-oriented approach that uses few verbal mediators, that is brief and demonstrably effective, and that can be implemented by family or members of the patient's community in an immediate and practical way.

A good example of this specific sex therapy, where traditional Masters and Johnson therapy enables the problem to be seen as faulty learning that can be corrected by structuring new learning between the couple. Home assignments are carried out in the couple's own cultural and family setting, with adjustments made for the requirements of that culture. It is not essential to good outcome, however, that therapists and patient share the same set of beliefs.

Recent work carried out in the East End of London suggests that Asian couples respond every bit as well to this 'Western' approach as those in the indigenous population (d'Ardenne 1985). It will be only a matter of time before a systematic comparison is made of other behavioural methodologies.

Treatment outcome is measured by easily defined therapy goals and is much less likely to be affected by the quality of interaction between the doctor and the patient than more dynamic therapies.

It is important at this stage that GPs should be aware of the varying presentations of behavioural problems, both in a different cultural setting and in a transcultural context, that may make initial diagnosis difficult. It is only when these differences have been fully considered that we are entitled to say whether or not a behaviour is abnormal. This is aside even from considerations of language.

Philip Rack (1982) has written an immensely practical text for all health care professionals that offers a clear account of the difficulties encountered by these subcultures, and how they have been overcome.

At the very least all GPs should be aware of the basic tenets of the major religions and cultures in our ethnic minorities, the way they construe mental and physical illness and distress, how they handle major life events, and how they are likely to respond to outside professional intervention (Sampson 1983).

References

d'Ardenne, P. (1985) 'Sexual dysfunction in Asian couples', Paper presented at the Seventh International Congress of Sexology, New Delhi.
Argyle, M. (1967) *The Psychology if Interpersonal Behaviour*, Harmondsworth, Penguin
Bagarozzi, D. A. and Winter Giddings, C. (1983) 'Behavioural marital therapy:

empirical status, current practices, trends and future directions', *Clinical Social Work Journal, 11*, 263–9

Falloon, I. Lindley, P. and McDonald, R. (1974) *Social Training: A Manual*, London, Psychological Treatment Section, Maudsley Hospital

LoPiccolo, J. and Lobitz, W. C. (1972) 'The role of masturbation in the treatment of orgasmic dysfunction', *Archives of Sexual Behavior, 2*, 163–71

Masters, W. H. and Johnson, V. E. (1970) *Human Sexual Inadequacy*, London, Churchill

Rack, P. (1982) *Race, Culture and Mental Disorder*, London and New York, Tavistock

Sampson, A. C. M. (1982) *The Neglected Ethic: Cultural and Religious Factors in the Care of Patients*, London, McGraw-Hill

Semans, J. M. (1956) 'Premature ejaculation — a new approach', *Southern Medical Journal, 49*, 353–7

Trower, P. Bryant, B. and Argyle, M. (1978) *Social Skills and Mental Health*, London, Methuen

Recommended for Further Reading

Argyle, M. (ed.) (1981) *Social Skills and Health*, London, Methuen

Bancroft, J. *Human Sexuality and its Problems*, London, Churchill Livingston

Hawton, K. (1985) *Sex Therapy — A Practical Guide*, Oxford, Oxford University Press

Jehu, D. (1979) *Sexual Dysfunction. A behavioural approach to causation, assessment, and treatment*, Chichester, John Wiley

Priestley, P., McGuire, J., Flegg, D., Hemsley, V. and Welham, D. (1978) *Social Skills and Personal Problem Solving*, London, Tavistock

Books for Patients

Alberti, R. E. and Emmons, M. L. (1983) *Your Perfect Right*, San Luis, Impact

Delvin, D. (1974) *The Book of Love*, London, New English Library

Dickson, A. (1982) *A Woman in Your Own Right — assertiveness and you*, London, Quality Books

Kaplan, H. (1981) *The Illustrated Manual of Sex Therapy*, St Albans, Mayflower Book, Granada Publishing Ltd.

Equipment

Graded Vaginal Dilators' Suppliers: John Bell and Croyden, Wigmore Street, London W1

7 DISORDERS OF HABIT

Under this heading will be considered two main groups: motor habits such as tics and spasms; and disorders of appetite including eating disorders, problems with alcohol, drug misuse, smoking and gambling. Sleeping problems have been discussed with anxiety disorders, and enuresis and encopresis will be discussed later under problems of childhood, although all of these may also be legitimately regarded as habit disorders. These are a wide and somewhat disparate group of problems which cannot be easily fitted into one model of development or plan for modification.

Behaviourally, however, they may all be regarded as learned habits possibly with initial rewards but long term costs. These costs range in severity from mild social embarrassment in the case of some muscle spasms to an early painful death from lung cancer in the case of the smoker. Another way of saying the same thing is that reinforcement for repeating the habit is much more immediate than the reinforcement for controlling it. We have seen in Chapter 4 that reinforcement is much more effective when it is provided immediately. It is often the task of the therapist to try and devise strategies for overcoming this imbalance.

Another feature common to these conditions is the crucial importance of an accurate assessment of the problem — when and in what environment it is likely or unlikely to occur, with what consequences and with what associated thoughts and emotions. This analysis leads to accurate and appropriate baseline measurements which in turn may lead the sufferer to understand aspects of the problem which were purely automatic previously. This self-monitoring can lead to a rapid and often quite simple intervention or even promote change in itself.

Motor Habit Problems

There are as many types of motor habit problems as there are sufferers. Even the apparently commonly occurring ones such as eye blinking, nail biting and hair pulling will have individual features in each case, which emphasises the importance of assessment.

Functional Analysis

This should particularly emphasise any factors that make the problem more or less probable, such as nail-biting in the office or an increase in muscle spasm on Sundays when the children are at home to lunch. The problem may mainly affect the sufferer or be an irritation to others such as the teacher or different members of the household. An awareness that habits are often inadvertently reinforced by attention from others is important and should be explored. The removal of the problem may have extremely negative effects for the sufferer if it results in him being ignored or feeling insignificant.

Baseline Measurements

These are planned using the information gained from the functional analysis particularly with regard to expected frequency and severity of the habit. It is obviously impossible to count every occurrence of a muscle twitch which is frequent and repetitive. In these cases some form of time sampling or interval recording would have to be used. If these techniques are adopted it is useful to take samples at different times of the day and at week-ends when circumstances are likely to be different. Baseline records are probably most useful when taken by the sufferer as the process of self-monitoring may promote change in itself. Clearly, however, there are situations, for example with unconscious habits or handicapped children, where an independent observer must be used. The brief of the observer must always be clear and well defined as described in the section on data collection (Chapter 3).

Principles of Intervention.

The information produced by the interview and the baseline measurements should enable an hypothesis to be formed. A decision is then taken, if possible with the full cooperation of the patient, about the type of intervention most likely to prove effective.

Here there are a number of different possibilities. The habit may be seen to be largely secondary to another problem such as general or situational anxiety. Treatment of this may be all that is required. A local government worker had to pass urine whenever she was attending a committee meeting. She responded well to a very short programme consisting of an explanation of the likely anxiety-based mechanism of the problem and distraction by counting the number of times the chairman said 'of course'.

As mentioned earlier self-monitoring will often alleviate a habit by promoting an understanding of the muscular mechanism involved and producing a sense of perceived control of the problem. A tally counter of the sort which is used to record the attendance at jumble sales is extremely useful. In the USA it is possible to obtain these from golf professionals or specialist suppliers (see page 137). Unfortunately the only British equivalent is a rather more cumbersome and expensive version obtainable from city stationers.

It may be possible to alter the stimulus situations in which the problem occurs, for example, by eliminating long hours of boredom and inactivity, or to make it more difficult to perform the response for example by encouraging the wearing of gloves by a hair-puller. These factors will both be discussed in more detail when smoking is considered. With certain habit disorders, differential reinforcement of an alternative incompatible activity is also to be considered. This may be particularly useful with children or as part of a self-control programme. Nail-biters can sometimes be helped by learning to make a fist or squeeze the thumb between the index and middle fingers in response to a desire to bite. The parent ignores biting but notices and praises when the chosen alternative takes place.

Patients presenting with tight or recurrently sore throats in the absence of obvious infection are a fairly frequent problem in general practice. Acting on the hypothesis that this problem results from increased pharyngeal constrictor tone, treatment by relaxation training of the adjacent neck muscles, sometimes with the help of simple electro-myographic biofeedback, has produced considerable relief in a number of cases. (See Chapter 5 for information on biofeedback apparatus.)

The most specific and long-established behavioural method of treating habit spasms is by massed practice in which the patient deliberately learns to perform the tic or twitch for varying periods voluntarily. At its simplest, massed practice programmes are very easy to plan and initiate in primary care, as long therapist contact is unnecessary. There are probably a number of different elements contributing to the effectiveness of massed practice. First the subject learns in detail the component movements of the tic and thus brings it to some extent under voluntary control; second, repeated practice tends to extinguish the habit; and, third, relief from fatigue and boredom provides negative reinforcement on stopping. A number of other theoretical models have also been suggested to explain the manifest effectiveness of this rather improbable procedure. Once the muscle groups involved in the movements have been clearly identified by the patient it is often possible to involve the same or opposing muscles in an incompatible behaviour. This can be used to supplement or replace the massed practice if this proves to be insufficient in itself to eliminate the habit.

Appetite Disorders

Eating Problems

The main subject to be discussed under this heading is obesity, which presents a major and largely unsolved dilemma to the primary care team, who in turn often seem rather undecided whether to accept it as a medical problem or not. The twin scourges of anorexia nervosa and bulimia are becoming distressingly more common. Although their management lies mainly outside the scope of primary care, they deserve some mention if only because specialist resources in this field are becoming so overloaded that expert help is not always readily available.

Obesity. Many general practitioners feel uneasy when confronted with this problem. On the other hand it is a major health hazard directly causing a number of diseases and contributing to others which challenge the family doctor's preventive role. On the other hand it is realised that converting it into a *medical* disorder involving a passive patient and a doctor 'who has got to do something about it' distorts the nature of the problem and will usually be counterproductive in terms of successful management. Aside from these issues the problem is a vast one and it is debatable if one-to-one treatment, even if desirable, can be offered with the resources available.

In this context group treatments have numerous advantages. They can be organised by any member of the team who has the enthusiasm, particularly health visitors and practice or district nurses. This in itself to some extent weakens the dependent medical model which is further weakened by self-help support between group members who are all trying to cope with the same problem. It is possible to deal with more clients at one time and to go into aspects of the problem, for example relapse prevention strategies (Perri *et al.* 1984) in far greater depth than would be possible on an individual basis.

There are some snags. The group programme has to be fairly general and cannot be tailored to meet exactly the requirements indicated by the assessment of each individual's problem. It is quite possible, though, to incorporate some individual assessment and time during sessions for members' particular difficulties. The programme given below is derived from other workers (Stuart and Davis 1972; Mahoney and Mahoney 1976) with some individual modifications. It is not intended to be in any way definitive but merely to give an example of one programme which has been used in a NHS health centre in the UK.

Summary of a Group Weight Loss Programme

Framework Requirements

(1) Introduction. This consists of an initial talk to the potential group to enable them to decide if they wish to take part. It is explained that weight reduction is achieved by (a) planned reduction of eating in a sensible and manageable way, (b) increase of exercise to increase energy usage, and (c) control of various environmental factors influencing the other two. The disadvantages of crash diets, cranky diets, drugs and other pitfalls are discussed briefly. It is pointed out that the long term objective is a permanent method of controlling weight, tailored to the tastes and needs of the individual.

(2) Pre-Programme. Those who wish to take part then enter a two-week self-measurement period during which they try to maintain their previous habits in order to (a) provide a baseline of weight and diet, and (b) get clients used to the tools and procedures that they will be using throughout the programme.

(3) The Main Programme. This consists of three sections:

(a) An initial intensive supervision period with weekly meetings. This adjusts the diet to obtain a weight loss of 1–2 lbs per week and in so far as possible adapts the programme to suit individual lifestyle requirements.

(b) A longer supervision programme with monthly meetings to enable the target weight to be achieved at the proper rate.

(c) A final meeting for assessment of the content of the programme, evaluation of its benefits and long term planning for the members.

Material Required
One pack per client containing:
(1) Specimen baseline self-observation form.
   (a) Daily Food Intake   (b) Daily Exercise Expenditure.
(2) Calorie or unit value booklets or charts which can be of any type as long as they are accurate and fairly comprehensive.
(3) Planning charts for the main programme.
   (a) Food in calories or units   (b) Exercise in calories used.
(4) Advice sheets for helping to control environmental factors.
   (a) To suppress uncontrolled eating (Sheets 1 & 2)
   (b) To strengthen appropriate eating (Sheet 3)
   Each member should provide themselves with a book or a loose-leaf folder which they can use to reproduce these materials as necessary.
(5) A chart giving various forms of exercise in terms of calories expended.

Activity	Unit	Calories
Squash	1 hour	1650
Swimming	1 hour	600
Digging	1 hour	450
Tennis	1 hour	450
Dancing (Vigorous)	1 hour	400
Cycling	1 hour	400
Walking	1 hour	300
Running	3000 metres	200

Time Table (About 60–90 mins per session)
Pre Programme
Week 1 Weigh and agree final or intermediate target weight. (For the substantially overweight a final target weight may be dispiriting so an intermediate target may be desirable). Provide and introduce calorie or unit diet sheets. Provide and explain the baseline self-observation form which will be used to record all food and exercise during the baseline period. Although it is stressed that no attempt should be made to alter normal eating and exercise habits during this period of recording, it is best if weighing is only carried out at the sessions in early stages in order to avoid frenetic frequent weighings and between-weighing-machine variation. Later the client must use their own bathroom scales.
Week 2 Attitudes to weight, exercise and dieting are discussed

within the group and the opportunity used to talk about pitfalls and misconceptions including 'glandular trouble', crash diets, cranky diets and the place of anorectic drugs. The long term objective of a permanent improved method of eating is outlined. The previous week's self-observation forms are checked and any difficulties discussed.

The value of increasing exercise is discussed and members are asked, as homework, to consider consistent and measurable ways in which this could be done e.g. cycling to the station (10 mins) instead of taking the car. It is important that, if possible, additional exercise is taken in a form that the client enjoys and is therefore likely to continue.

Main Programme

Week 3 This is an extremely full session during which the dietary and exercise modifications designed to produce controlled weight loss are introduced. The initial eating reduction is somewhat arbitrary but usually a daily programme set at around 75 per cent of baseline calorie intake will be about right. Fine adjustment can be undertaken later. It is important that the programme contains all the client's favorite foods albeit in reduced quantities. Deliberate abstinence from much-loved foodstuffs leads to an unnatural dichotomy between 'good but unattractive' and 'bad but delicious' foods which makes the latter loom large in the client's mind and tempts him or her to lapse. This may contribute to the abstinence violation effect of one lapse resulting in a feeling of total failure. This will be considered in more detail when drug and alcohol problems are discussed.

If possible an increased exercise programme should be planned and introduced at the same time.

At the end of the sessions the first advice sheet (To help to make your diet work, Part 1) (see Figure 6.1) is distributed to be read before the next week.

Week 4 After weighing, the adjustments necessary to obtain the target 1–2 lbs weight loss, are made to the programme and any difficulties are discussed. The help of one group member to another is particularly useful in overcoming snags as such suggestions are more powerful than those of the leader. The achievements of the individual increased exercise programmes are then considered and an attempt made to obtain an increased exercise expenditure of 500 calories per day.

The first advice sheet is discussed together with its underlying philosophy of limiting or removing the cues for inappropriate eating. Often members will have suggestions which can usefully be considered by the group and perhaps added to the sheets. The second sheet (see Figure 6.1) is distributed at the end of the session.

Week 5 This is devoted to monitoring progress and adjusting the diet and exercise programmes, discussing difficulties and distributing the final advice sheet (Figure 6.1) which explores cues and methods for obtaining reinforcement for an appropriate life-style.

The question of relabelling emotions can be usefully considered at this session. It appears that many overweight people misinterpret emotions such as boredom, anxiety and tiredness as hunger. They can usefully be trained to ask themselves if there is an alternative explanation when they think that they feel hungry. Negative thoughts about such subjects as lack of willpower, relative inability to lose weight and excuses for not doing so are discussed in the group. These 'negative monologues' (Mahoney and Mahoney 1976) can be answered by 'appropriate monologues' in much the same way as negative automatic thoughts are answered by rational alternatives in the cognitive therapy of depression (Beck *et al.* 1979, see Chapter 8). For example

Situation	Negative Monologue	Appropriate Monologue
Seeking excuses	My family are all overweight — I shall never get rid of it	With the right eating habits everyone can lose — don't be too impatient.

Support from other group members is extremely useful in finding appropriate alternatives.

Deep muscle relaxation which has been considered in detail in Chapter 5 can usefully be taught at this point as an alternative response to eating which can be used to cope with anxiety, anger or frustration.

Week 6 After the usual assessment and adjustment, this session is used to determine which environmental cues each client finds most appropriate for him or herself and which emotions he or she may mislabel as hunger. As this is the last session of the intensive programme it is a good idea to suggest that the group takes a meal out together. This is a pleasant and appropriate setting to discuss the possible problems of public meals and hospitality.

Monthly Meetings These have no formal structure apart from progress monitoring and the discussion of difficulties and negative monologues. They are incorporated to continue group support and to enable long term target weights to be reached.

Final Meeting The difficulties of continuing without the support of the group are discussed and the problems of maintaining the changed pattern permanently. One technique which is worth mentioning is to reintroduce the full monitored programme for one month in every six as a refresher course.

Figure 6.1: Advice Sheets for Dieters

TO HELP YOU TO MAKE YOUR DIET WORK I

Eat all meals at a formally prepared table in one room. Concentrate on the meal and never do anything else e.g. read or watch TV at the same time as eating.
Use a smaller plate than usual.
Concentrate on chewing food slowly. Try to be the last to finish.
Have a salad before the meal to take the edge off your appetite.
Try a drink of water or unsweetened fruit juice before a meal to see if it reduces your appetite.
Do your shopping from a list and only take enough money to cover the things on that list.
Shop immediately after a meal when you are not hungry.
Avoid buying prepared high calorie foods, e.g. biscuits, crisps or pies. Therefore see that any high calorie foods you do buy need preparation and cooking. If possible keep them deep frozen.

TO HELP YOU MAKE YOUR DIET WORK II

Get your family and others around you to:

(1) Provide, or help you provide, suitable meals
(2) Help you keep a check on what you eat and encourage you when you are doing well.

Serve your food onto your plate before the meal – not from dishes on the table.
Leave the table as soon as you have finished. Never leave food out in view after meals.
Spread small portions over the plate making them look larger.
Eat three meals a day at planned intervals, never miss one.
Never get overtired.
Have something to do at all times e.g. book, records, gardening, sewing to distract you from eating through boredom.

TO HELP YOU MAKE YOUR DIET WORK III

Learn the full range and quantities of non-fattening foods from your chart and use them to give variety. Include occasional small quantities of fattening food to avoid craving.

Learn the amount of each which can be eaten so that portion size becomes second nature.
Have a reserve supply of non-fattening foods e.g. apples, tomatoes, beef extract for snacks or save something from a previous meal.

Anorexia Nervosa and Bulimia Nervosa. These interrelated problems will often require appropriate in-patient and specialist treatment. Some mention of them is made here as the general practitioner and other members of the primary care team do have an important role in early detection of the vulnerable patient. They may be able to prevent the problem assuming major proportions by taking early action to point out the dangers. Unfortunately the units specialising in the treatment of these problems are, in the UK, currently overwhelmed by the potential number of patients. Consequently early management or even all management may have to be given in rather inappropriate general hospital settings. Here the emphasis is often directed solely to obtaining sufficient weight gain to make discharge physically safe. This 'Strasbourg goose' approach may be necessary to preserve life but offers little in the way of help after discharge or help with the emotional and environmental factors that have been maintaining the condition.

Interview assessment should concentrate especially on the following points:

(1) What are the antecedents of bingeing or starving? Amongst these may be found loneliness, anxiety, depression or boredom on the one hand and certain physical situations like the presence of particular feared foods or returning to the family home on the other.

(2) What is the patient's and her family's attitude to food? Is it abundant and important in their lives? Was great store always set on finishing all food prepared and having second helpings?

(3) Has the patient ever been overweight and if so what were the attitudes of parents, peer-group and self to that?

(4) How many of these factors operate in her present life?

(5) Are there excessive or unreasonable academic expectations from the patient herself, her parents or others?

(6) Is the eating problem a form of avoidance of distasteful aspects of life or is it being rewarded by excessive attention? Is it being used to control or punish parents?

These points deserve special attention in the general scheme of assessment described earlier. After the interview patients should be asked to record baseline data with particular reference to:

(1) All food eaten, where it was eaten and at what time. The record should also have an anxiety rating. A brief description of the thoughts and circumstances of eating will serve to highlight any particularly dangerous times of day or foods likely to lead to bingeing.

(2) Encouraging both anorexics and bulimics to make lists of feared foods i.e. those likely to lead to bingeing, starving or self-induced vomiting, and of situations, e.g. being alone, which they find to be particularly difficult.

Once this information has been obtained, a programme can be drawn up. This might include amongst others the following elements:

(1) Measures to label correctly and to counteract associated factors such as anxiety, depression and social isolation. An attempt should be made to fill the gap left by abandoning the 'professional anorexic or bulimic career'. Many of these patients' lives revolve round their problem and there may be a real danger that they will become 'nothing people' if their problem disappears.

(2) A weight target should be set and instructions given to eat three meals per day with provision for appropriate snacks. An anorexic is more likely to be able to cooperate with a programme designed to lead to gradual weight gain which in turn allows her to come to terms with her changing shape. Frequently it is this resistance to 'becoming fat' that leads to the breakdown of home-based programmes. It is essential that the patient is allowed to discuss her fears about this without confrontation and preferably away from her parents. Bulimics who are within their recommended weight limits should aim to maintain this or possibly lose small amounts. It is sometimes helpful to ask the patient to make out a daily target diet in advance. Each item is ticked off in turn providing some sort of self-reward for each day successfully completed.

Many attempts at modification of these problems at home founder because the patients have learned a pattern of deception and denial over the years which they find it difficult to abandon. The therapist therefore cannot obtain reliable direct-observation data or adequately control the reinforcers. If these difficulties become insurmountable or the situation is deteriorating to the point of danger, admission is essential. It is possible, however, that the family doctor may be able to modify patient or family attitudes early in the condition in such a way as to prevent the intractable full-blown problem developing.

Smoking

It is unlikely that anyone reading this book will need convincing that smoking is extremely harmful and yet, alas, it is still extremely widespread. The evidence of successive reports by The Royal College of Physicians of London and the Surgeon General's department in the USA need not be reviewed here. There has been a net reduction of smoking in the USA and UK in recent years although it is uncertain which factors have brought this about. In the UK it may be that a general trend towards physical fitness and the cultivation of healthier living habits has been more effective than the pathetically small budget of the Health Education Council and the dedicated efforts of organisations like ASH in the face of massive tobacco advertising and the damaging models presented by parents, teachers and nurses. Doctors cannot be exempt from responsibility as, although they have stopping smoking in greater numbers than other professionals, the damage done by the smoking doctor as a model far outweighs that caused by most other groups. Such gains as have been made by older men and women stopping, have to an extent been offset by young women and girls who have taken up the habit in greater numbers. Most smokers start in their teens perhaps to assert themselves as independent and follow their group. It is possible that one of the unlooked-for effects of female emancipation is a greater readiness to smoke. The harmful effects of smoking seem irrelevant and remote at this age to both sexes. Later in life many smokers want to stop but find it difficult to to so. Many of these would-be non-smokers seek help from doctors, clinics or anti-smoking preparations.

On the surface it would appear that smoking prevention might be a particular fruitful field for the behaviour modifier. The cues are often clear-cut, the behaviour easily studied and measured and the potential reinforcers for quitting considerable in terms of money and health. If the therapist is also the patient's family doctor or a primary care colleague who is in a potential position to comment on matters of personal health so much the better. A survey of the multitude of techniques that have been used to achieve quitting however shows almost uniformly disappointing results. The best results have often been achieved by simple advice in a medical setting following an episode of illness like a myocardial infarct or in association with some chronic condition where smoking is likely to prove particularly harmful (Raw 1976; Russell *et al.* 1979). This seems to give some support to the theory that doctors are particularly well placed to influence the problem.

Apart from the giving of simple advice there is no clear view of the best approach. Recently great hopes have been raised by nicotine replacement therapy, usually with chewing gum (Nicorette). Although results were good under experimental conditions with about 40 per cent abstinent at one year follow-up, it seems that random prescription in the surgery is unlikely to do as well. This is probably because maximum effect is achieved only when the gum is part of an overall treatment plan.

In clinical practice it seems that the most promising results may be obtained using a group treatment package with Nicorette as an adjunct (Russell *et al.* 1980). The group scheme that follows was used by a general-practitioner-led group from a health centre and achieved 30 per cent abstinence at one year follow-up without the use of Nicorette.

Summary of a Group Non-smoking Programme

Introduction. As with the Weight Loss Programme the initial meeting is to explain the nature of the programme before a commitment is made. It is explained that during the first two weeks members study and learn about their own smoking behaviour by recording the circumstances of all the cigarettes they smoke. This is followed by a two-week reduction period during, or at the end of, which members contract to quit. Each member decides for himself whether to cut down generally during this period or to stop suddenly at the beginning. After the quitting date there are two more weekly meetings giving advice and support followed by monthly meetings up to six months.

Anybody is welcome to attend the first meeting to find out about the group without obligation. Those attending the second are asked to sign a contract to the effect that they will:

(1) Complete the group programme and attend at monthly intervals for five months afterwards.

(2) Stop smoking on or before the Quitting Date (four weeks later).

(3) Contribute a weekly money deposit (amount to be decided by the group) for the duration of the programme and the five months afterwards. This deposit will be returned at the final meeting (Repayment Date) to those who have not smoked between the Quitting Date and the Replacement Date. The group takes a decision about how the forfeits are to be used. One possibility is an unpopular charity, for example the League Against Cruel Sports in a keen hunting district or the British Field Sports Association if the group abhors blood sports. The complete deposit may be forfeited at the first lapse. It is better, however, if some provision is made for only a small cost for a single transgression. This lessens the abstinence violation effect of guilt and hopelessness in a situation which, if regarded only as a lapse, can still be redeemed.

The group leader agrees to provide the materials necessary for the programme. He co-ordinates the group's discussions and provides support to members during various difficulties that may occur.

Material Requirements. One pack per client containing:

(1) A specimen Daily Smoking Record Chart which can be copied to provide charts for each day until the Quitting Date.

(2) An ARU Smoking Questionnaire. This gives a comprehensive account of smoking behaviour and attitudes — see Figure 7.2.

(3) Contract Sheet.

(4) Summary Progress Chart.

(5) Three advice sheets which may be retained by the leader for distribution later in the programme.

Timetable for the group.

Week 1 The outline of the programme is explained. The Quitting Date is fixed. The purpose of the ARU Questionnaire and the Daily Chart is explained together with using the Desire Rating. Summary and Contract Forms are given out with Stop Smoking leaflets. An explanation is given about (i) the need for regular attendance by

Figure 7.2: ARU Smoking Questionnaire

Please leave empty

	1	**2**	**3**	**4**		**5**	**6**	**7**	**8**	**9**	**10**

Clinic: _____ ⊠ ☐ ☐ ☐   Client number: ☐ ☐ ☐ ☐   ☐ ☐

FULL NAME: _____   **DATE:** _____   **11-16**
Christian name   Surname

ADDRESS: _____

_____   **DATE OF BIRTH:** __/__/__
                                     day / month / year

_____   **AGE:** _____

TELEPHONE: Home _____   **SEX:**   **Male** ☐ 1   **17-18**

            Work _____   **Female** ☐ 2   **19**

1) Are you ...
Single .... ☐ 1
Married and living with spouse........ ☐ 2   **20**
Separated or divorced............... ☐ 3
Widowed .... ☐ 4
Other .... ☐ 5

2) Are you ...
please tick one only
in paid employment .... ☐ 1
a housewife .... ☐ 2
a full-time student .... ☐ 3   **21**
retired .... ☐ 4
unemployed .... ☐ 5
permanently sick or disabled .... ☐ 6

3) Which one of these descriptions best applies to your job, or applies to your last job if you are not working now? *please tick one only*

Please explain what you do in your work.
Unskilled or semi-skilled worker....... ☐ 1
Skilled worker or craftsman .... ☐ 2
Foreman, supervisor .... ☐ 3   **22**
Clerical, secretarial................. ☐ 4
Professional, managerial, administrative ☐ 5
Have never had paid employment...... ☐ 6

_____

4) If you are (or have been) married, which one of these descriptions best applies to your husband or wife's present job, or last job if not working now? *please tick one only*

Please explain what he/she does in their work.
Unskilled or semi-skilled worker....... ☐ 1
Skilled worker or craftsman .... ☐ 2
Foreman, supervisor .... ☐ 3   **23**
Clerical, secretarial................. ☐ 4
Professional, managerial, administrative ☐ 5
Have never had paid employment...... ☐ 6

_____

5) Are you allowed to smoke at work?
Yes whenever I want to .... ☐ 1
Yes, but only during breaks........ ☐ 2   **24**
No, not at all.................... ☐ 3

6) How old were you when you started smoking regularly (one a day or more)?   (give age in years)   **25-26**

7) Over the past year, how many cigarettes a day have you **usually** smoked? _____   **27-28**

How much does this vary
from day to day?   The **least** I smoke in a day _____   **29-30**

                                    The **most** I smoke in a day _____   **31-32**

---

8) What type of cigarettes do you   Filter tipped . . . . □ 1
   normally smoke?   Plain . . . . □ 2   **33**
                                         Hand-rolled . . . . □ 3

If you smoke hand-rolled cigarettes   **34**
about how many ounces of tobacco do
you use per day?   _____   □

---

9) What is the full brand name of   _____   **35-37**
   your usual cigarette?
                                                                                              □
                                       (For instance "Embassy" is not a full brand name   □
                                       but "Embassy Extra Mild King Size" is)   □

                        Is it? Low tar . . . . □ 1
                                Low to middle tar . . . . □ 2
                                Middle tar . . . . □ 3
                                Middle to high tar . . . . □ 4   **38**
                                High tar . . . . □ 5
                                Don't know . . . . □ 6

                        Is it? King size . . . . □ 1
                                Regular size . . . . □ 2   **39**
                                Small size . . . . □ 3

---

10) When you smoke cigarettes,   A lot . . . . □ 1
    do you inhale . . .   A fair amount . . . . □ 2   **40**
                                        Just a little . . . . □ 3
                                        Not at all . . . . □ 4   **41-42**

---

11) Do you smoke . . .   A pipe . . . . □   □
    tick appropriate boxes if you do   Cigars . . . . □
                                                                                              43
If so, how much each week?   Pipe _____ oz per week   □
                                        Cigars _____ per week   **44-46**

---

12) How enjoyable is smoking for you?   Extremely enjoyable . . . . □ 1
                                         Fairly enjoyable . . . . □ 2   **47**
                                         Slightly enjoyable . . . . □ 3
                                         Not at all enjoyable . . . . □ 4

---

13) How unpleasant do you find it if   Extremely unpleasant . . . . □ 1
    you can't smoke for an hour or two? Fairly unpleasant . . . . □ 2   **48**
                                         Slightly unpleasant . . . . □ 3
                                         Not at all unpleasant . . . . □ 4

---

14) Do you think you are addicted   Extremely . . . . □ 1
    to smoking?   Fairly . . . . □ 2
                                         Slightly . . . . □ 3   **49**
                                         Not at all . . . . □ 4
                                         Don't know . . . . □ 5

---

15) If you wanted to stop   Very easy . . . . □ 1
    smoking altogether, how   Fairly easy . . . . □ 2   **50**
    difficult would you find it?   Fairly difficult . . . . □ 3
                                         Very difficult . . . . □ 4

---

16) When you wake up do you usually smoke   YES . . . . □ 1
    before your first cup of tea or coffee? NO . . . . □ 2   **51**

17) On occasions when you can't smoke or you haven't got any cigarettes (tobacco) on you, do you feel a craving for one? *please tick one only*	Never .... □ 1 Hardly ever .... □ 2 Occasionally .... □ 3 Frequently .... □ 4 Always....................... □ 5	52
18) Is the person who is most important to you a smoker?	YES......................... □ 1 NO .... □ 2	53
19) What does this person feel about your smoking?	Objects strongly............... □ 1 Prefers if I don't.............. □ 2 Doesn't mind .... □ 3 Encourages me to smoke .... □ 4	54
20) About how many times have you tried seriously to stop smoking **over the past 5 years**?	Never .... □ 1 Once........................ □ 2 2-4 times .... □ 3 5 or more times................. □ 4	55
21) Not counting times when you were ill or in hospital, what is the longest time you have ever gone without smoking **over the past 5 years**?	Less than 1 day .... □ 1 1-6 days .... □ 2 1-4 weeks .... □ 3 1-3 months .... □ 4 4-6 months .... □ 5 7-11 months .... □ 6 1-3 years.................... □ 7 More than 3 years .... □ 8	56
22) Do you have any health problems which **you** think are related to your smoking?	YES......................... □ 1 NO .... □ 2	57
If the answer is YES, are the problems mainly to do with ...	Your heart .... □ 1 Your chest .... □ 2 Something else .... □ 3	58
23) If you succeed in stopping smoking altogether, do **you** think you will be healthier? a) in the **short-term**:	Much healthier .... □ 1 A little healthier.............. □ 2 No difference.................. □ 3	59
b) in the **long-term**:	Much healthier .... □ 1 A little healthier.............. □ 2 No difference.................. □ 3	60
24) What is your **main** reason for wanting to stop smoking? *please tick one only*	Your health .... □ 1 The expense................... □ 2 It's a dirty habit.............. □ 3 Not fair on other people.......... □ 4 Don't like being addicted .... □ 5 Some other reason.............. □ 6	61
25) How much do you want to stop smoking altogether?	Very much indeed .... □ 1 Quite a lot................... □ 2 Not very much .... □ 3 Not at all .... □ 4	62
26) Have you been feeling more depressed than usual over the past 3 months?	Not at all .... □ 1 Slightly..................... □ 2 Quite a bit .... □ 3 Very much .... □ 4	63 64-66
27) What is your weight?		

28) What is your height?   67-69

29) Are you worried about   Not at all worried . . . .   ☐ 1
    gaining weight if you   Slightly worried . . . .   ☐ 2
    stop smoking?   Fairly worried . . . .   ☐ 3
                              Very worried . . . .   ☐ 4   70

30) Do you expect to be under   Not at all . . . .   ☐ 1
    much pressure at home or   Slightly . . . .   ☐ 2   71
    work over the next three   Quite a bit . . . .   ☐ 3
    months?   Very much . . . .   ☐ 4

31) Do you think you will stop   Definitely . . . .   ☐ 1
    smoking for at least a year? Probably . . . .   ☐ 2   72
                                Probably not . . . .   ☐ 3
                                Definitely not . . . .   ☐ 4

32) How did you find out   Friend . . . .   ☐ 1
    about this centre?   Newspaper/magazine . . . .   ☐ 2   73
                                Television/radio . . . .   ☐ 3
                                A doctor . . . .   ☐ 4
                                Other . . . .   ☐ 5

    If 'other' please say how.   _____   74

    Please make sure you have answered **ALL** the questions.   79-80

                                                                   Card number:

© Martin Raw, Michael Russell, Richard Eiser, Stephen Sutton, Martin Jarvis

The ARU Smoking Questionnaire is copyright and we gratefully acknowledge the
permission of the copyright holders Dr. M.A.H. Russell of the Addiction Research
Unit, Institute of Psychiatry, 101 Denmark Hill, London, SE5 8AF, and Martin Raw
of the Department of Psychology, St George's Hospital, Tooting, London, to whom
all enquiries about it should be directed.

those who decide to become group members; and (ii) quitting, not
reduction, becoming the goal. During the pre-quitting period a
Desire Scale of 0 = no desire to 5 = most severe craving is used when
monitoring smoking.

Week 2 The returning participants are congratulated upon their
decision and welcomed. Completed Contracts, ARU Questionnaires and Daily Charts are collected and discussed. The goal of
eliminating Ratings 1 and 2 cigarettes on the Desire Scale is
discussed. The option of rapid quitting is considered. Group
partners (buddies) are selected with the object of providing each
member with a kindred spirit who can be contacted if the going gets
tough. Partners also provide each member with somebody who can
keep them informed if a meeting is unavoidably missed. Telling
friends about the decision to quit is suggested. Joint treasurers are
appointed to hold the money deposits in a bank account. The details
of the money deposits and destiny of forfeits are settled.

Week 3 Daily Charts and the reduction obtained are discussed together with the elimination of Desire Ratings 3 and 4. Deposits are collected and the arrangements checked. The first hand-out, 'The Smoker's Habits,' is distributed.

Week 4 Daily Charts and the reduction obtained are discussed. Rating 5 is eliminated before the Quitting Date the following week. Money for deposits is collected. Ways of helping to stop are discussed amongst the group and, if wanted and available, an outside speaker can be asked to talk about how he stopped. 'Lengthening the Chain' is distributed.

Week 5 The Quitting Date. Everybody should have stopped by this date. Usually those still attending will have done so but some time can be taken strengthening the resolve of any lame ducks. Methods of helping the new non-smoker avoid excessive weight gain are considered. Money deposits are collected and if time permits a Health Education slide programme can be shown. Negative thoughts and difficult situations are discussed in order to generate relapse prevention strategies (Marlatt and George 1984). The hand-outs on 'Withdrawal Symptoms' and 'Remaining a Non-smoker' are distributed.

Week 6 The success rate is discussed and any special tips or difficulties. This meeting produced 'The Dottle Bottle' which is an extremely simple portable aversion therapy apparatus. It consists of the contents of a bar ashtray after a busy evening emptied into a wide-neck bottle and macerated with a little water. Carried in the pocket, it can be opened and smelt every time the desire to smoke is felt. At first suggested by a group member as a joke it was later adopted widely as a serious aid. If time permits a film may be shown and the venue for the bar or pub meeting decided.

Week 7 Final meeting of the intensive series is held in a bar or a pub. This is to enable the members to experience a normally difficult, high-probability smoking situation whilst still having the support of the group. Similar problems are discussed, the money deposits are collected and arrangements are made for the subsequent meetings.

Extended Meetings. These are held every month up to six months. The money deposit continues to be collected at the same rate but now four weeks at a time. It is repaid in the prescribed manner at the final meeting after six months. The purpose of these extended meetings is to protect against the danger period for restarting which seems to be at its height between six weeks and six months.

Running groups of this sort is a time-consuming and quite demanding pastime. It does however have a number of rewards and can be enjoyable. It is a moot point whether the use of professional time is cost effective when only small groups of up to 16 people can be involved at one time. Ideally it should be possible to hand over the running of subsequent groups to 'lay graduates' of the earlier ones.

THE SMOKER'S HABITS

Study your Daily Smoking Record Chart. Make a note of particular activities associated with particular cigarettes. There may be coffee cigarettes, after a meal cigarettes, driving cigarettes, telephone cigarettes and so on. Each of these cigarettes has the same Desire Rating each day. Work through the week blocking out one or more extra habit cigarettes in each Desire Rating group each day. For example on Monday you knock out the coffee cigarettes, Tuesday you knock out the coffee and the after breakfast cigarettes, Wednesday you knock out the coffee, the after breakfast and the telephone cigarettes and so on.

The following tips may be helpful:

The Coffee Cigarette. Many smokers have the first cigarette with the first cup of coffee in the morning and all cups of coffee may carry a 5 rating. To beat it (1) change to tea or some other drink, (2) change your way of flavouring coffee, for example drink it without sugar if you have been used to sugar in the past, or (3) munch a tea biscuit or anything else you fancy.

The After Breakfast Cigarette. This could be a coffee cigarette or it could simply be a cigarette smoked while having a think about the day ahead. To beat it, change your habit by (1) going for a quick walk or jog, (2) if you are not athletic carry a paperback and have a quick read, or (3) use any other method you can think of to prevent 'dead time' developing.

The Driver's Cigarette. Some drivers believe that a cigarette helps them to relax at the wheel and makes them a better driver. There is no basis for this, in fact smoking whilst driving is actually dangerous. To beat it (1) turn on and concentrate on the car radio, (2) try to carry a passenger so that you can talk, (3) chew gum or a hard sweet.

The Waiting Cigarette. Read, exercise or chew a sweet. Watch others smoking and list your benefits from stopping, which they lack.

The Telephone Cigarette. (1) Doodle on a pad, (2) answer the phone in a different physical position, (3) play with an 'executive toy'.

The After Lunch Cigarette. Like the after breakfast cigarette, try to eliminate the dead time by changing your routine. Take walks, read the sports news or write a book on stopping smoking.

The Drinking Cigarette. This is often the toughest one to beat, particularly because your inhibitions and self-control are reduced when you drink. (1) Never carry your cigarettes or matches with you to a party — take only your rating form. If you allow yourself a cigarette you must cadge both it and a light. (2) 'phone your partner before any drinking session or during its early stages. (3) If you are fairly sure that there will be something to eat at the party, eat nothing beforehand and nibble often as you drink. (4) If all else fails, give up alcoholic drinks for a few months. This is hard but it may be the only way.

WITHDRAWAL SYMPTOMS

Weight gain. Although not strictly a withdrawal symptom, this can be a problem. Try to increase the amount of exercise that you take, it will also help your efforts to remain a non-smoker and prove to you that you are fitter than before. Find something that you enjoy — it is much more fun and you are more likely to keep it up. Diabetic sweets and drinks can be helpful.

Other Symptoms. Most other symptoms are mild and seldom last longer than a week. You may experience some of the following:

(1) Occasional dizziness because more oxygen is reaching your system.
(2) Headache.
(3) Hunger.
(4) Constipation. Drink extra water or fruit juice each day.
(5) Trembling and sweating. Both will subside as the body gets used to the non-smoking habit.
(6) Insomnia. You may actually need less sleep. Go to bed later and only when you feel tired.
(7) Nervousness or irritability. This is due to increased energy and is best dealt with by increasing activities.

You may also notice slower breathing, slower pulse and better taste and smell — all of which should be benefits.

LENGTHENING THE CHAIN

Smoking requires a series of physical movements which are often half-conscious and semi-automatic, for example you keep your cigarette in a certain place and find them in a certain way, you use the same method of lighting-up and you hold and smoke the cigarette in a particular way which you have been doing for years.

These movements form a chain which must be first studied and then lengthened or broken to lose the habit. Deliberately alter every part of the chain of habits that you can. For example:

Change brands. Choose a brand as different as possible from your normal brand.

Buy cigarettes in a new place. Never again use the familiar machine, garage or sweet shop. Get them in a shop you have never used before.

Keep your cigarettes in a new place. If they have been in a pocket or a handbag, keep them on a shelf or in the desk drawer.

Make it hard to get to the packet and get a cigarette. Wrap your rating form round the packet with tight rubber bands. Ideally lock the packet in the boot of the car and put the key in a locked locker two blocks away.

Change your way of lighting-up. If you use a lighter, change to matches and vice-versa. Light-up left handed which will be awkward. This is the main idea.

Change your lip grip.
Change your ash-tray system. Keep ash-trays away from your desk or chair or even get rid of them altogether and use a water filled saucer as a temporary measure. This is evidence that you are serious about giving up.

REMAINING A NON-SMOKER

(1) Never offer cigarettes to anybody else, for example, at a party.
(2) Never buy or carry cigarettes for anybody else.
(3) Never light a cigarette for anybody else. Say in your most charming way 'I'm sorry but I'm a non-smoker'.
(4) Don't keep ash-trays in view around your house. Only produce them if you see somebody lighting-up.
(5) Never give an ash-tray, lighter or any other smoking equipment as a present.
(6) Never buy duty-free cigarettes for people when you go abroad.
ALWAYS CALL YOURSELF A NON-SMOKER NOT AN EX-SMOKER.
SAY 'I DON'T SMOKE', NOT 'I'VE GIVEN UP'.

Alcohol and Other Drug Misuse

Alcohol

The alcoholic or potentially alcoholic patient presents a particularly difficult problem in primary care. The general practitioner has an opportunity of identifying a potential problem and offering advice early if he enquires routinely about alcohol use amongst his patients. He is often accused of neglecting this opportunity by the mass media and special interest organisations. He may realise, however, that merely identifying the problem is of little use if the patient continues to deny it himself and refuses to accept help, or the resources available to provide help are inappropriate or inadequate.

Notoriously many drinkers are unwilling to accept that they have a problem until it is well advanced. This attitude is compounded by the traditional illness model of the problem adopted by the profession and organisations like Alcoholics Anonymous, useful as they often are. The model emphasises that alcoholism is a disease which, once acquired, is lifelong. The sufferer is always one drink from the gutter ('one drink, one drunk'). The only treatment is directed towards a goal of total abstinence with the threat of loss of control always looming large. This goal, it is said, can only be achieved initially by means of lengthy in-patient therapy disruptive to career, family and self-esteem alike. Small wonder that many who privately suspect that they are developing a mild drinking problem prefer to deny it until they can do so no longer.

The above model may be useful for the severely dependent alcoholic who has had daily withdrawal symptoms for at least six months, who engages in withdrawal drinking and whose drinking repertoire has become narrowed to a stereotyped pattern. It is, however, counter-productive in the much larger group of drinkers, including those commonly seen in primary care, who are only mildly to moderately dependent. This group are characterised at the most by mild or moderate withdrawal symptoms a few times a week for less than six months and only the beginning of narrowing of the repertoire. They do not exhibit a 'priming effect' if one drink is taken (Hodgson *et al.* 1979). To encourage them to believe that disaster will follow a single drink is not only untrue but damaging as it encourages the belief that all is lost if any lapse from abstinence occurs. This belief may help the initial cessation of the problem but it actually hinders the rather more important objective of maintaining long-term change. It may increase the Abstinence Violation Effect (Marlatt and George 1984) which occurs when someone committed to abstinence finds himself unable to cope with a particularly high risk situation. He crosses the 'forbidden line', perceives himself as having failed totally in his endeavour and gives up. In reality all that has happened is one lapse which affects the person's ability to continue his programme only in his own perception.

Controlled drinking programmes have the great advantage that the AVE is much less likely to be a problem. Even where abstinence is the goal as much time as possible should be spent on relapse prevention (RP) strategies. It will be apparent that RP and AVE are important not only in the management of drinking problems but also in other forms of drug abuse including smoking.

Assessment. This will depend upon the type of presentation. Is the problem acknowledged and understood by the patient? Is the patient there to find out whether a problem he himself suspects in fact exists? Does the doctor suspect a problem which the patient has not accepted?

In the last two situations the Drinkwatchers (Ruzeck 1984) unit system is the most helpful rule of thumb:

1 unit alcohol = half pint of beer = 1 glass of wine = 1 glass of sherry = 1 single whisky.
Too much = more than 30 units per week for men
= more than 20 units per week for women.

If these levels are being consistently exceeded then there is a potential or actual problem. This information alone will be very helpful to many patients.

Further assessment, once it has been decided that there is a problem, will consist of a standard behavioural analysis as described in Chapter 2 to determine the environmental factors influencing the patient and the problem. Of particular value are the following factors:

A narrowing of the repertoire of drinking behaviour
Salience of drink-seeking behaviour
Increased tolerance to alcohol
Repeated withdrawal symptoms
Repeated relief or avoidance of withdrawal symptoms by further drinking
Subjective awareness of compulsion to drink
Reinstatement of the previous elements after abstinence

Further assessment can be by means of the Severity of Alcohol Dependence Questionnaire (SADQ) (Stockwell *et al.* 1979) which is divided into five sections dealing respectively with (i) physical symptoms (ii) affective symptoms (iii) craving and relief drinking (iv) daily consumption and (v) recurrence of symptoms after abstinence. As well as giving detailed factorial information, the questionnaire serves to distinguish mild to moderate dependence in those with scores up to 35 from severe dependence at scores of 36 and above. For the clinical reasons explained at the beginning of this section this distinction may be extremely important.

Goal Choice. From the information now available it should be possible to assist the patient in deciding whether he chooses a goal of controlled drinking or whether abstinence is more desirable and appropriate. If the former, the type of controlled drinking must be clearly defined.

Intervention. Some, particularly the severely dependent patient, will need to be referred to specialised agencies at this time. If successful with these he may require more help at the primary care level later particularly with relapse prevention.

With the others many different intervention elements may be needed. Self-monitoring for stimulus recognition and control is important so that the high risk situations may be identified and alternative ways of coping rehearsed. Elements of social skills training will help the patient learn to refuse alcoholic drinks without embarrassment. The type of non-alcoholic drinks available may be discussed so that an appropriate choice may be made in advance of need. It is important to consider and reframe the Abstinence Violation Effect mentioned earlier and adjustments in life style should be considered.

Alcoholics Anonymous have a long and honoured place in the management of this problem and branches exist in all areas and can be contacted through the telephone book. For the reasons discussed above they may not always be the most suitable agency. In Britain Drinkwatchers (Accept Services; address on p. 137) publish a lot of information about controlling drinking and run groups where the sensible drinking approach is advocated. Unfortunately they are not available in all areas.

BBC Further Education programmes 'Dealing with Drink' for helpers and 'What's your poison' for drinkers were both accompanied by useful books which take a broad approach to the problem. They are now out of print but may be obtained from libraries.

The Scottish Health Education Group publish an excellent pocket-sized behaviourally based kit for GPs to give patients whom they suspect are drinking too much. It is entitled DRAMS (Drinking Reasonably And Moderately with Self-control). The kit consists of a medical record card for the doctor and a booklet for the patient. The latter contains information on the medical and non-medical effects of alcohol, information about how to cut down and specimen diary sheets.

Other Drugs

The number of other substances that can be abused is legion and the problem is becoming daily a more important one. In many cases the substance is either dangerous, illegal or uncontrollable or all three so that controlled use is not an available option. Apart from that, however, most of the factors operating with alcohol problems, particularly the Relapse Prevention model and the importance of the Abstinence Violation Effect apply as well to other substances. Recognition of the problem and early straightforward advice about ways of stopping may be very effective.

Figure 7.3: Severity of Alcohol Dependence Questionnaire

S.A D Q

NAME ....

AGE ....

SEX ....

First of all, we would like you to recall a recent month when you were drinking heavily in a way which, for you, was fairly typical of a heavy drinking period. Please fill in the month and the year.

MONTH......................... YEAR...............

We would like to know more about your drinking during this time **and during other periods when your drinking was similar.** We want to know how often you experienced certain feelings. Please reply to each statement by putting a circle round ALMOST NEVER or SOMETIMES or OFTEN or NEARLY ALWAYS after each question.

First we want to know about the physical symptoms that you have experienced **first thing in the morning** during these typical periods of **heavy drinking.**

PLEASE ANSWER EVERY QUESTION

1. During a heavy drinking period, I wake up feeling sweaty.
   ALMOST NEVER   SOMETIMES   OFTEN   NEARLY ALWAYS

2. During a heavy drinking period, my hands shake first thing in the morning.
   ALMOST NEVER   SOMETIMES   OFTEN   NEARLY ALWAYS

3. During a heavy drinking period, my whole body shakes violently first thing in the morning if I don't have a drink.
   ALMOST NEVER   SOMETIMES   OFTEN   NEARLY ALWAYS

4. During a heavy drinking period, I wake up absolutely drenched in sweat.
   ALMOST NEVER   SOMETIMES   OFTEN   NEARLY ALWAYS

The following statements refer to moods and states of mind you may have experienced **first thing in the morning** during these periods of **heavy drinking.**

5. When I'm drinking heavily, I dread waking up in the morning.
   ALMOST NEVER   SOMETIMES   OFTEN   NEARLY ALWAYS

6. During a heavy drinking period, I am frightened of meeting people first thing in the morning.
   ALMOST NEVER   SOMETIMES   OFTEN   NEARLY ALWAYS

7. During a heavy drinking period, I feel at the edge of despair when I awake.
   ALMOST NEVER   SOMETIMES   OFTEN   NEARLY ALWAYS

8. During a heavy drinking period, I feel very frightened when I awake.
   ALMOST NEVER   SOMETIMES   OFTEN   NEARLY ALWAYS

PLEASE ANSWER EVERY QUESTION

The following statements also refer to the recent period **when your drinking was heavy,** and to periods like it.

9. During a heavy drinking period, I like to have a morning drink.
    ALMOST NEVER   SOMETIMES   OFTEN   NEARLY ALWAYS

10. During a heavy drinking period, I always gulp my first few morning drinks down as quickly as possible.
    ALMOST NEVER   SOMETIMES   OFTEN   NEARLY ALWAYS

11. During a heavy drinking period, I drink in the morning to get rid of the shakes.
    ALMOST NEVER   SOMETIMES   OFTEN   NEARLY ALWAYS

12. During a heavy drinking period, I have a very strong craving for a drink when I awake.
    ALMOST NEVER   SOMETIMES   OFTEN   NEARLY ALWAYS

Again the following statements refer to the **recent period of heavy drinking** and the periods like it.

13. During a heavy drinking period, I drink more than a quarter of a bottle of spirits per day (4 doubles or 1 bottle of wine or 4 pints of beer).
    ALMOST NEVER   SOMETIMES   OFTEN   NEARLY ALWAYS

14. During a heavy drinking period, I drink more than half a bottle of spirits per day (or 2 bottles of wine or 8 pints of beer).
    ALMOST NEVER   SOMETIMES   OFTEN   NEARLY ALWAYS

15. During a heavy drinking period, I drink more than one bottle of spirits per day (or 4 bottles of wine or 15 pints of beer).
    ALMOST NEVER   SOMETIMES   OFTEN   NEARLY ALWAYS

16. During a heavy drinking period, I drink more than two bottles of spirits per day (or 8 bottles of wine or 30 pints of beer).
    ALMOST NEVER   SOMETIMES   OFTEN   NEARLY ALWAYS

IMAGINE THE FOLLOWING SITUATION:
  (1) You have been COMPLETELY off drink for a FEW WEEKS,
  (2) You then drink VERY HEAVILY for TWO DAYS,

HOW WOULD YOU FEEL THE **MORNING AFTER** THOSE TWO DAYS OF HEAVY DRINKING?

17. I would start to sweat.
    NOT AT ALL   SLIGHTLY   MODERATELY   QUITE A LOT

18. My hands would shake.
    NOT AT ALL   SLIGHTLY   MODERATELY   QUITE A LOT

19. My body would shake.
    NOT AT ALL   SLIGHTLY   MODERATELY   QUITE A LOT

20. I would be craving for a drink.
    NOT AT ALL   SLIGHTLY   MODERATELY   QUITE A LOT

Source: Reprinted by kind permission of Prof. Ray Hodgson. Dept. of Clinical Psychology, Whitchurch Hospital, Whitchurch, Cardiff, and colleagues to whom all enquiries should be addressed.

References

Hodgson, R., Rankin, H. and Stockwell, T. (1979) 'Alcohol dependence and the priming effect', *Behaviour Research and Therapy, 17*, 379–87
Mahoney, M. J. and Mahoney, K. (1976) *Permanent Weight Control — A total solution to the dieter's dilemma*, New York, Norton and Co.
Marlatt, G. A. and George, W. H. (1984), 'Relapse prevention: Introduction and overview of the model', *British Journal of Addiction, 79*, 261–73
Perri, G. Shapiro, R. M. Ludwig, W. W., Twentyman, C. T. and McAdoo, W. G. (1984) 'Maintenance strategies for the treatment of obesity: an evaluation of relapse prevention training and post-treatment contact by mail and telephone', *Journal of Consulting and Clinical Psychology, 52*, 404–13
Raw, M. (1976) 'Persuading people to stop smoking', *Behaviour Research and Therapy, 14*, 77–101
Russell, M. A. H., Raw, M. and Jarvis, M. J. (1980) 'Clinical use of nicotine chewing gum', *British Medical Journal, 28*, 1599–602
Russell, M. A. H., Wilson, C., Taylor, C. and Baker, C. D. (1979) 'Effect of general practitioners' advice against smoking', *British Medical Journal, 2*, 231–5
Ruzek, J. *Drinkwatchers Handbook*, London, Accept Publications
Stockwell, T., Hodgson, R., Edwards, G., Taylor, C. and Rankin, H. 'The development of a questionnaire to measure severity of alcohol dependence', *British Journal of Addiction, 74*, 79–87
Stuart, R. B. and Davis, B. (1972) *Slim Chance in a Fat World*, Illinois, Research Press

Recommended for Further Reading

Heather, N. and Robertson, I. (1983) *Controlled Drinking*, London, Methuen
Raw, M. and Heller, J. (1984) *Helping People to Stop Smoking*, London, Health Education Council
Sobell, M. B. and Sobell, L. C. (1978) *Behavioral Treatment of Alcohol Problems*, New York, Plenum

Books for Patients

Oswald, I. and Adam, K. (1983) *Get a Better Night's Sleep. Positive health guide*, London, Martin Dunitz
East, R., Towers, B. and Moreton, W. (1982) *No Smoke: A self-help handbook for people who want to give up smoking*. Published by the authors at Kingston Polytechnic, Kingston, Surrey
Halhuber, C. (trans by N. Fowler) *Cigarette End: Do it yourself programme for stopping smoking for ever*. Wellingborough, Thorsons
Robertson, I. and Heather, N. 'So you want to cut down your drinking' adapted as 'Your drinking and your health' part of the DRAMS package for use by GPs. Published by Scottish Health Education Group, Woodburn House, Canaan Lane, Edinburgh EH10 4SG, Scotland.
Orbach, S. (1978) *Fat is a Feminist Issue* and (1982) *Fat is a Feminist Issue 2*, London, Hamlyn

Useful Addresses

Accept Services (UK), Accept Clinic, 200 Seagrave Road, London SW6 1RQ. Advice on controlled drinking.

ASH (Action on Smoking and Health) 5–11 Mortimer Street, London W1N 7RH. Supply of non-smoking leaflets.

Scottish Health Education Group, Woodburn House, Canaan Lane, Edinburgh EG10 4SG

Equipment

Tally Wrist Counters obtainable from the Behavior Research Company, Box 3351, Kansas City, Kansas 66103, USA

Nicotine Chewing Gum 'Nicorette' manufactured by AB Leo, Sweden. Supplied in the UK by Lundbeck Ltd., Lundbeck House, Hastings Street, Luton, Bedfordshire.

8 COGNITIVE-BEHAVIOURAL MANAGEMENT IN DEPRESSION

The psychological treatment of depression has evoked more interest in recent years than almost any other subject in the cognitive-behavioural field. It may seem rather a luxury to extend this interest into primary care as, unlike most of the other problem areas that we have covered, the general practitioner already has available to him effective and respected methods of treatment. It is not our contention that anti-depressant drug treatment should be abandoned in favour of an exclusively psychological approach, rather that there are several important advantages in being able to combine the two or in having a choice of therapies.

Amongst certain groups of patients and the news media, drug treatment of all forms of psychiatric disorder is increasingly being questioned and criticised. Whilst anxiety over benzodiazepines seems well-founded, it seems illogical and dangerous to tar antidepressants with the same brush. Ill-informed criticism may actually prevent depressed patients receiving the treatment that they need and deserve. Drug treatment is, however, likely to be more convincing and logical to the patient if it forms part of a regime that recognises that the patient's self-image and way of life outside the consulting room are important and shows concern for his thoughts and behaviour. When the whole problem is being tackled, the drugs may seem more acceptable and the oft-heard criticism 'I went to my doctor but all he did was to give me tablets' can be avoided.

History of Cognitive Behaviour Therapy for Depression

In 1974 Seligman and his co-workers described changes in animals subjected to uncontrollable shock and other aversive events (Seligman 1975, see Chapter 1). These animals developed lack of motivation to initiate escape and were slow to learn control when it became available. They also developed stomach ulcers and other evidence of emotional change. To explain these changes, Seligman proposed the theory of 'learned helplessness' which, he suggested, occurred when an organism had no control over outcomes of unpleasant events.

138

The practical application of this theoretical work was provided by Beck and his colleagues (Beck *et al.* 1979, see Chapter 4) who in successive publications have developed systems of treatment based on the modification of activities and thoughts of depressed patients (Cognitive Behaviour Therapy — CBT). As first presented, these systems were seen as alternatives to drugs and required extensive therapist training and many hours of treatment. More recently Blackburn and her colleagues (Blackburn *et al.* 1981) in Scotland have shown advantages in combined drug and CBT in hospital outpatients. A GP patient group in the same study did equally well on the combination and CBT alone, both being superior to drugs alone. Many workers are now interested in separating out the essential elements of the CBT package with a view to much shorter, simpler interventions which would be suitable for use in the consulting room as an adjunct to traditional methods of treatment (Teasdale 1985).

Principles of Effective Treatment

Depression may be seen as a response to current experiences perceived as highly aversive and uncontrollable. The depression itself then modifies perceptions of current events, recall of memories and significance of symptoms in such a way that the negative aspects are selected, thereby increasing the depression by a vicious circle feedback. Negative aspects are regarded by the depressed patient as being due to global, permanent defects and inadequacies in himself as a person. The positive aspects of life, if noticed at all, will be attributed to transient chance external circumstances.

The factors operating to maintain depression once it is established include:

(1) Major life difficulties and stressors — which would be aversive for anybody whether depressed or not.
(2) Minor life problems such as domestic, child rearing and work difficulties which seem highly aversive and uncontrollable to the depressed person but not to the non-depressed.
(3) Memories of past depressing experiences which surface in the form of depressive ruminations if the depressed person is not otherwise occupied.
(4) The depressed state itself.

Different techniques may be required to treat each of these but the last, i.e. depression about depression, is probably the most important target for psychological approaches. First, in order to counteract the prevailing view that the depression is due to personal inadequacy, information must be given explaining the symptoms as those of a well-understood psychological state. This state is experienced by many and occurs as a natural reaction to certain circumstances affecting behaviour, thoughts, mood and bodily functions. It can be reduced by learning certain techniques which are under the patient's own control.

Second, a structured framework must be provided in which the patient learns and practises the appropriate coping techniques.

Third, the programme should provide ample feedback and monitoring so that the patient recognises the effects of his acquired skills.

By these steps the 'depression about depression' is reduced and a sense of control over his problem is returned to the patient.

In addition to these steps the first three factors may require additional techniques. These include the development of problem-solving skills and help in specific areas where difficulties exist such as in marriage or in employment.

These elements described above by Teasdale seem to be common to the effective psychological treatments for depression. For the sake of consistency, the theory and practice which are now described in detail are adapted to the requirements of primary care from all the work of Beck (Beck *et al.* 1979, see Chapter 4) and his co-workers.

The Cognitive Theory of Depression

This depends upon three components:

(1) The *cognitive triad* of *negative automatic thoughts* concerning the depressive himself (e.g. 'I'm no good at anything'), the environment he lives in (e.g. 'Nobody can get a job in this place') and the future (e.g. 'It will never get any better')

(2) *Thinking errors* — examples include *all or nothing thinking* (e.g. 'If I don't get this contract I'm a total failure'), *overgeneralisation* (e.g. 'I'm always miserable at weekends'), *discounting the positive* (e.g. 'Nothing went right today'), *jumping to conclusions* (e.g. 'Other mothers never find it difficult to keep their children happy'), *catastrophising* (e.g. 'Even if I do win the pools the cheque

will get lost in the post'), *global judgements* (e.g. 'I got that wrong so I must be useless'), and *personalisations* (e.g. 'Everybody in my house always gets ill').

(3) *Assumptions* These are underlying attitudes which are organised from past experience and produced to influence the way in which new situations and pieces of information are handled. They include the 'shoulds' and 'ought tos', the 'I must have . . .' or 'I need . . .' and the 'would be terrible if . . .' statements. The assumptions often imply unrecognised or half-recognised values which none the less exert a very powerful and restricting influence on a person's thinking.

Assessment

This must include:

(i) the *symptoms* of mood, thoughts and behaviour including any thoughts of suicide;
(ii) the effect of the depressed state on work, home and family;
(iii) other problems;
(iv) evidence of the cognitive triad;
(v) duration, precipitants and consequences.

From this information a problem list can be drawn up. The patient is then consulted as to which problem seems most important or urgent.

An explanation of the approach is given with, if possible, a simple experiment to show how thoughts can affect mood. This can be done by getting the patient first to think about a recent depressing time or experience, describe his mood and then transfer to a neutral or pleasant activity such as describing sights seen from the window, demonstrating that the mood will usually change with this distraction.

Assessment of initial severity is aided by getting the patient to complete the Beck Depression Inventory (Figure 8.1) at the first visit; this is then repeated regularly in order to monitor progress. The BDI consists of 21 items each containing four or five alternative statements. It can easily be completed in a few minutes before or during a session. The maximum score is 63, mild depression scores 14–20, moderate 21–26, severe over 26. It should not be used to

Figure 8.1: Beck Inventory

Name   Date

On this questionnaire are groups of statements. Please read each group of statements carefully. Then pick out the one statement in each group which best describes the way you have been feeling the PAST WEEK. INCLUDING TODAY: Circle the number beside the statement you picked. If several statements in the group seem to apply equally well, circle each one. Be sure to read all the statements in each group before making your choice.

1   0   I do not feel sad.
     1   I feel sad.
     2   I am sad all the time and I can't snap out of it.
     3   I am so sad or unhappy that I can't stand it.

2   0   I am not particularly discouraged about the future.
     1   I feel discouraged about the future.
     2   I feel I have nothing to look forward to.
     3   I feel that the future is hopeless and that things cannot improve.

3   0   I do not feel like a failure.
     1   I feel that I have failed more than the average person.
     2   As I look back on my life, all I can see is a lot of failures.
     3   I feel I am a complete failure as a person.

4   0   I get as much satisfaction out of things as I used to.
     1   I don't enjoy things the way I used to.
     2   I don't get real satisfaction out of anything any more.
     3   I am dissatisfied or bored with everything.

5   0   I don't feel particularly guilty.
     1   I feel guilty a good part of the time.
     2   I feel quite guilty most of the time.
     3   I feel guilty all of the time.

6   0   I don't feel I am being punished.
     1   I feel I may be punished.
     2   I expect to be punished.
     3   I feel I am being punished.

7   0   I don't feel disappointed in myself.
     1   I am disappointed in myself.
     2   I am disgusted with myself.
     3   I hate myself.

8   0   I don't feel I am any worse than anybody else.
     1   I am critical of myself for my weaknesses or mistakes.
     2   I blame myself all the time for my faults.
     3   I blame myself for everything bad that happens.

9   0   I don't have any thoughts of killing myself.
     1   I have thoughts of killing myself, but I would not carry them out.
     2   I would like to kill myself.
     3   I would kill myself if I had the chance.

10   0   I don't cry any more than usual.
     1   I cry more now than I used to.
     2   I cry all the time now.
     3   I used to be able to cry, but now I can't cry even though I want to.

11   0   I am no more irritated now than I ever am.
     1   I get annoyed or irritated more easily than I used to.
     2   I feel irritated all the time now.
     3   I don't get irritated at all by the things that used to irritate me.

12   0   I have not lost interest in other people.
     1   I am less interested in other people than I used to be.
     2   I have lost most of my interest in other people.
     3   I have lost all my interest in other people.

13   0   I make decisions about as well as I ever could.
     1   I put off making decisions more than I used to.
     2   I have greater difficulty in making decisions than before.
     3   I can't make decisions at all anymore.

14   0   I don't feel I look any worse than I used to.
     1   I am worried that I am looking old or unattractive.
     2   I feel that there are permanent changes in my appearance that make me look
         unattractive.
     3   I believe that I look ugly.

15   0   I can work about as well as before.
     1   It takes an extra effort to get started at doing something.
     2   I have to push myself very hard to do anything.
     3   I can't do any work at all.

16   0   I can sleep as well as usual.
     1   I don't sleep as well as I used to.
     2   I wake up 1-2 hours earlier than usual and find it hard to get back to sleep.
     3   I wake up several hours earlier than I used to and cannot get back to sleep.

17   0   I don't get more tired than usual.
     1   I get tired more easily than I used to.
     2   I get tired from doing almost anything.
     3   I am too tired to do anything.

18   0   My appetite is no worse than usual.
     1   My appetite is not as good as it used to be.
     2   My appetite is much worse now.
     3   I have no appetite at all anymore.

19   0   I haven't lost much weight, if any, lately.   I am purposely trying
     1   I have lost more than 5 pounds.   to lose weight by eating less.
     2   I have lost more than 10 pounds.
     3   I have lost more than 15 pounds.   Yes _____ No _____

20   0   I am no more worried about my health than usual.
     1   I am worried about physical problems such as aches and pains: or
         upset stomach: or constipation.
     2   I am very worried about physical problems and it's hard to think of
         much else.
     3   I am so worried about my physical problems that I cannot think
         about anything else.

21   0   I have not noticed any recent change in my interest in sex.
     1   I am less interested in sex than I used to be.
     2   I am much less interested in sex now.
     3   I have lost interest in sex completely.

---

diagnose depression, only to measure severity once it is diagnosed.

Beck publishes a patients' booklet 'Coping with Depression' which is obtainable from the Center for Cognitive Therapy Philadelphia, and serves as an introduction to the method.

Planning Treatment

The overall objectives of therapy are:
(1) To expand the patient's positive activities by carefully graded tasks and, from this basis,
(2) To demonstrate, monitor, modify faulty thinking and attitudes and arrive at more reasonable and hopeful alternatives.

Activity Scheduling

Depending on the level of depression, it is usual first to focus on activities. It is important to gauge the current level of the patient's activities and to find out what he has given up that he previously found satisfying and enjoyable. The severely depressed patient may find taking a bath or making a pot of tea a challenging task. Even simple activities must often be broken down into shorter, simpler components so that success, which is vital, can be achieved. For the first week or so he is merely asked to fill in a record sheet showing how he spends each hour of the day (Figure 8.2). Using this record as a baseline it is then possible to agree, week by week, gradually more extensive positive target activities, always advancing slowly enough to see that the targets are met. If a target is not met, it is put to the patient that this is not a 'failure' but merely a useful opportunity of gaining more information which will be of help in the future.

As soon as the records are understood and are being properly completed a second stage is introduced whereby each activity is rated on a 1–5 scale for Mastery and Pleasure or, if these terms seem alien to the normal language of the patient, alternatives such as Competence and Satisfaction may be substituted. This enables the patient to concentrate more on the positive aspect of his activities as it can be used to provide evidence that he is selectively attending to the negative and discounting the positive. If the assessments are clearly too low or apparently inaccurate these can be challenged.

Experience gained from activity scheduling can be used to plan a timetable which increases the opportunity for satisfying events or reintroduces those which were previously satisfying but which have

Figure 8.2: Weekly Activity Schedule

NAME .... WEEK BEGINNING ....

	Monday	Tuesday	Wednesday	Thursday	Friday	Saturday	Sunday
9-10							
10-11							
11-12							
12-1							
1-2							
2-3							
3-4							
4-5							
5-6							
6-7							
7-8							
8-12							

been allowed to lapse. These changes are not too time-consuming as much of the work is done by the patient at home. They should however be carefully negotiated as sometimes previous enthusiasms have become associated with the onset of depression and their reintroduction may not be feasible or therapeutic. Under these circumstances an alternative is to look to those subjects in which he has in the past been only mildly interested or to those that seem attractive but have never been explored.

As much time as is available during the session should be used in dealing with the blocks to progress. These may be chiefly of two types: (i) thoughts getting in the way of carrying out assignments, which can be explored and if possible dealt with in advance; and (ii) upsets during the homework period preventing progress e.g. rows at home, unexpected adverse events, drinking bouts, etc. It may be powerfully helpful to suggest to the patient in advance that some such difficulties may be expected and to rehearse his possible response to them.

The Cognitive Component

Recording Automatic Thoughts. Teaching the patient to identify, count and challenge negative automatic thoughts is central to the cognitive component of the treatment. It is explained that the best way is by means of a *record of negative automatic thoughts* on which is written the date and time, the emotion or feeling, the situation and the automatic thoughts associated with that situation. These thoughts may initially be hard to recognise and occur as images or meanings as well as words. Often considerable patient practice is required in the actual situation before thoughts can be accurately identified, as they are recurrent, fleeting and automatic. Paradoxically they may have become so much a normal part of the patient's thinking that he fails to recognise them as a separate phenomenon. Once recognised, these thoughts can be counted and the patient will often come to realise that the more of them he has in a particular day the worse he feels.

Answering Thoughts. Once a reliable record of thoughts is being produced, a start can be made with challenging and answering them. This again is done largely between sessions but guidance as to the procedure used will be needed. There are a number of different techniques that can be used but most revolve round four groups of questions:

(1) Does the evidence support the way you think or is it against it? What objective evidence do you have to back it up? Would somebody else accept that evidence?

Example:

Date/ Time	Situation	Feelings	Immediate Thought	Answer
10/3/9 a.m.	Office — Jim didn't say 'Good Morning'	Worthless	He must think I'm useless and has gone off me.	Perhaps he didn't notice or was concentrating on the balance sheet.

This is also an example of jumping to conclusions. Depressed people assume without any evidence that people are thinking critically about them (thought reading)

(2) What alternatives are there to the explanation (usually negative) that you have given? Is there another more positive alternative?

Example:

Date/ Time	Situation	Feelings	Immediate Thought	Answer
11/8/6 p.m.	Girl-friend refuses to go for a drink.	Sad	It's all over. She was bound to go off me.	Perhaps it was the only night she could wash her hair and she'll come out later in the week.

This is also an example of thinking in all-or-nothing terms and catastrophising (see thinking errors — below).

(3) What is the effect of thinking in this way? Does it help the situation? Does it help you get what you want out of life or is it getting in your way? Is there a more constructive way of thinking?

Example:

Thought I must always know all the answers and be able to show the juniors how to do it.
Advantage Enjoying feeling more knowledgeable than younger colleagues.
Disadvantage There's bound to come a time when I don't know all the answers and then I'll feel worthless. Nobody can know everything all the time.

Brooding over meaningless questions like 'Why is life so unfair?' 'Why didn't I make a different decision in the past?' 'Why do these things always happen to me?' is bound to be depressing as these questions have no useful answer and cannot help the solution of current problems.

(4) What thinking errors are you making? Some of these have been mentioned above. Others include: (a) condemning yourself on the basis of a single mistake 'I forgot Sue's birthday so I must be a hopeless husband'; (b) taking personally casual happenings 'They always run out of cornflakes at the supermarket the day I need them'; or (c) concentrating on the things which have gone wrong 'That was a really terrible day because the car wouldn't start' but forgetting the boss congratulating you on your hard work on the new contract and Tracy winning the music prize.

Example:

Date/ Time	Situation	Feelings	Immediate Thought	Answer
11/2/11 a.m.	Boss said to be sure to finish job quickly	Anxious	I've got it wrong again. I'll be made redundant	It's an important job. He must think I'm reliable or he would have given it to one of the others

When examining faulty thinking the technique of *distancing* is easily learned and particularly helpful. *Distancing* may be spatial in which case the patient is asked to imagine his reactions to another person in the situation which he is facing, or it may be temporal in which case he is asked to imagine his own reactions during a previous (or future) period of his life.

Examples:

'Would you regard your friend Bill as a total failure as a husband if he forgot his wife's birthday?' This may lead to an exploration of the double standard used by the patient in evaluating his own actions and those of others.

'If you had had this bump with the car a year ago how would you have dealt with it?' It may turn out that the same event in a previous time would have produced a very different reaction.

The attitude to exploring thinking errors must be one of experimental cooperation rather than didactic instruction. Not all the hypotheses tried will be valid and there must be a readiness to reformulate ideas in the light of new data.

CBT in Primary Care

Although it may seem that this approach is too complex and time-consuming to be easily adaptable to the primary care setting, there are several compensating advantages:

(1) The techniques are easily broken down for use in very short contact sessions. One thought, thinking error or assumption can be examined at a time.
(2) The individual techniques can be usefully employed without a commitment to the whole package being necessary.

    With the severe depressive much time may have to be spent in activity recording, and scheduling. The cognitive elements of thought spotting and the correction of thinking errors, however, can often be introduced much more rapidly with the mild depression often seen in primary care.
(3) Much of the work is done by the patient himself between sessions.

The Use of Homework

The behavioural element of the treatment requires that the Weekly Activity Schedule is completed at home. Initially this simply records activities but subsequently it is used to plan new ones, firstly by introducing easily attained graded components and then by including a complete enhanced range of confidence-building items. Session time can be used to rehearse the problems which may be encountered in carrying out these schedules and discussing ways round those difficulties actually experienced in the previous week.

Progress in spotting, counting and challenging negative automatic thoughts and rating belief in them is more reliably assessed in homework where the patient is on his own away from the influence of the therapist.

An extremely important element of homework is the construction of experiments to test the validity of predictions. A depressed mother may believe she is a total failure 'because all the other mothers I know get their children to go to bed without a fuss but I can't'. After discussing the evidence for this assertion an experiment may be set up whereby the patient asks other mothers of her acquaintance whether they ever experience such difficulties. It may be that the patient will be much more relieved to find that they do. Even if it turns out that they don't it may become obvious that they do have problems in other areas of child rearing.

Experiments testing predictions should if possible be of the 'no-lose' variety so that even if the patient's negative prediction is supported the information can be used to help in further treatment. The negative results of a first experiment can be used to explore further thinking errors and once a different method of thinking is found a further experiment may be arranged, this time, possibly, with more positive results.

Assumptions

These form the third element of the cognitive model presented earlier. These are the basic beliefs which predispose somebody to depression. They are often tackled last, after symptoms have improved, mainly with the object of helping to prevent recurrence. Their origins are often deep in childhood-learning, when we first began to organise information about the world and set standards. They include the 'shoulds' and 'musts' by which we organise our thinking according to our underlying belief systems.

Some arise out of the identifiable folklore of childhood, for example 'you must finish all your jobs or mummy won't like you', 'you shouldn't answer back', 'nice girls don't do that' or 'you must work hard and pass all your exams'. Built in to all these examples is the idea that if you fail in any of these respects you are in some way worthless. Other assumptions come from more sophisticated and less overt learning by modelling or reinforcement. As well as 'shoulds' and 'musts' they include statements about the catastrophic or awful effects of events, ideas of human worth rated on some internal absolute scale and the necessity of certain things if any sort of happiness is to be found. In essence:

(i)   They are *untrue or irrational* — exaggerated, not supported by evidence or unreal.

(ii) They are *commands* — not conditional or relative. Demands versus wishes, shoulds versus preferences, needs versus wants.

(iii) They *disturb emotions* by being extreme and overwhelming. Depression versus unhappiness, anger versus irritation, anxiety versus concern.

(iv) They do not help *attain goals* as they perpetually get in the way.

Beck (1976) specified some of the assumptions frequently found in depression:

(i)   'In order to be happy, I have to be successful in whatever I undertake'.

(ii) 'To be happy, I must be accepted by all people at all times'.

(iii) 'If I make a mistake it means that I am inept'.

(iv) 'I can't live without you'.

(v)   'If somebody disagrees with me, it means he doesn't like me.'

(vi) 'My value as a person depends on what others think of me.'

Exposing the nature of these assumptions and the potential that they have for damage may in itself promote their change. More specifically, however, they may be tackled by the vertical arrow technique in which a statement is explored by examining the meaning to the patient at deeper and deeper levels until the underlying assumption is uncovered.

Example:

'I've had a row with my wife. I feel terrible'
↓
(What does that mean to you?)
↓
'It means I've upset her and she'll feel miserable'
↓
(If that's true what does it mean to you?)
↓

'It means I'm a lousy husband'

↓

(If that's true what does it say about you?)

↓

'A lousy husband is a worthless person'
i.e. My estimation of my worth as a person depends on success in every aspect of every relationship.

Other techniques include experiments to see what happens if the patient does not for once follow his particular 'shoulds' which will often show that no dire consequences occur. This can be done either in reality or in rehearsal.

References

Beck, A. T. (1976) *Cognitive Therapy and the Emotional Disorders*, New York, International Universities Press

Blackburn, I. M., Bishop, S., Glen, A. I., Whalley, J. J. and Christie, J. E. (1981) 'The efficacy of cognitive therapy in depression: A treatment trial using cognitive therapy and pharmacotherapy, each alone and in combination', *British Journal of Psychiatry, 139*, 181–9

Teasdale, J. (1985) 'Psychological treatments for depression: How do they work', *Behaviour Research and Therapy, 23*, 157–65

Recommended for Further Reading

Beck, A. T., Shaw, A. J., Rush, B. F. and Emery, G. (1979) *Cognitive Therapy of Depression*, Chichester, John Wiley

Williams, J., Mark, G. (1984) *The Psychological Treatment of Depression, A guide to the theory and practice of cognitive behaviour therapy*, London and Canberra, Croom Helm

Books for Patients

Beck, A. T. and Greenberg, R. L. (1974) *Coping with Depression*. New York, Institute for Rational Living

Goldberg, D. P. B. (1984) *Depression*, London, Churchill Livingston

Useful Address

Center for Cognitive Therapy, 133 South 36th Street, Philadelphia, Pennsylvania 19104, USA

9 BEHAVIOURAL MEDICINE I: THE MEDICAL SETTING

This chapter considers the behaviour of clinicians as well as patients and how the two interact. The GP is no longer a lone figure but has been joined by nurses, midwives, health visitors and sometimes others. This team widens the scope of treatment but increases the risk of anonymity, remoteness and bureaucracy. The bigger the team the more difficult is good communication. This is one reason why the subject has already received a lot of attention from experienced authors (Pendleton and Hasler 1983; Byrne and Long 1976) and is a major concern of the Royal College of General Practitioners (RCGP 1972). Another is that communication and understanding are closely linked with adherence to treatment.

Adherence to Treatment Regimes

Doctors find the failure of patients to follow their advice puzzling, frustrating and irritating. After all, why should a patient seek their help and fail to follow their advice? A number of studies, however, have rated non-adherence at between 40 per cent and 50 per cent for a wide range of treatments of many different conditions (Ley 1982a).

Why Do We Fail?

The reasons for this paradox are complex and have not been fully explored (Maguire 1984). Several considerations are important:

(1) The patient may not understand the nature or the significance of the condition. For example, a woman with post-coital bleeding is less likely to follow advice to see a gynaecologist if she believes the condition is due to muscle strain and is ignorant of the possibility of cancer.

(2) The patient may not understand the nature and effect of the treatment. A young woman needing hysterectomy for fibroids may refuse surgery if she believes she will be unsexed and has not been told her ovaries will be conserved.

(3) The patient may expect adverse effects from treatment. A depressed patient is less likely to take antidepressants if she thinks

them to be tranquillisers which she has been led to believe from the media are unfailingly habituating.

(4) The patient may be unprepared for the complexities of the advice given. A patient who feels tired and is asking for a tonic may genuinely expect a 'magic bullet' which will cure her at once. She may be unprepared for the suggestion that her problems have many factors. These may involve her children, job, husband, lifestyle and menstrual pattern which will all need to be considered if rational answers are to be found.

(5) The same patient in the previous example may understand the advice but be completely without the resources to carry it out for lack of mobility, money or housing.

(6) In their thinking doctors recognise two types of patient, those that follow their advice and get better or at least benefit and those who reject it and remain ill or get worse. They are much less ready to come to terms with the other two possible groups, i.e. those who follow advice and don't benefit and those who reject it and still get better. A moment's reflection is enough to realise that both these groups are sizeable. Operant theory, which has been discussed in Chapter 4, clearly indicates the importance of these groups. Cooperation is extinguished in the third group and non-cooperation reinforced in the fourth. Personal or hearsay experience in the first two groups will increase the likelihood of medical advice being followed. The opposite, of course, is true of the others. The man who is told his chest pain is indigestion and will respond to antacids is less likely to take them if his father received the same advice and dropped dead of a heart attack shortly afterwards.

These factors influencing treatment adherence are summarised in the Health Belief Model:

Belief about susceptibility to
   disease increases
Belief about the likely severity
   of disease increases   Likelihood
Belief about the likely benefit of   of adherence
   treatment increases
Belief about likely barriers to
   treatment decreases
(Becker and Rosenstock 1984)

Several other factors also predict non-adherence:

(1) Duration and complexity of the regime
(2) Patients' general dissatisfaction with the service
(3) Lack of supportive follow-up

An out-patient study in an hypertension clinic found that drop-out rate was related to waiting time and non-availability and variations in staff. There is no reason why these effects should not be the same in primary care. Increasing off duty and decreasing use of personal lists may well therefore be interfering with successful management.

Effects are not only clinical. A recent survey indicated that probably 20 per cent and possibly 25 per cent of all hospital admissions were due to lapses in treatment (Ausburn 1981). The cost is substantial.

In spite of the evidence, however, many clinicians still give the problem scant attention.

What Can Be Done?

Both practice organisation and communication in the consultation can be improved.

The Organisation of the Practice. This can be subjected to a behavioural assessment. The questions to be answered are: What are the problems in the way the practice is working at present? What triggers produce these problems? What are their consequences and to whom — staff or patients? What improves them or makes them worse? What has been tried already? What would be the effect of change? What would be reasonable goals and how could these best be achieved?

Baseline measurements resemble a practice audit but with particular emphasis on the behaviour to be changed. As with other kinds of baseline recording, it is useful to employ more than one observer. This could be a role for a patient liaison group as well as staff members (Hutton and Robins 1985).

Possible changes might include:

(1) The design or re-design of patient information cards or booklets to explain to patients the way the practice works and what services are available.
(2) A staff information handbook giving the preferred way of handling routine and occasional problems. These might

include daily home visit requests, complaints from patients and collapse in the waiting room.

(3) The introduction of personal lists, where these do not exist already, in order to help one patient get to know one doctor and vice versa.

(4) The rationalisation of weekly timetables to ensure a spread of availability over the week. It may be helpful to publish time-tables with the patient booklet so that patients can always know when their doctor or health visitor is likely to be avail-able.

The Consultation. Most clinicians think that they are good communicators. Criticism from patients is uncommon but Ley (1982b) found that on direct enquiry a median of 35 per cent of patients expressed dissatisfaction with communications with their GP. There seem to be problems with particular types of patients. Couples, adolescents and medically trained people were all found difficult, by doctors themselves. Particular types of problem also seem to cause difficulties for both doctors and patients. Both groups were uncomfortable with sexual and drug abuse problems. Doctors tend to prefer somatic to psychological diagnoses which perhaps reflects the strong bias of medical teaching which still all too often stresses that psychological diagnosis should not be entertained until a physical one has been excluded. This is a spurious order of priorities and excludes the possibility of physical, psychological and social factors all being present.

Patients also prefer a 'somatic' ticket of entry into the system. One reason for this is a reflection of the doctor's own usual bias. Another is that patients fear to be thought weak or, even worse, mad, and these days fear being put on tranquillisers worst of all. The patient may also believe that co-existing physical conditions will be disre-garded and not receive proper treatment.

The traditional scheme of medical interviewing taught to the clinician medical student on his first day on the wards is also to blame. It is rigid, highly physically biased and completely directed by the doctor who asks a set routine of questions (Byrne and Long 1976). Enquiries about family, home, job and the impact or interpretation of the problem are usually scanty or absent altogether. It is too soon to tell if new GPs, with the benefit of vocational training and the triaxial emphasis of the MRCGP exam, will permanently adopt different methods. The benefits of similar thinking are already apparent in psychiatric nurse training.

There are three main areas in which the consultation can be improved:

(1) Providing an interview that is satisfactory in the patient's estimation:
(2) Elucidating accurately the patient's problem(s);
(3) Giving information about management which is likely to be remembered.

Satisfaction with the Consultation. This can be secured in the following ways:

(1) A friendly rather than business manner on the part of the doctor.
(2) An understanding by the doctor of the patient's real concerns.
(3) A consultation that does not thwart the expectations of the patient. (Korsch *et al.* 1968)

Accurate Identification of Problems. Symptoms must be clarified beyond the mere label to find out what they actually mean, when and where they occur and what other factors affect them. Typical examples would be 'can't sleep' and 'giddy attacks' neither of which yields any useful information until it is explored further. This has already been discussed in detail in Chapter 2.

Goldberg and Huxley (1980, p. 80) identified ten definable and teachable behaviours which predicted the family doctor's success as a case detector. These are, at the outset (of an interview):

(1) Makes immediate eye contact
(2) Clarifies the presenting complaint
(3) Uses directive questions for physical complaints
(4) Uses 'open to closed' clones, i.e. the interview starts with open questions of the 'How have things been?' 'Are there any other worries?' 'How has this affected you?' type and then goes on to find out in detail what are the factors relevant to each symptom by closed, direct questioning of the more traditional kind

and, during the interview:

(5) Empathetic style (frequency) i.e. how often the doctor appears to understand the patient's feelings or put himself in the patient's place by his comments or questions

(6) Sensitive to verbal cues, i.e. he can change his line of enquiry in response to some half-dropped hint

(7) Sensitive to non-verbal cues i.e. as above but in response to a gesture or a grimace

(8) Doesn't read notes during history. This is a very common vice and yet it is the simplest thing in the world to say politely to the patient 'Would you mind if I just had a minute to catch up on/remind myself of your notes?'

(9) Can deal with overtalkativeness. Being able to listen to the patient does not imply sitting in silence whilst the irrelevant complaints about distant relatives or domestic pets are described.

(10) Asks fewer questions about past history. We have stressed before the importance of a predominantly here-and-now approach although we do not deny that past history can be extremely relevant and important

We would add to these that a question about how the patient sees his problem, and how it is affecting his daily life should be considered in every clinical interview.

Management. Finally the patient must know what he has to do. First, is he able and willing to respond to the offered regime? The old joke of the wheel-chair-bound patient being told to take more exercise is often sadly true. Rheumatology and respiratory clinics advise patients to lose weight or stop smoking without any attempt to consider how they might do it. The patient must have the resources in his repertory or if not he must be helped to obtain them. It follows that any advice is much more likely to be effective if it is compatible with the patient's existing lifestyle or preferences. Second, the patient must remember the advice if he is to follow it. Much information given in consultations is forgotten. A number of factors help recall: (Becker and Rosenstock 1984).

(1) Important information should be stressed and given first.

(2) Instructions should be simple and given in simple language whether written or verbal. Newspapers are good at this; doctors and, sadly, psychologists often are not.

(3) Instructions can be repeated at the same or different consultations. The patient may be encouraged to go through them himself but his dignity should not be offended.

(4) Advice should be specific e.g. 'Walk a mile a day' not 'take more exercise' or 'drink a half pint of water morning and evening' not 'have plenty of fluids'.

(5) Checks should be made that he has understood and should give him an opportunity to say if he hasn't.

(6) The advice should be arranged in a stated order, for example 'I am going to tell you what is wrong, what I am going to do, what you should do and what I expect will happen. Now first, what's wrong . . .'.

Hospital advice often seems less well understood than primary care management and time can usefully be spent checking that hospital instructions have been understood when the patient returns to the primary care. This may become more necessary as treatment becomes more sophisticated.

The Elderly Patient. There are a number of additional techniques which are particularly helpful with the elderly patient who may find remembering to follow instructions particularly difficult. These can also sometimes be used with the younger age group.

(1) When remembering to take medicines, a container where the day's dose can be put into compartments marked 'breakfast', 'lunch', 'tea' and 'before bed' by the patient or a carer is extremely useful. Such containers can sometimes be made by grandsons in carpentry classes.

(2) The doctor should try to give instructions to a relative or friend as well as the patient.

(3) It is important to make sure the patient can take the form of medicine prescribed i.e. open containers or swallow pills.

(4) Patients should be encouraged to destroy or, preferably, return old medicines — many elderly patients' medicine cupboards contain truly horrifying quantities of unused drugs.

Special Situations in Medicine

There are a number of situations in medicine which place particular requirements on communications. Most of them involve doctors working with patients in a particular setting but the final section will deal with the inter-professional relationship between doctors and psychologists working in primary care or with primary care patients.

The Sick Role

Certain patients attempt to cope with distress by becoming ill. Failure to recognise this will lead to a frustrated doctor and a disillusioned patient. Physical symptoms arising in these circumstances are never likely to respond to medical treatment unless their true cause is recognised and appropriate management provided.

Certain patients have entrenched attitudes towards their condition that seem to preclude any possibility of recovery. Such patients consume medical time and resources without achieving progress. They are, in a sense, sticking to the rules of the game. This demands that in exchange for the privileges of the sick role such as being excused work and receiving extra family attention, they must be seen to cooperate with expert, usually medical, advice. Whereas it is entirely reasonable that ill or disabled patients enter, at least temporarily, the sick role, there are a number of factors which may contribute to the patient remaining in it once the original need has passed. The reinforcers of the sick role may include:

(1) Increased attention from other family members
(2) Avoidance of the aversiveness of normal working life
(3) Perceived difficulties in recovering, for example:
    (i)   Side effects of drugs
    (ii) Painful operations
    (iii) Difficulties in relearning the skills of normal life
    (iv) Lack of interest outside the illness
    (v) Pleasant effects on mood of drugs e.g. analgesics or tranquillisers

Assessment. It is always worthwhile to take a fresh look at the sick role patient. The first decision is whether there is a major problem that justifies the effort of intervention. Second, a clear idea must be obtained of who is to benefit from any intervention — is it the patient himself or, for example, a spouse or other carer? The reinforcing factors must be determined and a decision taken as to which, if any, can be changed. Other social or emotional factors not previously noted must be investigated. Enquiry into the nature and result of any previous attempts to help the problem is also worthwhile. The effect on all parties of a successful attempt at modification is considered. Finally, clear goals must be established, usually in positive terms, for example, getting a paid job, being able to walk to school and fetch the grandchildren or being able to play golf once a week. As always it cannot be stressed too strongly that these goals must be those of the patient, however bizarre they may seem, not those of the therapist. If the initial goals are out of reach smaller intermediate steps can be negotiated.

Intervention. Time spent with these patients on exploring the rationale of a tentative programme and obtaining their understanding and cooperation in the steps that are being contemplated is essential. Without this the chances of success are slim indeed. In particular the following must be considered:

(1) The long term prognosis
(2) The benefits to be obtained by the programme in terms of life style and quality
(3) The difficulties and blocks which may be experienced, as seen by both the patient and the doctor

The next element in the programme is the changing of unhelpful attitudes in spouses, relatives and friends. Any behaviour reinforcing invalidism will need modifying and relatives' cooperation must be obtained to change circle A to circle B

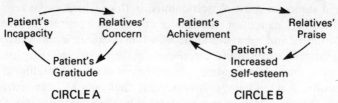

At this point consideration must also be given to whether the relatives' own self-esteem may suffer in this change.

The third element will usually be the graded re-introduction of activities shaping behaviour in the direction of the pre-set goals.

There are two major sources of reinforcement for these activities:

(1) The achievements in themselves as perceived by the patient with the aid of as much feedback as can be mustered from those around him.
(2) Direct reinforcement from family and friends who in turn may need some reinforcement and rehearsal from the doctor or other professional.

This can be an exhausting process leaving the therapist feeling like a burnt-out cheer leader but if the first gains are achieved the others often follow more easily. The guidelines to success are that the regime should ideally be as simple as possible, as short as possible and involve the minimum possible change in the patient's life style *but* if it has to be more complex one step must be taken at a time. If it has to be longer, there must be very frequent reviews of progress and if it has to involve several different items to be changed, again one step at a time is taken, with sensitivity to blocks so that these may not result in loss of confidence.

Many other intervention strategies may be required as part of the package and some of these have been covered elsewhere. In particular those discussed when the management of pain is considered in the next chapter may have a place in the management of any form of problematic sick behaviour.

Pregnancy, Childbirth and the Puerperium

The explosion of literature in the behavioural medicine field has left maternity care relatively untouched. The reasons for this are unclear but may be associated with the transient nature of pregnancy and the rigid stance of most obstetric units, both of which make research difficult. Change in the management of pregnancy involves attitudinal and behavioural modification in obstetric and midwifery hierarchies often more interested in their concepts of obstetric 'safety' than in the treatment of parturient women as intelligent and sensitive human beings. It is possible that only by demonstrating that obstetric safety is indeed affected by these considerations that progress will be made. There is already some evidence that this is so. It has been demonstrated that high levels of anxiety in pregnancy and labour affect the incidence of somatic complaints in pregnancy, the incidence of premature labour and the number of obstetric complications (Crandon 1979). It has also been shown that antenatal preparation does reduce the pain experience in childbirth possibly by increasing mothers' sense of personal control over events (Brewin and Bradley 1982). It has also been shown that relaxation rather than medication or hospitalisation can be effectively used to control raised blood pressure during pregnancy (Little *et al.* 1984).

Several other measures, some already routine at certain centres, seem helpful. These are:

During the antenatal period:

(1) As much *information* as possible concerning the physiology and management of pregnancy, involving not only talks, films and question-and-answer sessions for both parents but also feed-back on the various procedures. These would include allowing the mother to see the baby on a real-time ultrasound scanner with expert and sensitive comments (Reading and Cox 1982) on the features seen and an explanation of the nature and purpose of blood tests, all in easily understood language.

(2) Dealing with *negative thoughts and feelings* about being able to cope with labour, motherhood or related subjects by (i) allowing time and opportunity for them to be expressed, for example 'How do you feel about having the baby?' 'Are there any worries or problems?' and (ii) employing the cognitive techniques described in Chapter 8 for modifying them.

(3) *Physical relaxation training.* This is routine in obstetric practices but it is important to consider with individual patients how they are going to use it in labour and also cue it to other sources of tension such as early difficulties in breast feeding. A very important adjunct to relaxation for decreasing mothers' anxiety is to expose them as much as possible to the labour ward or delivery suite during pregnancy. This may be rejected on the grounds that it cannot easily be accomplished within the hospital organisation. We see it, however, as an extremely important desensitisation exercise, as there can be few things more anxiety-provoking than to find yourself in a vulnerable and highly apprehensive condition surrounded by unfamiliar sights and sounds loaded with personal threat.

(4) Measures to increase *perception of control* over the pregnancy by both the mother herself and by her attendants. These include cooperation over various measures of antenatal care such as vaginal examinations, blood tests, scans and amniocentesis so that they are chosen by a fully informed patient, not inflicted on her. Various

options about the management of labour should be discussed — Where is it to take place? Who is to help and be present? What are the preferred methods of pain relief and what is available? Are induction of labour and episiotomy likely to be used and, if so, does the patient understand them and has she strong feelings about them? Does she understand the various options for the position at delivery and does she have a preference?

During labour and delivery:

If the measures suggested above have been taken during the antenatal period, there may be little to do in labour except implement and adjust them as circumstances dictate. If for any reason proper discussion has not taken place some of the choices will have to be made when labour has already started. This is second best, but much better than inflicting a state of helplessness upon the mother.

One major problem is that in most of North America and many parts of Europe, the primary care team has no involvement with or influence upon labour. We see the involvement of community midwives and, if possible, GPs in all stages of obstetric care including labour to have real advantages. Such involvement, (i) ensures that decisions and discussions taken in the antenatal period have a direct bearing on the conduct of the labour and (ii) secures the attendance of consistent staff known to the mother which we have seen is an important correlate of good communication.

During the puerperium:

Four factors have been identified as predictors of *post natal depression* (Elliot 1985): (i) past history of neurotic depression; (ii) past history of post natal depression; (iii) poor quality of the marital relationship; and (iv) anxiety during the first trimester of pregnancy. Perhaps rather surprisingly, obstetric and demographic factors do not seem to have much influence. The degree to which we can modify post natal depression by attention to these factors must remain an open question but it would seem logical to try and improve at least the fourth and possibly the third. Management of this distressing form of depression has normally been by means of physical treatments. Cognitive therapy, perhaps in groups, may certainly have a place. Further research is necessary to clarify the ideal approach. For the more usual and fortunate mother whose puerperium is only troubled by the third to sixth day 'blues' at the most, some attention should be given to the problems of *adjustment to the changed state*. A chance to discuss methods of adjusting to the altered environment for both mother and father brought about by the arrival of the baby may uncover practical, emotional and cognitive problems. Amongst the latter the idea that 'mother love' is instant and overwhelming is a common assumption of many mothers. They suffer severe distress and make extremely negative self-evaluations when it doesn't arrive. For example 'If I am not overwhelmed by love for that screaming pink thing, wet at both ends, then I must be lacking in essential feelings. This make me a useless mother, therefore a worthless woman, therefore a defective person, i.e. some sort of monster'. These sorts of assumptions, expressed here by the vertical arrow technique (q.v. Chapter 8) seem common in normal new mothers and much distress can be saved if they are examined logically and put into context.

Anxiety about the health of the baby can also usefully be explored. Some problem-solving on practical questions like breast feeding, family planning and return to work may be necessary.

Abortion

Spontaneous abortions are a form of bereavement and many of the considerations dealt with under that heading will apply. Induced abortions are also a form of more complex bereavement although if undertaken under the best possible conditions it seems that guilt and self-blame are less common than are traditionally supposed. Important factors in minimising adverse reactions are:

(1) The mother should feel fully responsible for the decision. The wife who bows to the wishes of her husband or the teenager who obeys her parents' orders are particularly at risk.
(2) The termination is carried out as early as possible since emotional adjustments become more difficult later.
(3) The matter is considerately handled by GP, surgeon and clinic or hospital staff. This should not need saying today but sadly, insensitive remarks are still too often a source of guilt and distress.

Preparation for Stressful Medical Procedures

The role of psychological preparation for stressful medical procedures has, in contrast to childbirth, received a good deal of attention recently (Mathews and Ridgeway 1984). The questions that we must try and answer are:

(1) Is psychological preparation of use in the type of medical procedures undertaken by GPs and if so in which?
(2) Has the GP a role to play in the preparation for hospital treatment and if so, what role?

Almost all the research that has been undertaken to date has involved hospital populations and much of it has been done with patients about to undergo surgery, who form a reasonably homogenous group which can be studied with scientific rigour. There are, however, two problems for the clinician that arise with these studies: Any assessment and intervention by hospital teams must take place (i) after the admission to hospital which may in itself be a more stressful event than the surgery, and (ii) in the very limited time available between the admission and the operation.

It is, however, interesting to summarise these studies, which in themselves provide a number of important leads about the direction of possible future primary care research and interventions. The methods of preparation attempted, have included:

(i) Information about the procedure to be undertaken, i.e. what is done, who will do it and how it will be done. This appears to affect outcome only very weakly if at all.
(ii) Information about the physical sensations to be experienced i.e. 'you will feel sick, a burning pain' etc.
(iii) Behavioural instruction i.e. 'you should walk 330 yds', 'hold your side when you cough' etc., which seems to have more effect than the two previous techniques.
(iv) Relaxation, either general or cued to specific situations or symptoms, has been discussed in the previous sections and appears to produce rather equivocal results
(v) Cognitive coping techniques which involve identifying any anxiety provoking thoughts and finding an answer to them. For example 'I am afraid they will find cancer when they do the operation.' This might be answered with 'It's a common operation which several of my friends have had. None of them have had cancer so why should I have it.'

The consensus of opinion is that the last technique of preparation is the most effective and the most universally applicable. It is also unfortunately the most difficult to use as measures such as information booklets or tapes need very careful design.

It seems that the information techniques must be used with care as a percentage of patients cope well with stress naturally by avoidance and distraction. These will not be helped and may actually find it more difficult to cope if provided with unsolicited information.

The published work outside the hospital surgical setting has been mainly in connection with dentistry (Anderson and Masur 1983) apart from one paper where sensory and procedural information was given when IUCDs were fitted (Newton and Reading 1977). The outcome measures in these studies were mainly self-report scales of pain with the occasional physiological measure such as GSR (Galvanic Skin Response) There have been a number of papers reporting positive results. It would seem worthwhile to use these techniques, with evaluation, more extensively for primary care procedures such as injections of soft tissue and joints, vaginal examinations, IUCD fitting and possibly in obstetrics.

Another interesting but unexplored area is that of providing training in coping techniques for hospital patients well before admission. This would seem to have two possible advantages. First the techniques could be practised before the distractions and anxieties of admission arrived, and secondly much more time would be available for their perfection. This has yet to be attempted.

Terminal Care

Previous parts of this chapter have dealt with subjects where the practice manager and the midwife are likely to be the most concerned. In the care of the terminally ill, however, the district nursing sister is likely to carry most responsibility. The techniques and procedures described here can be seen as one aspect, or as an extension of, the nursing process. Much of the progress in the care of the terminally ill in recent years has been brought about by the hospice service. The methods described in this section were pioneered by Lunt (1978; Lunt and Jenkins 1983) working in a hospice in Southampton. Very little adaptation is required to make them entirely suitable for use in the community as no special facilities are required.

In outline, the approach is based on the philosophy that the terminal period should be regarded as a part of life not merely as a preparation for death. The dying patient has a number of problems associated with a number of aspirations which, with help, can be converted in many cases into realistic goals. Not all problems will be associated with goals and not all goals will be realistic but even the impossible ones may be achievable in part, if they are broken down into components, for example — see Figure 9.1.

Figure 9.1: Goal Setting

Mr S. Richards aet. 82. Diagnosis: Disseminated Ca. Stomach

Problem Area Mobility Problem	Goal	Secondary Goals	
Too weak to walk	Walk downstairs and into garden (not achievable)	(i) see his roses (ii) stop daughter having to bring food up	(achievable with room rearrangement + wheelchair)
		(iii) Go to Chelsea Flower Show	(? achievable with wheelchair)

Assessment. This is carried out by means of an assessment form which groups the problems into various sections and then determines goal areas, priority, current status of problem and strengths and resources (see Figure 9.2).

Identified problems are listed in the various sections in the left hand column with goals in the next column. Priority is assessed as 1

Figure 9.2: Assessment Form

Problems	Goal Areas	Priority	Current Symptom Status	Strengths and Resources
Symptoms				
Self-care				
Mobility				
Sleep				
Recreation/ Leisure				
Family				
Work/ Employment				
Financial				
Information on illness				
Other				

= attention now or 2 = can be reviewed later. Current symptom status gives the original or baseline state which may be adequately described under the 'problem' heading or need amplification, for example: What does the weakness affect? What housework is impossible? Strengths and resources outline special factors such as motivation — Mr Richards in the example quoted was a life-long keen gardener — or special resources such as available friends, special equipment or skills (patient's or others').

Once the assessment has been completed a coordination meeting between the patient, the family or other home carers and the professional e.g. district nursing sister and GP at which resources and methods are discussed and an optional plan evolved. A patient's daily diary which can conveniently be written on the same form as the Weekly Activity Schedule (see Chapter 8) is used to keep track of progress towards the goals. Assessments are made at previously agreed intervals, which may be determined by the nature of the patient's illness, at which progress is determined according to the following scale:

-2	-1	0	$+1$	$+2$
Much worse than expected.	Worse than expected.	Expected outcome.	Better than expected.	Much better than expected.

In the light of these results, goals can be reset and new ones devised for as long as the illness lasts. There are a number of variations on the basic plan which can be used when the situation demands. For example, some of the goals may involve the aspirations of relatives such as having a night out or taking a short holiday, as well as those of the patient. The above techniques may be useful in the management of any chronic illness or disablement.

Grief

After a death, the attention of the primary care team is directed to the bereaved spouse and family. The components, no longer regarded as stages, of the grief reaction are now well recognised and consist of the following (Parkes 1972):

Shock, which is associated with numbness, unreality and apathy.
Disorganisation, which frequently follows the supreme effort of the funeral when the bereaved person may collapse into a state of helplessness.

Denial, which is associated with searching for the dead person and the distressing idea that he is still present, provoked by the misinterpretation of sights, e.g. a person in similar clothes in the street or, more commonly, sounds e.g. the noise of the dog in the kitchen is the dead husband making the tea. Although presumably originally a defence mechanism, the continual correction of these false interpretations is often one of the most painful components of early grief.

Depression, with feelings of pining and despair usually represents a progression to a more realistic phase and evidence that the 'work' of grieving is indeed being done as the person is coming face to face with the impossibility of bringing back the dead.

Guilt often occurs, whether justified or not, with its concurrent obsessional thoughts of what might or should have been done for the dead person.

Anxiety is caused by fears, sometimes realistic, of changed life circumstances, e.g. loneliness or finance problems and also by a type of fear about fear e.g. of being unable to cope with the situation or of going mad.

Aggression may take many forms. It may be directed against a friend or relatives who have 'not helped' or who still have spouses. It is commonly directed against those doctors or hospitals that cared for the dead person. In this context it presents special problems to the GP and his colleagues who may feel a considerable conflict of roles and interests. Finally it may be directed at the dead person — 'How dare he/she leave me like this to fend for myself!'

Resolution and acceptance occur when the farewells are finally said and the huge gap left by the dead person, like the wake of a ship, gradually fills. This allows the final battle phase of reintegration into a life without him or her to begin.

Management of normal grief is essentially passive and involves allowing time for the patient to work through his reaction with its sudden changes from component to component and then often back again. Patience is needed for the sometimes endless repetitive discussions of various aspects. A permissive approach is required to let the more sensitive issues like delusions of physical presence and fears of impending insanity to be raised. Ramsay (1977) has viewed grief as a special kind of specific fear or phobia. This model can be used in helping with normal bereavement as any tendency to avoidance can be countered by gentle persuasion to return to the real work which is to keep in contact with the feared stimulus i.e. the fact of loss.

An awareness of the risk factors predisposing to morbid grief is also important. These are (Raphael 1978):

(1) an unsupportive social network — originally described amongst widows and probably more important for them as many men have work or social contacts.
(2) another crisis occurring at the same time, e.g. the break-up of a daughter's marriage.
(3) 'traumatic' circumstances surrounding the death which may involve the actual final illness, the treatment received or family factors.
(4) a pre-existing marital problem, e.g. an insecure or over-dependent relationship.

Prevention and Management of Pathological Grief. (Ramsay 1977) following the model of morbid grief as a phobic reaction, has very successfully introduced a system of therapy based on the flooding technique used with phobias (q.v.). He argues that morbid grief is characterised by avoidance of the stimuli, e.g. objects, places or people associated with the dead person which blocks the resolution of the problem by preventing the 'work' being done. His therapy therefore consists of bringing the patient into contact with objects and places associated with the dead person and eliciting the avoided emotions over a long period until they subside and the patient is ready to accept the lost person as really dead and say good-bye to them. This is extremely simple in principle but there are two factors which limit the usefulness of the technique in primary care. First it is a time-intensive process, typically demanding several hours per day, each day, until the desired goal is obtained. Second, and connected with the first, is that the emotions aroused are extremely strong. Anybody attempting this technique must be sure in advance that they have the time, the personal expertise and resources to see it through. Once started there is no turning back. Its use in primary care should be not ruled out but it is clearly not a technique for the inexperienced, the faint-hearted or the hurried.

As with other types of phobia, a graded approach may be used. This sets progressively more difficult goals, week by week, repeating them until they can be done without undue discomfort. For example one week's goal might be to contact a mutual friend not seen since the bereavement, the next to tidy out a room with memories and a third to look at a photograph of the dead person.

In summary the primary care worker whether health visitor, district nursing sister or GP should:

(1) be aware of the risk factors leading to morbid grief;
(2) when dealing with normal grief remain largely a permissive listener but be aware that they are involved in a desensitisation (see Chapter 5) process and be prepared to redirect the patient towards the 'work' which must be done;
(3) be aware of the graded approach and powerful flooding therapy for morbid grief and be prepared to refer the patient appropriately. It is never too late.

Referral and the Liaison with Clinical Psychologists

It is obvious that primary care workers will often have neither the experience, time nor resources to undertake cognitive-behavioural treatment for all the different types of problem for which the approach is suitable. Whilst we feel that there are no areas where referral is mandatory, as competence and enthusiasm differ so much, a number of different conditions have already been mentioned where referral is usually the preferred course. This presents the difficulty of obtaining expert treatment as there is a wide variation in the facilities available. The most usual recourse for a GP faced with an emotional problem which he feels is outside his scope is referral to a psychiatrist. This may be appropriate if available psychiatrists are interested and skilled in behaviour therapy. Many however have little training in this field. It is true, of course, that most psychiatric teams include clinical psychologists and problems can always be re-referred. There may, however, be a reluctance to do this and anyway it seems an unnecessarily complicated way of achieving treatment. We feel that referral direct to the clinical psychologist (or sometimes behavioural nurse therapist) is almost always preferable.

Clinical psychologists' training demands that they first obtain a good basic degree. Most then have a period of relevant work experience before proceeding to a postgraduate course leading to a Master's and sometimes later Doctor's degree in the applied clinical speciality. Their training, therefore, although non-medical, is as long and detailed as any medical course. Once qualified they enjoy clinical autonomy although they may, of course, want to consult with doctors on purely medical aspects of care.

Recently there has been an extension of their work from hospital departments into primary care and in most districts referrals are now accepted direct from GPs and other primary care workers. In some cases clinical psychologists have physically moved out of hospitals to work as part of the primary care team. There has been some discussion of the validity of this move. Definite advantages have been demonstrated (Robson *et al.* 1984) but it is unlikely to become widespread in view of current restrictions on manpower and money.

Whether the clinical psychologist is working in the same building or in the local department, there are certain rules for the liaison that apply. From the referrer, e.g. GP or health visitor, the clinical psychologist has a right to expect:

(1) A written referral stating the problem for which advice is being sought and some idea of the desired outcome. Methods of treatment, however, are the responsibility of the clinical psychologist and should not be specified.

(2) Adequate assurance that everything possible has been done to diagnose, investigate and stabilise any purely medical problems. As psychologists are not medically qualified, it is extremely unnerving for them to find that the patient that they have been treating for tension headaches or somatising anxiety has in fact got a cerebral tumour or ischaemic heart disease.

(3) Contact and cooperation over drugs is expected. Drug treatment, psychotropic or otherwise, does not rule out any form of cognitive-behavioural intervention. It is clearly necessary, however, to know what is being prescribed and in what dosage. Cooperation in drug reduction is also essential.

We are principally concerned in this book with treatment approaches and therefore we have discussed the clinical psychologists' role in this context. We should point out that they also have a considerable part to play in teaching, research and the planning of services, all of which lie beyond our scope.

References

Anderson, K. O. and Masur, F. T. (1983) 'Psychological preparation for invasive medical and dental procedures,' *Journal of Behavioural Medicine, 6,* 1–40

Ausburn, L. (1981) 'Patient compliance with medical regimes' in J. Sheppard (ed.) *Behavioural Medicine*, Lidcombe, NWS, Cumberland College of Health Sciences

Becker, M. H. and Rosenstock, I. M. (1984) 'Compliance with medical advice' in A. Steptoe and A. M. Mathews (eds.) *Health Care and Human Behaviour*, London, Academic Press

Brewin, C. and Bradley, C. (1982) 'Perceived control and experience of childbirth', *British Journal of Clinical Psychology, 21*, 263–9

Byrne, P. S. and Long, B. E. (1976) *Doctors talking to Patients*, London, HMSO

Crandon, A. J. (1979) 'Maternal anxiety and obstetric complications' (109–11) and 'Maternal anxiety and neonatal well-being' (113–5), *Journal of Psychosomatic Research, 23*, 109–15

Elliot, S. A. (1985) 'Pregnancy and after' in S. Rachman (ed.) *Contributions to Medical Psychology, Vol. 3*, Oxford, Pergamon

Goldberg, D. and Huxley, P. (1980) *Mental Illness in the Community*, London, Tavistock

Hutton, A. and Robins, S. (1985) 'What the patient wants from patient participation', *Journal of the Royal College of General Practitioners, 35*, 133–5

Korsh, B. M., Gozzi, E. K. and Francis, V. (1968) 'Gaps in Doctor-patient communication: Doctor-patient interaction and patient satisfaction', *Paediatrics, 42*, 855–71

Ley, P. (1982a) 'Satisfaction, compliance and communication', *British Journal of Clinical Psychology, 21*, 241–54

Ley, P. (1982b) 'Giving information to patients' in J. R. Eiser (ed.) *Social Psychology and Behavioral Medicine*, New York, Wiley

Little, B., Hayworth, J., Benson, P., Hall, F., Beard, R. W., Dewhurst, J. and Priest, R. G. (1984) 'Treatment of hypertension in pregnancy by relaxation and feedback', *Lancet 1*, 8382, 865–7

Lunt, B. (1978) 'The goal setting approach in continuing care', Paper presented at the Annual Therapeutics Conference at St Christopher's Hospice, Sydenham, England, 17 November 1978

Lunt, B. and Jenkins, J. (1983) 'Goal setting in terminal care: a method of recording treatment aims and priorities', *Journal of Advanced Nursing, 8*, 495–505

Maguire, P. (1984) 'Communication skills and patient care' in A. Steptoe and A. M. Mathews (eds.) *Health Care and Human Behaviour*, London, Academic Press

Mathews, A. M. and Ridgeway, V. (1984) 'Psychological preparation for surgery' in A. Steptoe and A. M. Mathews (eds.) *Health Care and Human Behaviour*, London, Academic Press

Newton, J. R. and Reading, A. E. (1977) 'The effects of psychological preparation on pain at intrauterine device insertion', *Contraception, 16*, 523–32

Parkes, C. M. (1972) *Bereavement*, Harmondsworth, Penguin

Pendleton, D. and Hasler, J. (1983) *Doctor-Patient Communication*, London, Academic Press

Pendleton, D., Schofield, T., Tate, P. and Havelock, P. (1984) *The Consultation. An approach to learning and teaching*, Oxford, Oxford University Press

Ramsay, R. W. (1977) 'Behavioural approaches to bereavement', *Behaviour Research and Therapy, 15*, 131–5

Raphael, B. (1978) 'Mourning and the prevention of melancholia', *British Journal of Medical Psychology, 51*, 303–10

Reading, A. E. and Cox, D. N. (1982) 'The effects of ultrasound examination on maternal anxiety levels', *Journal of Behavioural Medicine, 5*, 237–47

Robson, M. H., France, R. and Bland, M. (1984) 'Clinical psychologist in primary care: controlled clinical and economic evaluation', *British Medical Journal, 288*, 1805–8

Royal College of General Practitioners (1972) *The Future General Practitioner. Learning and Teaching*. London, British Medical Journal

Recommended for Further Reading

Liddell, A. (ed.) (1984) *The Practice of Clinical Psychology in Great Britain*, Chichester, John Wiley

Parkes, C. M. (1983) *Recovery from Bereavement*, London, Harper and Row

Pendleton, D., Schofield, T., Tate, P. and Havelock, P. (1984) *The Consultation. An approach to Learning and Teaching*, Oxford, Oxford University Press

Sackett, D. L. and Haynes, R. B. (1976) *Compliance with Therapeutic Regimes*, Baltimore, The Johns Hopkins University Press

Stedeford, A. (1984) *Facing Death — Patients, families and professionals*, London, Heinemann.

10 BEHAVIOURAL MEDICINE II: TREATMENT OF SPECIFIC DISORDERS

Psychological interventions have been found to have a place in the management of organic medical disorders at three separate but inter-related levels. First, they can be used to increase the effectiveness of conventional treatment, for example by improving adherence, augmenting effects as in analgesia or improving communication, some aspects of which have been discussed in the last chapter. Second, they may be used to modify the psycho-social effect of various conditions and, third, they may be used as an alternative to more traditional kinds of therapy. We now come to consider the second and third groups in connection with a number of specific problems.

Essential Hypertension

There is now fairly conclusive evidence that stress in the form of adverse life conditions contributes to the incidence of essential hypertension in some people. It may be that inherited predisposition and personality variables such as seeing particular situations as more threatening than other people do, also play a part. It seems that the need to cope actively with a stressor is important as, for example, it has been shown that air traffic controllers are more prone to high blood pressure than aircrew working in the same environment but without the requirement of alertness and responsibility (Cobb and Rose 1973). The mechanisms involved are the subject of substantial but often somewhat confusing research fraught with difficulties of measurement, multifactorial aetiologies and confounding reactive effects concerned with such variables as whether the diagnosis is known to the patient. At the present time it appears that a sympathetic nervous system mechanism is involved which is comforting to those of us who, in ignorance, have been using this explanation to our patients for some years. Excellent review papers exist (Johnston 1984; Steptoe 1980) and it seems unnecessary to explore matters further here.

Management

The place of cognitive-behavioural strategies in the management of hypertension is less confused than in aetiology. The outstanding work is that of Patel. In her most recent study (Patel *et al.* 1985) she identified by screening 192 men and women aged 35–64 with two or more of the following coronary risk factors:

(1) Blood pressure more than 140/90
(2) Plasma cholesterol concentration more than 6.3 mmol/litre
(3) Current smoking more than 10 cigarettes per day.

The subjects were randomised into two groups. Both received health education leaflets but the treatment group, in addition, received eight, one-hour group sessions teaching breathing exercises, relaxation, meditation and stress management.

At four-year follow up, the control group reported more angina, and more needed treatment for hypertension and its complications. Incidence of ischaemic heart disease, fatal myocardial infarction, or electrocardiographic evidence of ischaemia was also significantly greater in the control group.

These results were impressive particularly when the extremely modest gains for drug treatment of mild hypertensives are considered (Medical Research Council Working Party 1985).

The techniques used by Patel include Jacobson Relaxation, GSR feedback and cueing relaxation into stressful situations in daily life.

A number of other well-controlled studies (see Johnston 1984 for a review) have demonstrated that relaxation-based techniques are not only effective but that the blood pressure reduction generalises into the working environment and persists for up to 15 months following treatment. Other workers have obtained positive effects with simple relaxation which appears to be as effective as biofeedback. The latter has a number of technical drawbacks as continuing methods of monitoring the pressure itself or its correlates such as pulse transit time require sophisticated and perhaps alarming apparatus, which is not likely to be available in primary care.

The main difficulty following relaxation training is to secure continuing cooperation as only the more obsessional find it easy to continue practice once the initial enthusiasm has worn off. This would, however, seem to be important, as long term effects last well with the initial treatment but sometimes cannot easily be regained by reintroducing relaxation once it has lapsed.

Attempts to modify the hypertensive patient's lifestyle have also received a good deal of attention. The value of stopping smoking and reducing weight is obvious and methods of achieving these objectives have already been discussed in Chapter 7 as have techniques aiding cooperation with drug treatment. Patients may be trained to identify situations in which their blood pressure is likely to increase by keeping a situation and blood pressure (self-estimated) diary. These situations can then be managed by a variety of techniques. For example, if a patient finds that his weekly interview with his boss is a high BP period, training in assertion may help him get his point of view across more effectively and thus indirectly lower his BP. Similar techniques can be used for other stress-related situations as alternatives to cued relaxation. Work in this area is hampered by the absence of a simple and cheap BP apparatus which would enable patients to measure their own BP frequently and unobtrusively and also by the technical difficulties in carrying out evaluation research in complex situations.

A booklet containing information about high blood pressure can be usefully given out to patients and may include sections on (i) how the heart and circulation function, (ii) the nature of hypertension, (iii) drug treatment and its side effects, (iv) the role of weight, diet and salt consumption, (v) smoking and alcohol, (vi) stress and (vii) timetable organisation, rest, sport, exercise and holidays.

Clinically there is strong evidence that the measures described above have a beneficial effect on raised blood pressure. This is a field, however, where non-specific effects abound and hard data are difficult to obtain so that all results must be interpreted with caution. The situation is further complicated by the case made by Steptoe (1980) that the maximum benefits from all the behavioural measures are likely to be found, not when the condition is fully established, but in the antecedent stage of labile blood pressure which precedes established hypertension. At this stage it is felt that there is greater cardiac rather than vascular involvement and this is better subject to behavioural intervention. The snag is, of course, in clinical terms that such patients seldom present for treatment.

Ischaemic Heart Disease

For convenience, the place of cognitive-behavioural measures in connection with ischaemic heart disease may be considered under three headings corresponding to before, during and after the myocardial infarct.

Prevention and Modification of Risk Factors

These form an important primary care task and can be performed in a number of different ways. The 'opportunist' advice about smoking, diet or life-style during a consultation for another, usually minor, problem is one useful method and the running of groups aimed at the correction of specific problems is another. In both these settings advice can be made effective if its importance is emphasised and coupled to some suggestions as to how it might be more easily put into practice. The overweight, under-exercised, two-packets-a-day business man might be helped by a programme involving cutting down or stopping smoking and buying a bicycle to cycle to work or the station. The savings on smoking would pay off the cost of the bicycle. The ride would help reduce weight, increase exercise and demonstrate increased lung function thus providing three potential areas of reinforcement. Naturally such a programme must be negotiated, not imposed. If, however, the patient finds it acceptable, he is likely to be favourably influenced by his doctor's practical involvement with the details of the scheme.

The major risk factor of hypertension in coronary artery disease has already been discussed. Coronary prone Type A behaviour raises some of the same issues related to stress. It is unique amongst the risk factors in that it is an entirely psychological state. It has received a good deal of attention from behaviour therapists. The term originated from the work of Friedman and Rosenman (1974) and has been succinctly defined by Johnston (1982) as 'being characterised by a chronic struggle to achieve more and more in less and less time'. The Type A person is thrusting, ambitious, time-pressured, decisive and becomes readily hostile when thwarted. There is a strong but unproven suspicion that such behaviour is actually reinforced and shaped-up by life in western urban societies, which may be one reason for the epidemic of CHD at present being experienced.

Attempts at modifying Type A behaviour have centred on two main treatment packages. The first involves stress control undertaken in the same way as anxiety management. Deep muscle relaxation is taught and the patient taught to identify stressful situations. The relaxation is then paired to the situations, first in imagination and then in real life. The demonstrated effects of this technique are fairly weak but it does have the advantage that it incidentally teaches self-monitoring and it is suitable for the sort of group use that is feasible in primary care (Suinn 1975; Suinn and Bloom 1978). The second package involves a full range of cognitive techniques including self-monitoring but also challenging dysfunctional thoughts and assumptions, environmental restructuring and self-reinforcement as well as the more purely behavioural techniques of assertive training and behavioural rehearsal. These techniques have been described in other chapters. This package has been found to be the more powerful and has also been used with groups (Thoresen *et al.* 1982). Such groups could be undertaken at a health centre or group practice but would require considerable expertise and commitment on the part of the leader.

Care During the Attack

In most cases today this will be a task for the coronary care unit rather than the community team. It is however worth noting that amongst other findings, the extensive Vanderbilt/Holy Cross project in the USA (Cromwell *et al.* 1977) found that outcome was influenced best if patients received a lot of *information* about their condition but only if this was coupled with high *participation* in the form of monitoring their own ECGs, doing isometric exercises and generally being encouraged to take part in their own management, or high *distraction* in the form of TV, books, visiting etc. Better informed patients actually did worse if they could not share in their own management.

Aftercare and Rehabilitation

This is the area in which most practical work has been done. Coronary rehabilitation programmes are now available in many areas and are often in the hands of interested primary care workers. They usually consist of three main elements (i) monitoring the physical condition which has the additional psychological function of providing feedback and increasing confidence; (ii) graded physical exercise which as well as restoring physical fitness also helps rebuild confidence and the sense of control over the problem; and (iii) offering a counselling service that is overtly psychological. This service includes (i) life-style advice to eliminate risk factors; (ii) problem-solving related to the changed situation including employment and hobbies; (iii) allowing anxieties about the future to be expressed; (iv) advising about the resumption of sexual activities;

and (v) perhaps most important, avoiding the pitfalls of over-protection by spouse, friend and even, although less commonly today, doctor. This last is particularly important as helplessness and its associated hopelessness is a predictor of poor survival rates after myocardial infarction (Cromwell *et al.* 1977) whereas the much-feared unwise overactivity seems to be relatively unimportant.

Bronchial Asthma

At the outset bronchial asthma presents a paradox. Since the dawn of psychosomatic medicine it has often been regarded as a prime example of a stress-related condition. Many clinicians, including those who are not in other respects particularly psychologically orientated, believe strongly that emotional factors are a major aetiological factor. For this reason there have been attempts at behavioural treatment of asthma, usually based on various stress and anxiety management techniques, often involving relaxation. The outcome of these has sometimes been promising but there has been a good deal of variability in terms of results, even on the same outcome measurements such as peak flow rate, forced expiratory volume and inhaler use. This is perhaps not surprising when it is considered that relaxation is thought to work by reducing sympathetic and increasing parasympathetic activity which in simple effect would tend to exacerbate the asthmatic attack. That some benefits *have* been observed is probably due more to a non-specific anxiolytic action rather than a direct effect.

Problems also beset the other popular method of direct intervention which has been voluntary control of pulmonary function aided by biofeedback. Suitable apparatus giving continuous readings is extremely cumbersome and would be impracticable for general clinic, let alone primary care, use.

More promising, although technically less exciting, is to look at ways of improving behaviour problems related to the asthma, rather than the primary condition (Steptoe 1984). An asthmatic patient, particularly a child (and asthma is most prevalent in children), faces a major series of difficulties. He has a frightening, disabling illness which may strike embarrassingly and unexpectedly. It makes him different from other children, often dependent on medication and, not infrequently, periodic hospital admissions. Even if there is only a small psychological element in the aetiology, the emotional consequences of the condition are huge. We have already seen that anxiety reduction measures although largely ineffective in modifying the onset of attacks may have some ability to reduce the consequent anxious thoughts and feelings. Many individual patients are understandably panic-stricken by their condition and for these, even if not for experimental groups, a variety of anxiety management techniques which have been described in Chapter 5 can be strikingly effective.

The chief goal in treatment is to strive towards a life which is as normal as possible for the patient, his parents and sometimes school or employer as well. As much information as possible about the condition is the first step. This can be achieved by leaflets and membership of the local asthma society. Opportunities should be made for queries and worries to be discussed. A plan for dealing with acute attacks can be discussed in advance with the advisability of obtaining special equipment such as home nebulisers and peak flow gauges. It is important to be explicit about any restrictions on the patient's way of life mainly with the object of avoiding unnecessary ones. Overprotection is an ever present danger for the asthmatic and recent concentration on the dangers of the condition with such things as schemes for direct admission to hospital, however necessary in purely physical terms, can only make this danger worse.

The Management of Pain

Pain may be defined as an unpleasant bodily sensation usually, but not always, associated with tissue damage. Early conceptualisations of pain regarded it as a simple response in which pain receptors activated fibres in the peripheral nerves which in turn conducted impulses through the central nervous system to be received in the cerebral cortex. A great deal of practical evidence, however, indicated the inadequacy of such an explanation. for example, soldiers in battle suffered ghastly injuries which went unnoticed by them until they left the battlefield. Many other examples from more everyday experience indicated that multiple factors influenced the amount of pain experienced. A one-to-one relationship with tissue damage could not be sustained. From 1963 onwards Melzack (1973) studied these other factors and developed the 'gate-control model' to explain them. The model is a complex one but in essence suggests that nerve impulses from the tissues have to pass through a 'gate' situated in the dorsal horns of the spinal column, at which point they become modified by descending influences from the brain, some of which open and some of which close the postulated gate. These influences include:

(1) Mood and emotions. Depression, fear, sadness and anxiety lower the pain threshold and happiness, relaxation and feelings of well-being raise it.
(2) Motivation. A striving to overcome the pain and find ways of coping will in itself raise the threshold.
(3) Distraction. this explains the battlefield phenomenon mentioned above. Powerful distractions have a profound effect on modifying the experience of pain.
(4) Interpretation. A patient having a splinter removed in a treatment room may suffer the same amount of tissue damage as a detainee having a nail removed by the secret police. It is likely that their experience of pain will be quite different.
(5) Past experience. Previous experience of the same kind of pain or injury and its outcome influence the reaction to the present situation.
(6) Past learning history — individual or cultural. We model our own perceptions and behaviour on those around us and this has been shown experimentally to effect the amount of pain experienced.

Different cultures cope with pain in different ways which also affects the experience. The British require considerable quantities of analgesic drugs but are not expected to show much overt emotion when subjected to a painful experience. With the Italians, for example, the situation is reversed in that they mistrust the drugs but are encouraged to cry out and indulge in self-expression. Such factors will modify the amount of pain and the way it is experienced. Returning to the individual, the consequences of his reaction to pain will have a powerful operant effect. If, for example, attention and warm concern are offered by members of the family only in response to pain this will have a considerable influence in shaping up pain behaviour and also affect the amount of pain experienced.

This list is by no means exhaustive but serves to indicate that pain is a multi-faceted problem.

Assessment

The interview should include special enquiry into the factors mentioned above. Baseline observation follows. This often includes a record of date and time, situation, intensity of pain rated out of 10 or 100, associated thoughts and feelings, medication and outcome. There are various ways of collecting this information which will depend on the type of pain. Sometimes a graph will serve best, sometimes a diary-record is needed.

Intervention

As always, the type of intervention must be determined by the assessment data and the initial hypothesis. There are, however, three main cognitive behavioural approaches to pain which have been researched and used clinically (Turner and Chapman 1982). These are:

Applied Relaxation. (Linton 1982). This is effective with specific painful situations such as dental extractions or injections. Instruction in general relaxation is given first as has been described previously. This is then adapted to differential relaxation, without a tension phase, which is first rehearsed in an imagined painful situation and finally used in the real life setting. The same approach can be used with long-standing or chronic pain with a particular level of pain being the cue for the relaxation sequence. Electromyographic feedback using a simple apparatus such as the Aleph-One Myosone 404 or portable M59 can be used to provide the patient with information about the state of muscular tension. We have found this to be particularly useful where the patient finds it difficult to accept the rationale of pain relief by muscular relaxation or where specific muscle groups such as the jaw, the back or the sterno-mastoid are involved. An extension of this method is to use hypnotism, but this lies outside the scope of our discussion here.

The Operant Approach. This approach was pioneered by Fordyce (1976). It concentrates on pain behaviour and there is still considerable discussion as to whether pain experience is actually affected. It seems that there probably is a modest reduction of the amount of pain felt but the main advantage of the approach is in enabling the patient to lead a more satisfying life.

The treatment plan contains the following elements:

(1) Analgesic medication is arranged on a time schedule not given p.r.n. With the patient's permission, medication may be given in a liquid form so that the active ingredient can be reduced without the patient's knowledge. This eliminates a certain amount of reactive anxiety.

(2) A graded exercise programme is devised in relation to the pain and disability experienced by the patient. The initial level is set well below the pre-treatment amount of activity and extremely small increments are used. In this way confidence is built up and it is often possible to reach activity levels which would have been inconceivable at the outset. Reward rests are made contingent on target exercise periods being achieved and not, as previously, on complaints of pain.

(3) Relatives and friends are encouraged to reinforce progress, activity and 'up time', i.e. the time spent out of bed engaged on activities.

One of the problems of this type of programme is that it has largely been used in hospital with professional staff. It is possible to adapt these techniques to the home but only if there is cooperation from the relatives in providing reinforcement for various 'well behaviours' and a neutral attitude to 'pain behaviours'. In many of these patients' pain complaints they have often been substantially reinforced by sympathy, concern and offers of medication. In some cases this may be the patient's only enduring way of getting any attention at all and therefore the changes required of both the patient and his family for a new pattern to be established may be substantial. These considerations limit the effectiveness of this type of programme in the home but the difficulties may be overcome by the active involvement of as many of the family as possible in such tasks as charting 'up time', timing exercise sessions and arranging outings.

The Cognitive Method (Turk *et al.* 1983). It has been noted that such factors as distraction, interpretation and mood affect the way pain is experienced and to these must be added the fact that pain is reduced when the sufferer feels that he can exercise control over it. These observations have been employed by Meichenbaum and his colleagues to produce a treatment package which is a modification of the same workers' stress inoculation training. In summary, the patient first develops a number of coping strategies with the help of the therapist which might include:

(i) Distraction — very much as described in the chapter on anxiety management. The patient distracts himself from the pain by reciting poetry, solving problems, listing the sports teams in a league. He may also concentrate on aspects of people or things in his surroundings such as those wearing brown shoes, the number of cars in the road, etc.

(ii) He focuses on his own sensations including the pain and analysis and measures it 'like a scientist'. This appears to increase the perception of control.

(iii) He manipulates the imagery surrounding the experience of the pain. At its simplest this may consist of just imagining himself lying on a beach in Spain. More sophisticated methods involve reinterpreting the pain as trivial, e.g. 'just cramp' or 'like tingling' or suggesting that it is unreal or a long way away. Finally the pain can be incorporated in elaborate fantasy exercises like spy stories or television adventures. This is particularly useful in children who have a rich fantasy life and will meet the therapist half way.

The coping strategies are then incorporated into a timetable for coping with the pain:

(i) Preparing for the pain. Instead of nagging worry, the plan to deal with the pain, using the coping techniques, is rehearsed with self-encouragement.

(ii) Confronting the pain. The onset of the pain is the cue to relax and put the chosen strategy into operation, again associated with some calming self-statements.

(iii) The critical moments. The ability of the chosen strategy to control the pain is monitored. If needed, one strategy can be changed for another, e.g. reciting Kubla Khan to escaping from the KGB. Self-reminders are given that the object is to stay in control of the pain not eliminate it.

(iv) After the pain has passed. The way of coping with it is rehearsed and self-reinforcement statements like 'Well done — you managed it' are made. A record written down of the experience is also useful as this can be used for self-reinforcement on the next occasion.

This may seem an extremely complicated and sophisticated package to be recommended for use in primary care but it does have a number of advantages over the others. First, unlike the operant programme, it does not required trained staff. Second, once he has got the idea, the patient is able to do much of the work for himself and hopefully enter into the self-help spirit of the exercise. Third, it is almost endlessly adaptable to suit most sorts of pain and the main principles can be incorporated in a hand-out that the patient can keep for reference and discuss when he attends. Fourth, simplifications are possible when the whole package is not required. Finally, the experimental evidence indicates that it is probably more effective than the alternatives.

Deliberately, no mention has been made of the vexed question of outstanding compensation lawsuits for injury as reinforcers of pain behaviour. They are undoubtedly very powerful and it may be difficult to attempt any sort of programme whilst this factor is operating. Unfortunately it is outside our scope to modify it, which would involve some profound changes in the working of the legal system, e.g. no-blame compensation and rapid provisional case settlement.

Specific Types of Pain

Headaches

Although more than 15 types of headaches have been described, those most suitable for behavioural treatment may be divided into tension headaches and migraine.

Tension Headache. It was uncritically accepted for many years that tension headaches were associated with sustained contraction of skeletal muscles, in particular the frontalis and temporalis. Treatment was therefore given by encouraging EMG feedback-aided relaxation of these muscles which was often associated with subjective improvement. Recent work from Philips (1980) has pointed out that definite EMG abnormalities can only be demonstrated in a minority of tension headache sufferers and that many of the improvements noted as a result of EMG feedback training were probably due to non-specific factors. She points out that headache, like other sorts of pain, promotes behaviour patterns influenced by the factors which have been discussed in the last section. They cannot be regarded as merely a manifestation of altered muscle potentials. For practical purposes EMG biofeedback from the frontalis muscle may be worth a try, where facilities exist, as a small group will derive a specific benefit. The non-specific effects may be worthwhile in the remainder, but the more general pain modification strategies should also be considered.

Migraine. This is classically described as a unilateral throbbing pain associated with visual distortion, nausea and vomiting. There are, however, many different types, some differing quite widely from the classical description. The distinction from tension and other types of headache is not always easy. The pathology of the condition indicates an initial vasoconstriction phase associated with the prodromal symptoms followed by a vasodilation phase associated with the throbbing headache. The vascular aetiology of the condition produced an early enthusiasm for biofeedback therapy based on skin temperature or blood volume. Papers on these techniques continue to appear sporadically (Gauthier 1983) which show that these techniques are effective. Comparable results, however, can be obtained without expensive equipment by relaxation training coupled with anxiety management techniques. These deal with high stress trigger situations and assertion and inter-personal skills training may also be needed when these are deficient (Mitchell and White 1977).

Recurrent Non-infective Sore Throat

A group of recurrent sufferers from sore throats exist where there is no evidence of infection or other local lesion. They do appear to improve with specific throat relaxation exercises with or without the addition of EMG feedback from the sterno-mastoid area. It is proposed that high crico-pharyngeal muscle tone may be a factor in the throat discomfort which is then exacerbated by repetitive swallowing. Experimental evidence in support of this is lacking but a similar treatment has been shown to be effective in the much less common spasmodic torticollis involving muscles in the same area (Martin 1982). The problem is a relatively common one in primary care and further investigation would be worthwhile.

Primary Dysmenorrhoea

Relaxation training associated with EMG biofeedback from the lower abdominal muscles has been shown to be more effective than relaxation alone in the treatment of this condition (Bennink *et al.* 1982). We have no experience of using these techniques in primary care but in view of the prevalence of the problem and the relative ineffectiveness and unpopularity of many drug treatments it would seem to be a promising area to explore.

Skin Disorders

The emotional component in the aetiology of various skin disorders has been recognised for many years. As with asthma there may be some doubt as to the degree to which emotional factors are primary causes rather than secondary consequences of the eczema group of conditions. The continued general use of the term neurodermatosis, however, implies that the psychological component of at least these members of the group is widely accepted.

Many eczema sufferers are children and the first essential of management is education of both patient, if feasible, and parents. Explanation of the nature of the condition, the likely causative factors, the natural history, any necessary or, particularly, unnecessary restrictions and finally what can, and even more important what cannot, be done in the way of treatment, is essential. Cooperation, understanding and agreement of parents about the treatment plan is even more necessary in these cases than in other medical conditions.

Many parents of eczema sufferers are anxious and sometimes feel guilty about their child's condition. This in turn may have an adverse effect on the clinical course by adding to the child's anxiety and thus his scratching. Specific anxiety-reduction measures for both parents and child may be needed but even more necessary is a tactful approach to the problem.

A number of specific measures have been applied. The most useful are, (i) the extinction of scratching coupled to the reinforcement of scratching-free periods which may be gradually lengthened, and (ii) relaxation as an alternative response to scratching (Pinkerton *et al.* 1982). Skin sufferers not unnaturally often have rather low self-esteem and therefore adjuvant treatment in the form of assertive training, self-reinforcement or other cognitive measures may be needed.

Gastro-intestinal Problems

Anorexia, bulimia and encopresis are discussed elsewhere in this book. Other gastro-intestinal conditions which have received attention are peptic ulcer and irritable bowel syndrome although in both cases the experimental literature is surprisingly small.

Peptic Ulcer

This is one of the original psychosomatic conditions that has always been widely attributed to stress. Amongst the few studies, success has been reported for EMG-aided relaxation training followed by *in vivo* practice, and more recently for a combination of anxiety management and assertive skills training (Brooks and Richardson 1980). It is puzzling that this important condition has not been the subject of more work. This may be because traditional medical treatment has a better track record than in, say, coronary heart disease. It has always been recognised, however, that neither drug nor surgical treatment does anything to alleviate the stress that contributed towards producing the condition in the first place. This is an area where worthwhile research could be undertaken in primary care.

Irritable Bowel Syndrome

This is the most commonly occurring gastro-intestinal condition although it has also not been subjected to much behavioural investigation. EMG feedback from the frontalis muscle has been successfully employed (Weinstock 1976) and although some improvement was obtained it is not clear why a muscle so far distant from the site of the problem was chosen. As with dysmenorrhoea mentioned earlier, it would seem logical to seek feedback from muscles adjacent to the offending organ which is usually situated in the left abdomen. As far as we can tell this has not been done with EMG feedback, although sound feedback is reported. Various multimodal single case studies have also been reported as yielding promising results. These usually depended on a combination of relaxation, assertive training and some form of cognitive restructuring.

References

Bennink, C. D., Hulst, L. L. and Benthem, J. A. (1982) 'The effects of EMG biofeedback and relaxation training on primary dysmenorrhea', *Journal of Behavioural Medicine, 5*, 329–41

Brooks, G. R. and Richardson, F. C. (1980) 'Emotional skills training: A treatment programme for duodenal ulcer', *Behavior Therapy, 11*, 198–207

Cobb, S. and Rose, R. M. (1973) 'Hypertension, peptic ulcer and diabetes in air traffic controllers', *Journal of the American Medical Association, 224*, 489–92

Cromwell, R. L., Butterfield, E. C., Brayfield, F. M. and Curry, J. J. (1977) *Acute Myocardial infarction: Reaction and recovery*, St Louis, Mosby

Fordyce, W. E. (1976) *Behavioral Methods for Chronic Pain and Illness*, St Louis, Mosby

Friedman, M. and Rosenman, R. H. (1974) *Type A Behavior and Your Heart*, New York, Knopf

Gauthier, J. (1983) 'Blood volume pulse biofeedback in the treatment of migraine headaches: A controlled evaluation', *Biofeedback and Self-regulation, 8*, 427–42

Johnston, D. W. (1982) 'Behavioural treatment in the reduction of coronary risk factors: Type A behaviour and blood pressure', *British Journal of Clinical Psychology, 21*, 281–94

Johnston, D. W. (1984) 'Biofeedback relaxation and related procedures in the treatment of psychophysiological disorders' in A. Steptoe and A. M. Mathews (eds.) *Health Care and Human Behaviour*, London, Academic Press

Linton, S. J. (1982) 'Applied relaxation as a method of coping with chronic pain: A therapist's guide', *Scandinavian Journal of Behaviour Therapy, 11*, 161–74

Martin, P. R. (1982) 'Spasmodic torticollis: A behavioral perspective', *Journal of Behavioral Medicine, 5*, 249–73

Medical Research Council Working Party (1985) 'MRC trial of treatment of mild hypertension: Principal results', *British Medical Journal, 291*, 97–104

Melzack, R. (1973) *The Puzzle of Pain*, New York, Basic Books

Mitchell, K. R. and White, R. G. (1977) 'Behavioral self management: An application to the problem of migraine headaches', *Behavior Therapy, 8*, 213–21

Patel, C., Marmot, M. G., Terry, D. J., Carruthers, M., Hunt, B. and Patel, M. (1985) 'Trial of relaxation in reducing coronary risk', *British Medical Journal, 290*, 1103–6

Philips, C. (1980) 'Recent developments in tension headache research' in S. Rachman (ed.) *Contributions to Medical Psychology*, Oxford and New York, Pergamon

Pinkerton, S., Hughes, H. and Wenrich, W. W. (1982) *Behavioural Medicine: Clinical Applications*, New York and Chiciester, John Wiley

Steptoe, A. (1980) 'Stress and medical disorders' in S. Rachman (ed.) *Contributions to Medical Psychology, Vol. 2*, Oxford and new York, Pergamon

Steptoe, A. (1984) 'Psychological aspects of bronchial asthma' in S. Rachman (ed.) *Contributions to Medical Psychology, Vol. 3*, Oxford and New York, Pergamon

Suinn, R. M. (1975) 'The cardiac stress management programme for Type A patients', *Cardiac Rehabilitation, 5*, 13–15

Suinn, R. M. and Bloom, L. J. (1978) 'Anxiety management training for pattern A behavior', *Journal of Behavioral Medicine, 1*, 25–35

Thoresen, C. E., Friedman, M., Gill, J. K. and Ulmer, D. K. (1982) 'The recurrent coronary prevention programme: Some preliminary findings', *Acta Medica Scandinavica*, Supplement No. 660, 172–92

Turk, D. C., Meichenbaum, D. and Genest, M. (1983) *Pain and Behavioral Medicine. A cognitive behavioral perspective*, New York, Guilford

Turner, J. A. and Chapman, C. R. (1982) 'Psychological interventions for chronic pain: A critical review I and II', *Pain, 12*, 1–46

Weinstock, S. A. (1976) 'The re-establishment of intestinal control in functional colitis', *Biofeedback and Self-regulation, 1*, 324

Recommended for Further Reading

Broome, A. and Wallace, L. (eds.) (1984) *Psychology and Gynaecological Problems*, London, Tavistock

Fordyce, W. E. (1976) *Behavioral Methods for Chronic Pain and Illness*, St Louis, Mosby

Steptoe, A. and Mathews, A. M. (eds.) (1984) *Health Care and Human Behaviour*, London, Academic Press

Melzack, R. (1973) *The Puzzle of Pain*, New York, Basic Books

Books for Patients

Wilkinson, M. (1982) *Migraine and Headaches*, London, Martin Dunitz

STUDY, WORK AND RETIREMENT

The problems considered in this chapter may seem rather remote from the content of normal primary medical care. They are included for three reasons. First, the GP is often the only independent person who can be approached when difficulties about them arise. Second, the more common clinical problems including anxiety, depression and psychosomatic disorders often have their origins in the life transitions associated with learning, working or ceasing to work. Third, in our experience, simple behavioural counselling based mainly on the approaches and techniques which have already been discussed is often extremely effective in helping people with preoccupations about their jobs.

We shall not concern ourselves with institutional or organisational aspects such as classroom behaviour, job applicant selection and industrial planning which, although highly important, are beyond our competence and scope. Our interest is in problems affecting the individual which may become apparent in the consulting room. A number of threads run through the chapter. Amongst these are ways of coping with stress induced by the outside world, the setting of realistic goals and the need to develop tolerance to imperfect situations.

The referral of these problems to specialists is surprisingly difficult. Universities often do have clinical psychologists available to students for consultation but the educational psychology service in schools, at least in the UK, is usually too overloaded with other tasks to be readily accessible to this sort of problem. For the most part industrial psychologists seem more involved with organisational problems than the individual needs of workers, although there is some evidence that this is changing.

Study and Examination Difficulties

Study problems present frequently to family doctors particularly around the school and college examination months. Often they simply take the form of a request for medication but a little further investigation may reveal problems and anxieties amenable to behavioural intervention. Examinations present a high degree of stress, and some associated anxiety is both useful and universal. Fear related to such fundamentally threatening evaluations can, however, easily become excessive, and all the anxiety management techniques previously discussed may be useful.

There are, however, some aspects which deserve special consideration:

Concentration Problems in Reading and Revision

Students commonly complain that concentration and memory have become impaired. Discussion of the maintaining factors and maintenance of a baseline study diary will often show that concentration is not so much lost as simply diverted onto less threatening or more interesting activities. Alternatively, high levels of anxiety may prevent learning because of distracting worrying thoughts.

In order to counteract this, the student may be advised:

(1) to limit study to short bursts of, say, 10–30 minutes interspersed with equally short breaks. Periods should end once the mind begins to wander but every effort should be made to complete a small section successfully and then get ready for the next by deciding on what to do and preparing the relevant books and notes.

(2) to tackle reading in an organised logical sequence. A useful scheme is to (i) *survey* the material rapidly; (ii) formulate a *question* that might be asked or set on the subject; (iii) *read* the passage fully; (v) *recite* the answer to the question; and (v) *review* the important points of the material. This can be memorised as SQ3R (Beneke and Harris 1972)

(3) to see that the physical surroundings give the best conditions for study, e.g. a desk or table that is clear of other material and a place in the room that does not give a view out of the window and that is well away from the record player.

(4) to organise a proper sleeping routine. Most people have a preference for studying early in the morning or late into the night but it is inadvisable for this to be taken to extremes as students become overtired or sleep during the day. Conditioning is such that a person who regularly takes an afternoon nap and then has to tackle an afternoon exam may find it hard to stay awake for long enough to finish the paper. Those who study, particularly if they study in their bedroom, should try to cover the books or desk and change to another activity for 30 minutes or so before going to bed. The other

strategies for sleep disorders described in Chapter 5 may also be helpful.

(5) to consider how to use breaks — possibly to have a hot drink, make a phone call, do household chores or take exercise. Particularly when exams are near, many students take very little physical exercise but a swim or a run is not time-consuming and can be very effective in dissipating anxiety and agitation.

Note-taking and Essay Writing

Note-taking generally develops along idiosyncratic lines during the course of school and college life, but difficulties still often arise particularly in the transition from school lessons to college lectures and note taking from books. In lectures it is important to sit near the front and have a separate book or folder for each subject. Note-taking can be restricted to picking out important facts. Alternatively an attempt may be made to record everything, which is then checked over and reduced to the main points soon afterwards. The former is probably usually preferable but the latter may be necessary in some situations, particularly where suitable printed texts are not available.

Note-taking from books should normally be confined to *recitation*, i.e. the question-answering phase of SQ3R. Many of the more conscientious students make far too many notes, losing sight of the aim of the reading and ending up with merely a precis of the printed text. Wherever possible, apart from quotations, notes should be made in the student's own words as this forces him to work out and re-express the meaning. Also the original author's sentence structure may be difficult to learn. This may create one block to essay writing. Another may occur when note-taking has been over-inclusive, providing the student with too much material.

Once blocks have been identified, it is often helpful to suggest that an outline essay plan is made before reading. This is followed by a linked question for each section, the answering notes for which are then expanded into the final essay. Other students find that blocks in essay writing are sometimes easily lifted by first speaking into a tape recorder and directing the content as if to a fellow student rather than a senior expert.

The Revision Period and Examination Problems

Exam difficulties may present as a phobia of the actual test situation itself or as anxiety related to lack of skill.

The examination phobic may suffer from worrying thoughts about the coming ordeal, provoking severe panic during the revision period and physiological disturbances such as sleepless nights. These may be treated by imaginal desensitisation (described in Chapter 5, p. 67) aided by coping self-statements. The hierarchy used in this situation might include items like:

(i)   Thinking about the exam
(ii) The night before
(iii) The morning before
(iv) Entering the exam room

The student should be relaxed, presented with the scene and then asked to switch to positive coping statements such as:

(i)   I have worked steadily, I know enough to pass.
(ii) If I panic I will only have to take them at another time.
(iii) If I remain fairly calm, I shall do better.
(iv) I must concentrate on controlling my breathing and the tension in my arms.

In some cases anxiety about examinations leads to overbreathing and related symptoms of fainting, sickness and general panic which can be managed by demonstrating the linking relationship and teaching controlled breathing as described in Chapter 5. It is important that all these techniques are practised sitting in an upright chair similar to the examination setting.

Anxiety related to lack of skill may be realistic in students who have not taken examinations before or who have always repeated similar mistakes without attempts at correction. In these cases help may be needed with:

(i)   Revision techniques:
(ii) Practise timed question in various types.

Revision requires an extension of the study methods already covered. It should aim for a gradual condensing of information from copious notes to a single page per topic and then perhaps to a few key points. If these are well learnt they are not easily forgotten in a panic and can act as cues to further details once writing has started. If the intended paper has a choice of questions, topics can be listed and selected giving a better chance of an adequate answer to, say, three out of ten questions.

Practice timed questions can be answered at home with, perhaps, a relative acting as invigilator. First attempts should be at an easy question, then a more difficult one and finally a simulated hurried final question with only 20 minutes left. Practice should stress the importance of getting down facts without lengthy introductions and conclusions. Good literary essay writers often find this difficult. Later practice might include (i) a very difficult question; (ii) a question on a topic not revised; (iii) starting one question and then being asked to change to another; (iv) making very brief notes in case time runs out – even after this programme! Surprisingly, even senior students sometimes have to be reminded of the importance of attempting each question. Beta blockers are the drugs of choice if needed to supplement these techniques or in last minute emergency.

The Driving Test

Intended driving test candidates often attend the surgery asking for tranquillisers to help them overcome nervousness. Most commonly they are older people who have never experienced, or have got out of the habit of, taking tests. To provide tranquillisers for this purpose is dangerous and to take them without careful preparation is probably illegal.

Beta blockers, however, can be used without drowsiness in this and other examinations. It is often enough for a candidate to have a few in his pocket 'in case' although if they are likely to be used they should be tried beforehand to check their efficacy and inspire confidence. A simple desensitisation programme to the test circumstances and many repeated practice tests with the usual instructor, including making and mentally dismissing mistakes, will often achieve good results and render any drugs unnecessary.

Problems at Work

Although sometimes the presenting complaint, work problems more usually come to light when enquiring into the circumstances surrounding tiredness, snappiness or too frequent physical illnesses. They are commonly related to either interpersonal problems with colleagues or to the now fashionable burn-out syndrome. (Rigler and Bongar 1979).

Interpersonal Problems

These may occur with bosses, peers or subordinates. Assessment should try to pinpoint clearly the behaviour causing the difficulty. Who is doing what to whom? Where and how often? What triggers the problem? Who benefits from the present situation and how could it be altered? What would be the result of that alteration? All of these must be established clearly out of the pervading sense of injustice that usually surrounds these problems. Further information is then obtained by a baseline record which can contain any items thought to be relevant. A useful starting point is to ask the patient to record anything which irritates him at work, how it started, who was there, and what the result was. This may be enough to form an hypothesis or may indicate where further information is needed.

When problems arise with bosses, there is frequently a sense of helplessness on the part of the junior and an assumption that nothing can be done. In fact few bosses are as unreasonable as they may seem. They are often content, however, to continue with the *status quo* (including their own bad habits) either because there is a hidden reward or because they are ignorant of consequences like staff inefficiency or dissatisfaction. To take an example: Sid, a section leader, is criticised by Mr Power, the works director, for not having drawings for the biscuit plant ready on time. Sid knows the reasons for this are (i) the commission for the plans sat on Mr Power's desk for two weeks before being passed to Sid and (ii) that an experienced draughtsman in his section had just been replaced by a junior with no training in this type of project. Sid says nothing about it because, in spite of a feeling of injustice and frustration, he thinks that it is his job to 'deliver the goods' and not to 'whine to the bosses'.

Analysis of the problem showed (i) communication failure between Sid and Mr Power; (ii) submissive attitudes and behaviour by Sid; (iii) Mr Power's behaviour inappropriately reinforced, as he was able to get on with other work, play golf or take long lunches without any apparent penalty for failing to pass the commission on to Sid.

Sid originally consulted his GP wanting tranquillisers for tiredness and edginess. After this analysis, he booked an interview with Mr Power at which, maintaining good eye contact, he asked for his boss's experience and help in dealing with some problems (thereby reinforcing Mr Power's status). He explained how tight time was on certain jobs (prompting quicker delivery of commissions from Mr Power) and said that this was particularly true with inexperienced staff. He asked if Mr Power could use his influence in getting preliminary training for new draughtsmen. This Mr Power promised to do and added his own suggestion that if this proved impossible, extra time must be allowed for jobs in those sections with inexperienced staff.

Future commissions were passed on promptly. When Sid delivered the drawings back on time, he always remarked to Mr Power that is was easier to do the work now that he had enough time (reinforcing Mr Power's new behaviour). Staff pre-training was instituted.

It should be noted that in this example the subordinate has got the desired change without being critical, aggressive or servile. He has merely spoken his own opinions clearly and encouraged the behaviour he wanted. This sort of programme takes a little longer than the five-minute consultation but it avoids a miserable patient and endless requests for psychotropic drugs. It is also much more fun for the doctor.

Problems with the peer group in work may be concerned with social skills difficulties (Chapter 6) or involve unrealistic goals or unhelpful assumptions. A young woman working with entirely male colleagues in a male-dominated engineering field became tense and exhausted. Assessment of thoughts showed that she believed that she must be perfect at every part of her job or the men would say that a woman was unsuitable for the work. Exploring this attitude showed that, although there was some truth in it, the men would not assume her sex accounted for every minor lapse and that thinking in this way was unhelpful as perfection was impossible. The way was thus prepared for cue controlled shoulder relaxation. The patient and her work rapidly improved.

Promotion brings special problems particularly in its requirements for more strategic planning, delegation and different modes of communication. A recently promoted sales manager was depressed as he found himself edgy and overstressed. He concluded that he had reached his potential as a (very good) sales representative and that his promotion had been a mistake. This added to his depression. Assessment showed that he was attempting to do both jobs — his present and former one — and as a result had had no chance to plan the strategy of his new responsibilities and thus was staggering from crisis to crisis.

The first stage of intervention was to list the things he might leave subordinates to do by themselves and the possible consequences either for good or bad. In fact nothing further was needed from the GP as the patient saw what was happening, began delegating tasks and found time for planning. He carried out the whole programme with no further prompting. This case was a striking example of the rule that if behavioural assessment is adequate, change can often be obtained with little further trouble.

Job Burn-out

We use this term a little reluctantly both because it is a fashionable label and because it really only groups together a number of problem features of work which are far from new. These are loss of drive, dissatisfaction, depression, increased liability to illness and absenteeism and increasing inefficiency. Commonly the person is able and enthusiastic in the early stages of his career. He finds himself becoming increasingly dissatisfied with the job, exhausted physically and despondent and cynical psychologically. Pessimism and self doubts grow and eventually he becomes obsessed with his frustrations and the need to find a 'way out'. Sometimes this 'way out' will be a change of job or environment and the problems may improve but, unfortunately, often this adaptive solution seems impossible and 'the way out' will be alcohol, depressive illness, drugs, suicide or coronary thrombosis.

Additional circumstances such as family demands or environmental pressures such as poor housing, financial difficulties or excessive commuting predispose to burn-out and relaxations such as sport or hobbies will protect against it. Triggers often come from within work itself such as missed promotion or difficult colleagues. Most important is change in the firm such as mergers, contractions or altered management structure with known and trusted colleagues replaced by threatening unknowns.

Assessment will consist of an interview determining the factors discussed above and a stress diary recording all events felt to be disturbing for, say, one week.

The first stage of behavioural management overlaps assessment and consists of understanding and monitoring the problem. As with many problems, change is much easier to obtain early before the worst features of the downward spiral have developed. Thus early problem recognition is particularly important. If more is needed, the following strategies may be useful:

(1) Attempt to modify the environment, if possible, with attention to such factors as additional office space, more staff, change of job, improved travel, flexitime (but see later warning) or job sharing.

(2) Attend to unhelpful thoughts and attitudes by listing them and then attempting to answer or modify them (as with depression), for example:

Thought	Logical Answer
This is a nothing job — dead end and worthless.	It is boring a lot of the time but I have some good friends and the odd joke. It's better than nothing — stick to it and perhaps I can change later. I can concentrate on hobbies for now.

(3) Challenge perfectionist attitudes and learn to tolerate an imperfect self in an imperfect world.

(4) Invest physically and mentally in outside interests.

(5) Modify the timetable by allowing more time in the morning, cutting overtime or extra work and incorporating reward breaks in the day.

Changing Jobs and Redundancy

These are deliberately grouped together as it is often helpful if redundancy can be looked at as a change of occupation rather than the loss of it. A list of assets and liabilities can be drawn up in both circumstances and a problem-solving approach used to minimise the drawbacks and take advantage of the assets. This can then be converted into a task list including items dealing with finance, requirements, conditions of work or leisure and the availability of resources such as job vacancies or adult classes. By using this technique the multiple problems associated with redundancy may seem a little less dire.

Shift Work and Flexitime

Shift work is a common cause of multiple problems including sleep disorders, digestive troubles, fatigue and irritability which are probably associated with disturbance of the normal 24-hour pattern known as the *circadian rhythm*. In addition there are further problems associated with disruption of family, social and leisure activities. Night work appears to have a more adverse effect on physical health and afternoon and evening shifts disrupt home and recreation. The fixed-shift worker eventually will usually adapt to his changed circumstances in both body and life-style whereas the unfortunate rotating shift worker is denied this opportunity with a consequent higher incidence of stress-related problems (Landy 1985). Interventions may be directed to changing the working pattern with its associated difficulties or to modifying its adverse effects by using stress control techniques already discussed.

Flexitime implies a variable working week usually incorporating a core of obligatory hours with the rest to be made up at the worker's discretion. Although not possible in all types of work, it does give the worker a greater degree of control over his life and avoids, to some extent, the problem of incompatible timetables between spouses. The disadvantages of it are that it may obliterate the normal breaks in the day, perhaps allowing no time for lunch or a walk but more time to flop in front of the television or worry about the day's activities, resulting in later insomnia.

Retirement

As with redundancy this may be approached in the spirit of changing a job rather than leaving one. Unlike redundancy, for many people the prospect is pleasurable and much more time is available for planning.

Five years before retirement, the changes that it will bring may begin to be considered and plans laid. Consideration should be given to:

(1) moving or staying — and if a move is contemplated, the advantages and disadvantages in terms of housing, services including medicine, cost and access to relatives;
(2) a general financial prediction including income from pensions and other sources, costs and savings in moving house, keeping a car or not, the cost of increased leisure, the effect of inflation and the changes in basic living costs;
(3) the social effects in the losing, or possibly gaining, of friends and everyday contacts like tradesmen in the neighbourhood;
(4) the opportunities for recreation, sports and new interests to be developed.
(5) some specific exercises like the swopping of roles, with the wife changing the fuses and filling in the income tax form and the husband cooking the dinner and doing the washing;

(6) the availability of special investments and concessions like cheap travel for retired people;

(7) the importance of making wills and their provisions.

In an area or practice with substantial numbers of people on the verge of retirement, a group to discuss all these topics can usefully be run from a practice or health centre with outside authorities speaking at different meetings on relevant subjects.

References

Beneke, W. N. and Harris, M. B. (1972) 'Teaching self control of study behavior', *Behaviour Research and Therapy, 10*, 35–41

Landy, F. (1985) *Psychology of Work Behavior*, Homewood, Ill., Dorsey Press

Riglar, D. and Bongar, B. (1979) 'Occupational "Burn-out"' in D. J. Oborne, M. M. Gruneberg and J. R. Eiser (eds.) *Research in Psychology and Medicine*, London and New York, Academic Press

Recommended for Further Reading

Veninga, R. L. and Spradley, J. P. *The Work Stress Connection*, Boston, Little, Brown

Books for Patients

Hills, P. J. and Barlow, H. (1980) *Effective Study Skills*, London, Pan Books

Honey, P. (1980) *Solving People's Problems*, London, McGraw Hill

The Consumer Association (1983) *Approaching Retirement*, London, Consumers Association, 14 Buckingham Street, London WC2N

Open University (1979) *Preparing to Study*, Milton Keynes, Open University Press

12 CHILDREN AND THE ELDERLY

Many of the most effective behavioural interventions in primary care are with children. There are several reasons for this. First, children learn, unlearn and relearn with a rapidity that their elders envy; secondly, a parent or teacher is almost always at hand to act as a co-therapist; and thirdly, the reinforcers of a child's behaviour are much easier to control than those of an adult. The last is probably the most important factor but it also highlights a potential ethical problem as the very dependency of children on adults makes them particularly vulnerable to misdirected attempts at behaviour modification. For this reason the triangular nature of any therapy involving children must always be taken into account in a behavioural assessment. Otherwise, not only will the effectiveness of the intervention suffer but harm may occur through failure to distinguish parents' problems and needs from those of the child.

It is important to decide at the outset whether a problem exists at all. Many children are brought to the surgery by anxious parents with 'problems' which are in fact only less usual examples of the very wide variation of the normal. An explanation about the range of sleeping and eating patterns in infancy or rebellious behaviour in adolescence may be all that is needed. If a problem does exist, it is necessary to decide whether it belongs solely to parent, solely to the child or much more commonly, in varying proportions to each. A frequent example is the non-sleeping baby who may himself be miserable but is causing a far greater degree of distress to his fraught mother.

Once the nature, severity and functional determinants of the problem are plain, the advantages of treatment in primary care often become apparent, as it is possible to deal with problems away from school hours so that the intervention is kept as discreet and 'normal' as possible. Many problems with smaller children can receive attention before school age when the health visitor, with her knowledge of the home and family, is well placed to initiate or collaborate in treatment. This low-key approach enables potential problems to be recognised and helped at an early stage. This benefits both parent and child.

In general, programmes for children need to be rigid enough to work but not so inflexible that they become punishing for both child and parents. Parents are often so exhausted and at the end of their tether that initial changes must be kept small and very gradual for them to be able to cooperate consistently. Extra care must be taken in specifying target behaviours in steps which are clearly understood and which are possible in the prevailing circumstances. The most carefully thought-out toiletting programme will come to nothing if the youngster is unable to reach the door handle of the lavatory which is always kept shut. These sorts of problem are sometimes difficult to spot if programmes are run from the surgery or office without home visits by at least one member of the team. Equally it is important to see that a programme demands only behaviour that is age- and ability-appropriate and, if at all possible, already exists in the child's repertory. New behaviours can be built up by a variety of modelling, shaping and chaining procedures which have already been described in Chapter 4. Particularly in the limited time of primary care, however, reinforcing existing responses is clearly much more economical.

Most of the rest of this chapter will consider a number of specific problems which are amongst those most commonly seen in primary care. The techniques of assessment, data collection and basic methods of intervention have been described in Part One of this book. Some of the examples used there involve children. The reader is advised to refer back to these sections before considering individual problems. Many of the chapters in Part Two, notably those on anxiety-related problems and habit disorders, also contain much that is applicable to children as well as adults and may also be useful.

We will not deal specifically with classroom or institutional problems as these are outside our scope. It is, however, worth pointing out that a 'phone call to the school is usually very rewarding when dealing with any school-aged patient. Some schools will cooperate to a limited extent, if approached tactfully, in such things as record keeping and data collection but it should always be remembered when asking for this that teachers have a heavy work load. We have also not considered the topical and delicate subjects of physical, sexual and emotional abuse of children. We realise these areas are important but feel that referral to expert agencies is always necessary both because of the seriousness of the problems and the likelihood that any attempt at primary care intervention may risk damage to the long-term professional relationship with the family.

Although families will inevitably become involved in behavioural interventions with children, we do not feel competent to discuss formal family therapy and the interested reader is referred to specialised manuals.

Before dealing with some of the commonest specific problems, we are going to reconsider the concepts of reinforcement and Time Out (from positive reinforcement) and the way in which they are used in dealing with so many problems of children.

Reinforcement

The main principles governing the use of reinforcement as an instrument of behaviour change have been considered in Chapter 4. We return to it here not only because positive reinforcement is the most powerful instrument in changing children's behaviour but also because inappropriate reinforcement is often responsible for maintaining problems in the first place. Let us consider Kevin who is grizzling for sweets at the check-out of the supermarket. The most likely outcome is that sweets are given or are *sometimes* given. If Kevin never gets sweets in this situation he will soon realise that grizzling is unproductive. If sweets on the other hand are always forthcoming, Kevin is on a continuous schedule of positive reinforcement. If sweets are sometimes forthcoming, perhaps admixed with an occasional clip round the ear, he is on a variable ratio intermittent schedule of positive reinforcement which, as we have seen in Chapter 4, is more resistant to extinction than continuous schedules.

Two other points about this example are important. Firstly, even if sweets are not gained, mother's attention (and probably the rest of the queue's) certainly has been. He is thus provided with social as well as material reinforcement for grizzling. Secondly, if she gives way and buys the sweets, mother is being negatively reinforced because Kevin shuts up. There are therefore a number of very powerful supporting factors strengthening this particular behaviour pattern.

Parental attention is the strongest and most pervasive reinforcer of children's behaviour *even if that attention is critical or punishing*. It is unfortunate but true that it is usually easier for a child to gain attention by hitting the baby, pulling the cat's tail or putting jam on the hi-fi than by playing quietly with toys. When the toddler is quiet, mother is likely to sigh with relief and get on with the ironing or other jobs. To improve the situation the contingencies of reinforcement must be altered so that playing quietly with the toys gets the attention and praise of mother and, as far as safety allows, other less desirable activities are ignored. This process is known as differential reinforcement of other behaviour or DRO. If possible, the other behaviour should be incompatible with the problem, i.e. it should be impossible for the two to co-exist. This is particularly important when baby-hitting or fire-raising is involved as in these situations the reduction of behaviour by extinction, at least in its normal behavioural sense, is inappropriate.

It is important to look at the range of types of reinforcer that are available. It must be stressed that, with the exception of parental attention mentioned above which is virtually always effective, nothing can be assumed to be reinforcing until it has been tested in the situation under consideration. From the theoretical point of view it must be remembered that a reinforcer increases the likelihood or frequency of that behaviour occurring in the future. In practice this means that it is essential to discover what is in fact rewarding for the child in question *not* what the parent or the therapist *thinks* will be rewarding. Most of us can remember childhood 'treats' organised by well-meaning adults that were far from enjoyable to us.

There are some other general points. Parental praise and attention are very important. Some parents do not know how to give this and may need help with prompting and role play. This can present a problem in primary care where it is difficult for professionals to spend a lot of time in the patient's home. It is also very important to make sure that the child is able to perform the target behaviour. If not, he also will have to be taught perhaps using the methods described in Chapter 4. During assessment the distinction must therefore be made between skills deficits (i.e., not knowing) and performance deficits (i.e. knowing but not doing) in both child and parent.

A further problem with parental praise is that it can be overused. The first time somebody says 'well done — that's very good' is likely to be more effective than the fifteenth as anybody with a 'gushing' friend will agree. There is, therefore, a place for other rewards. The best are, of course, the natural consequence of the task, for example, the pleasure of making a toy or reading an exciting story, but these are often not available for manipulation. Other reinforcers may have to be linked to the behaviour and may be tangible, e.g. food or toys, or special treats or privileges, e.g. a game of football with father or half an hour's extra TV.

There are many varieties of points and token systems ranging from the common, and now sometimes overused, star-chart to sophisticated token economies where all goods and services must be bought by earnings. These programmes are really suitable for institutions but can be adapted for home use. Tokens are usually earned towards a 'back-up' reinforcer of which there are an infinite variety. The advantages of tokens are:

(1) They have great flexibility in that the ratio of tokens to the back-up reinforcer as well as the nature of the latter can be changed at will.
(2) They are more difficult to forget than social reinforcers, as the would-be recipient can prompt the deliverer.
(3) They are cheap per unit and always available.

It is useful to include other siblings in any sort of token system as this prevents disproportionate attention going to the identified problem child and also may produce all-round improvements in the way that the family functions.

Time-out

For practical purposes, time-out represents the most commonly used means of reducing unwanted activities and is usually used in conjunction with differential reinforcement of other behaviour, which has just been discussed. The routine for applying Time Out has been described in Chapter 4 but there are some further aspects which can be considered here. There has been some press and public criticism of Time Out as being too punishing and mechanical but this has usually been because it has been ill-applied or ill-understood by the critics. There is, after all, nothing very disturbing about removing a child from sources of reward for a short period of time. Many commonly used domestic punishments are much more severe, if less effective. Its effectiveness, particularly when coupled with DRO, means that in practice problems come quickly under control and the number of occasions on which it has been used usually decreases rapidly as long as the assessment has been correct. The following points should be borne in mind when using the technique:

(1) The procedure (see Chapter 4) should be meticulously followed and the Time Out situation must really be non-reinforcing not, for example, a relief from more boring activities.

(2) An explanation of the rules for Time Out (p. 41) is given when it is introduced. The reason for its use on a particular occasion is clearly stated both for the child's benefit and also to ensure that it is not used by the parent in a vague and slipshod manner.

(3) Release does not take place until the behaviour (e.g. tantrum) ceases or else release may inadvertently act as a reinforcer. It has been our experience that in simple family situations it may be enough to allow the child to release himself, without a fixed term, as long as the problem has ceased. This has not been experimentally tested.

(4) The timings given in Chapter 4 represent a consensus of opinion but essentially it seems that as short a time as possible can be used initially and only increased if it proves insufficient. If shorter periods are mixed with longer ones the former will be ineffective (Hobbs and Forehand 1977).

(5) Parents can usefully be asked to rehearse the Time Out procedure in the consulting room to make sure that they have understood it. The non-verbal part of the exercise in which the child is unemotionally but caringly removed from the problem situation to the Time Out area, without slamming or locking of doors, is particularly important.

Sleep Problems

The non-sleeping child presents a common and distressing problem. The child may seem tired and fractious but more important the mother is anxious, guilty and exhausted. Father, suffering also from lack of sleep, feels perplexed, powerless and sometimes ready to be angry with anybody within range including professional advisers. At the back of all this is the feeling that they must be defective as parents or, worse, that there is something the matter with their child. The first essential for GP or health visitor faced with this potentially explosive situation is to gain the confidence of the parents by listening to them and taking their problem seriously. Once trust has been established work can begin in earnest.

Assessment

The assessment phase starts with the behavioural analysis of the problem. A statement of the exact current difficulty is obtained together with details of the following:

(1) Bedtime and settling routine. Some parents have no consistent pattern and this often is associated with difficulties.
(2) Night waking, including frequency, duration and what action is taken.
(3) Daytime naps if any.
(4) Whether help has previously been obtained from outside and how the couple have tried to cope with the problem themselves.
(5) Whether the child has any other problems
(6) What the effect has been of the problem on the family as a whole.

An opportunity is then made for other family and emotional problems to be discussed with particular attention being given to any marital discord or sexual difficulties — a non-sleeping child is an excellent contraceptive.

The parents' attitude and feelings about the problem are then covered together with their expectations of the nature and effectiveness of various types of help. Often initially parents will simply be seeking drugs for the child. The advantages and disadvantages of sedatives must be discussed before other techniques will be willingly accepted. Finally, as has been implied, the presence or at the very least the cooperation of both parents must be obtained as no intervention can succeed in the face of opposition or simply lack of understanding of an absent husband or father.

After the assessment, it should be possible to form a preliminary hypothesis of the factors maintaining the settling or waking problem which can be confirmed by a baseline recording in the form of a sleep diary noting:

(1) Time to bed
(2) Time to sleep
(3) Time(s) awake in the night
     Action taken
     Time to sleep again

(4) Time of morning waking

(5) Time of parents to bed.

With this information, a plan of intervention can be formulated with agreed targets. These must be settled with the parents, having due regard as to what is tolerable and acceptable to them. For example, six hours of sleep per night with not more than one waking three times a week might be acceptable to one set of parents but not to another.

Methods of Achieving Change

These must be selected in accordance with the analysis of the problem. The following are amongst the techniques most often considered (see, further, Douglas and Richman 1982):

(1) Punishment is used in various forms and the sleepless child is at some risk of being battered. As a method of achieving change it has nothing to recommend it, as it is unpleasant, weak and temporary. It is also usually applied inconsistently.

(2) Extinction (i.e. ignoring the crying and sleeplessness) can be employed and if used consistently it is quick and effective. The snag is, however, that most parents simply cannot listen to their child crying. Unsuccessful attempts result in intermittent reinforcement as mother finds that she can stand the crying no longer and goes in. This is, as we have seen, a powerful way of strengthening behaviour. The assessment should show if extinction is a possibility by exploring both parents' attitude to listening to their child cry. If it *is* attempted, the rule for the parents must be *first time or not at all*, in other words they can go to the child as soon as he wakes but not after he has been crying for some time.

(3) Positive reinforcement, usually of quiet night behaviour rather than sleeping itself, can work well for the slightly older child. One three-year-old improved quickly once a morning drink brought by father was made contingent upon rapid night settling. The usual rules for reinforcement (see Chapter 4) apply. It is important to define exactly what is to be reinforced, e.g. 'staying in your own room', 'staying in your own bed' (which is difficult to observe) or 'not coming into our bedroom'. It is also important to make sure that the reinforcer can be delivered first thing in the morning to keep the necessary interval between task and reinforcer as short as possible.

(4) Graded approaches are usually the most useful as they do not

require the parents, who are often exhausted and demoralised, to do anything that is too unpleasant or difficult. The child's behaviour is changed gradually in very small steps. Short wakings are normal for most children but some cannot go back to sleep unless mother is present and for these this method is particularly suitable. Assessment will show the exact requirements of the individual situation but a typical programme might involve

(a) mother sleeping in the child's bed holding his hand
(b) mother sleeping in the child's bed without contact
(c) mother in bed but Teddy in between
(d) mother in another bed alongside
(e) mother in chair alongside
(f) mother in chair at other side of room
(g) mother outside the door in chair
(h) mother looking in before her own bedtime

The variations on this theme are infinite and the most important factor is achieving small enough steps. The use of a Teddy-bear or favourite toy during daytime naps may help to wean the child off mother's presence by providing a substitute stimulus for settling.

A similar technique can be used at bedtime when initial settling is a problem. Bedtime is first set very late. It is then progressively moved forward by 15 minutes each night until a satisfactory time is achieved.

(5) Bedtime routines are often absent or intermittent where children have difficulty in settling. Work to establish a regular programme is often helpful. A model sequence might be bath, cuddle, story, drink and settle. The cuddle should be placed early in the sequence if there is any fear that it is, or might become, the essential stimulus for settling (as described earlier).

(6) Drugs may be used with these programmes, particularly if parents' morale is very low. If possible, however, it is better to avoid them as they are often unpredictable, ineffective, difficult to stop and may increase thirst.

Nightmares, Night Terrors and Sleep Walking

These are all relatively common. The primary care worker's normal job is to explain this to the parents and reassure them that no permanent harm is likely to result. When this is insufficient, the circumstances suggest emotional problems, or if the symptoms are very severe referral may be indicated.

Feeding Difficulties

These are common and usually relatively easy to treat. Parents get extremely anxious when children refuse to eat and the child readily finds the coaxing and other bizarre attention very rewarding. Assessment concentrates on:

(1) Inappropriate feeding — is the child getting the wrong food, too much food or food at the wrong time?
(2) Attitudes and assumptions of parent about feeding. Some parents assume that food fads and refusal carry a grave health risk to the child. They may be unaware of normal variations between children, and at different times within the development of the same child.
(3) The functional analysis of eating or what happens before, during and after meals using the ABC model described in Chapter 2. This will reveal ways in which the refusal or fads are currently being cued or reinforced.

Management follows from the assessment. Usually it is sufficient to concentrate on eliminating the coaxing, anger and other disturbance caused by the problem. Parents are encouraged to serve food without fuss or comment and to remove it, also without comment, at the end of the meal if it has not been eaten. Praise and attention, possibly with the help of tokens or stars, are given if the meal is eaten without disturbance. It is important to warn parents that fuss at meal times will increase before it diminishes (the extinction burst) and that this storm must be weathered calmly. Snacks and sweet drinks must be eliminated or used only as a reward after the meal has been finished.

Obesity is still a considerable problem amongst children seen in primary care although parents have become more conscious of the advantages of breast feeding followed by a rational diet. Some parents, however, still seem to be unable to grasp these concepts and these same parents also often prove resistant to advice and education. Careful detailed instruction in food preparation from a dietician or health visitor coupled with a programmed increase in exercise seems to produce the best results. Many of the techniques described in the section on adult obesity may also be used with children.

Enuresis

Bed Wetting

This is also an extremely common childhood behaviour problem often presented to the GP or health visitor. It is fortunate that it also has one of the highest cure rates.

Assessment. This involves an accurate description of the duration and frequency of wetting and any factors making it better or worse. Special enquiry is made into stressful events such as birth of siblings, moving house or deaths of relatives or pets. These factors may have particular importance when wetting recurs after a period of dryness. Physical examination is essential both to discover the occasional relevant abnormality and as a prelude to explanation and reassurance. A mid stream specimen of urine should be taken as an important minority of enuretics have urinary infections. Baseline recording is by a chart, often using stars or pictures, which the child fills in himself. This in itself is a powerful means of change and, in many cases, when coupled with parental praise may be sufficient to solve the problem.

Management. Management starts with a discussion with the parents of the nature of the problem and its background. Many parents request help too early and it is useful to point out that 7 per cent of children are still bed wetting at seven years old and as many as 11 per cent at five. Some may have misconceptions that the problem is due to serious disease, bladder weakness or the need for circumcision. These myths may be discussed and dispelled. Previous attempts at management may have included:

(1) Punishment, which is unkind and ineffective;
(2) Restricting fluids which may send the child to bed uncomfortably thirsty and produce an irritable concentrated urine. It also begs the essential question of getting the child to respond to a full bladder and then learning to tolerate it.

(3) Lifting, which is ineffective as it is not related to the full bladder stimulus.

All of these should be considered and tactfully dismissed.

Once the decision is taken to go further with a programme the following techniques may be used:

(1) Monitoring and reinforcement with a star chart linked to a small back up reward for a pre arranged number of dry nights. This number can be varied as the programme advances.

(2) The buzzer, also known as the bell and pad or the Mowrer pad. A number of similar devices are available, all of which make a loud noise when activated by contact with urine. It is important to use an appliance that has adequate safety approval. Some of the best equipment uses a single pad with double aluminium tape. This has the advantage that it is easier for the child to reset in the night. The same range also provides an extra loud alarm for the child who has difficulty in waking, a pillow rocker for the child sharing a room and an extension alarm to lead to another room should this be required (see 'Equipment' at the end of chapter for details). The noise results in the child waking with a start that turns off the urine flow. The exact way in which this highly efficient apparatus works is unknown. It may make use of classical conditioning — pairing the full bladder sensation instead of the buzzer noise with waking. The negative reinforcement of avoiding the noise and the wet bed and positive reinforcement of being in a comfortable dry bed are also probably involved.

The procedure must be thoroughly rehearsed. *First* an explanation of the equipment and procedure is given to the child in a way that he can understand according to his age. *Second* he is shown how to assemble the apparatus in the order (i) mattress, (ii) waterproof sheet, (iii) buzzer sheet — correct way round, (iv) top bed sheet. *Third* the leads are connected to the buzzer which is switched on. *Fourth* the buzzer is made to sound by pouring some salt water over the sheets. *Fifth* he is shown how the buzzer is switched off. *Sixth* he repeats all the steps himself with appropriate prompting and praise.

When he wakes in the night he switches off the buzzer, goes to the toilet 'to finish if possible', takes the dry sheets from a previously arranged place, remakes the bed, switches alarm on again and gets back into it. Parents guide and encourage these steps.

A chart is kept recording not only wet and dry beds but also the size of the wet patch (initially) and whether the correct procedure has been achieved. It is important that the whole programme should be made fun and small back-up rewards incorporated. A suitable target is 14 consecutive dry nights. When this has been achieved relapse is minimised if an overlearning phase is incorporated. In this the child is given extra drinks at bedtime — one or two pints per night, according to age — and the routine continued until the target number of dry nights is again achieved. Surprisingly this usually happens quite quickly following the first phase.

Some snags may occur. The buzzer sheets get hard wear and particularly some types need frequent renewal if they are to work properly. Some children do not wake to the alarm in which case putting it in a tin will make it louder. Some turn it off before waking properly in which case it must be placed out of reach. If the child cannot turn off the urine stream when the alarm sounds, day time practice in the toilet stopping the stream when the buzzer sounds may help training. False alarms are sometimes a problem and as they are likely to weaken the programme every effort should be made to find the fault and stop them. (See Morgan 1981 for further reading.)

Day Time Wetting

This is often associated with (i) failure to detect full bladder signals until it is too late, (ii) inability to hold on once the signals are received, (iii) excessive distraction by other activities, and (iv) unattractive or over-public lavatories at schools without locking doors. Each of these situations requires its own management. Reception of bladder signals may be improved by practising waiting an extra five minutes after the urge is noticed. Holding on can be helped by waiting or stop-start exercises when passing water. Distraction may need concentration on discriminating bladder sensations by checking whether they are present at deliberately given intervals. A fixed timetable e.g. at break, before lunch, after lunch, etc. with gradual lengthening of the intervals can be effective. The school lavatories may require a diplomatic approach to the head teacher.

Soiling

This is, with a certain proviso, another extremely suitable problem for management in primary care as the behavioural and physical elements are often closely intertwined. The proviso is necessary as some soiling children have profound complicated emotional problems and for these intensive treatment may be needed. The most common type of soiling seen in primary care is retention of stools with overflow. This is caused by an initial failure to empty the bowel so that the rectum remains full although the urge passes. There may be many reasons for this — for example, hurry to do other things, a fissure *in ano* or the all too common unsuitable school lavatories. Once the urge has passed stool continues to accumulate so that the sphincter becomes overstretched and leaking takes place around the bolus. Any attempt to pass the stool mass is frustrated by painful overstretching or tearing.

The first step in management is to empty the rectum which usually requires an enema. This is followed by a high fibre diet and a suitable laxative agent such as docusate sodium syrup 25 mgms t.d.s (Dioctyl). From this point on the behavioural element of carefully charted regular toiletting with positive reinforcement from the parents takes over. The object is to train the child to detect when the rectum is full and go to the toilet immediately. This is then rewarded. It is important not to make 'clean pants' the target for reinforcement as this can promote a return to holding back.

Lack of control without retention is less common and may occur for a number of reasons. The very young child may simply not yet have learnt control or may temporarily have lost it. The occasional purely physical cause should not be ignored. Most serious are those children where persistent, usually secondary, encopresis is a symptom of personal or family stress. In these cases it is the underlying problem which must receive attention.

Where reinforcement alone is ineffective, more intensive methods are available. Overcorrection requires 30 minutes after each soiling to be spent in the child washing himself, his clothes and anything else soiled and then hanging them out to dry. Positive practice requires him to sit alone in a quiet room for ten minutes followed by ten minutes 'trying to go'. This sequence is repeated three times. Both these methods seem to us fairly punitive and we have not found them to be necessary in primary care.

Disruptive Behaviour

Many children only get attention when they make a nuisance of themselves. The shock and horror on the faces of bystanders and the confused embarrassment of mother are powerful rewards for having a tantrum. The overall object of any treatment is therefore to turn the situation round so that cooperative behaviour is rewarded and disruption is extinguished. Tantrums, disobedience and aggression occur in different circumstances but have features in common in both their origins and their management. *Tantrums* usually appear first and are so common as to be almost universal. The first question is to establish whether reassurance that they are within normal limits will solve the problem or whether something more is required.

Assessment follows the normal pattern (Chapter 2). Special points of importance are:

(1) The sort of situations that trigger the tantrums. Who is present? Where do they normally take place? A tantrum in a supermarket requires different handling from one in the kitchen.

(2) What does the child actually do during the tantrum? Can it be safely ignored or is there real danger? Screaming in the garden can be left; pulling the saucepans off the stove cannot.

(3) Exactly how does mother or do others react to the situation? How do they try to stop it? Does this method make matters better or worse?

Goals must be clear and achievable. In a severe case 30 minutes without a tantrum may be realistic initially. Baseline measurements produce a clearer perspective of the problem which often seems less overwhelming when accurately measured. They may also promote change by providing a calm alternative response for the mother. An ingenious variation on recording is for mother to write up the chart, which must be filled in, in detail *immediately* in the bedroom whilst Tommy is left to have his tantrum in the kitchen. (Hill 1985.) Management techniques include:

(1) Shaping and prompting mother's behaviour so that she can ignore (i.e. not reinforce) harmless tantrums and intervene firmly but calmly when this is necessary. Time often needs to be spent explaining that shouting or slapping can reinforce in that it provides attention.

(2) Identifying and shaping up activities that are incompatible with tantrums. These periods of quiet play are often seen by

mother as 'an opportunity to get on' and the child is therefore ignored during them. The necessity of joining in with the games or admiring the drawings must be explained. Role play can be helpful as some parents are unused to giving praise and constructive comment.

(3) Initiating new activities which are incompatible with tantrums. A four-year-old master of supermarket tantrums was encouraged to draw dogs by copying the pictures on a well known brand of pet food. These were then praised by mother and backed up by an ice cream for tea after a tantrum-free supermarket trip. This is an example of distraction and differential reinforcement of other behaviour (DRO). It is extremely simple to initiate quickly from the surgery.

(4) Time-out in the manner described in the beginning of this chapter and in Chapter 4.

Disobedience

This is also a frequent complaint and may be quite normal and require only reassurance. If the problem requires further attention it is important to focus on the frequency, consistency and type of commands which are being flouted. Direct observation is invaluable in these circumstances as self-report by the parents ('I always do that' or 'I never do that') is notoriously unreliable. Observation in the home is ideal but often impracticable and a lot can be learnt by watching the mother and child in the surgery or clinic room when, for example, clearing up toys. A count can be made of the number of alpha commands, which are defined as clear requests which allow time for a definite response that the child could reasonably be expected to make, e.g. 'Stop pulling Tracy's hair'. Beta commands are those that are unclear, contradictory or countermanded before the child has a chance to comply, e.g. 'I told you, you couldn't have a biscuit — oh well, you might as well eat it now'. These are also counted. Observation will often show that compliance problems are most common where mother uses a lot of beta commands. Management involves modelling and prompting the mother's commands so that the beta commands become fewer and that alpha commands predominate and are followed through so that obedience is obtained. Failure to obey may be managed by a period of time-out if repeated clear requests are unsuccessful.

Aggression

Aggression must be carefully assessed in relation to the family background and the nature of the relationships involved. Assessment should particularly look at:

(1) whether the child has been taught to be aggressive because mother or father are frequently aggressive themselves;
(2) whether a degree of aggression is necessary to achieve anything in that particular school or household;
(3) whether aggression on the part of the child is being met with more aggression on the part of the parents. This can lead to a vicious circle of coercive behaviour which can have two outcomes, both bad. The worst result is that the child is subjected to severe battering. The less bad, but also unfortunate, is that the parents give up, leaving the child in command of the situation. He has thus learnt that force is the best way of achieving results.

Intervention with these children relies heavily on the use of time-out which is an effective but non-violent response. At the same time everything possible must be done to reinforce cooperative, constructive behaviour.

Teenage Problems

The teenager who refuses to comply with parental rules is another problem which appears frequently in primary care. This must be seen in family terms and a joint interview with the whole family is an important part of the assessment. An attempt has to be made to distinguish between dangerous or genuinely unreasonable behaviour on the part of the youngster and failure of the parents to realise that he is developing into an adult and therefore some flexibility and adaption is needed.

The clinician acts as the 'honest broker' and must be careful to be seen to be fair to both sides. Problems are defined in terms acceptable to all, and everybody is allowed to state their personal goals. Acceptable joint goals are then developed. The most useful way of achieving this is by means of behavioural contracting in which the parties agree that a particular behaviour on the part of one will be met by a particular response. The rules for these contracts may be summarised as follows: (Stuart 1971):

(1) Within a family, rewards and affection must be earned and cannot be expected by anyone as a right.
(2) Everybody must be fairly compensated for their contribution.
(3) The more positive reinforcement given, the more will be received in return.
(4) Rather than being restrictive, contracts in fact create freedom because all parties know exactly where they stand and inconsistencies are ruled out.

The most frequent problem in setting up contracts is to restrain the authoritarian demands of parents. They are good at generating long lists of requirements but rather poor in seeing that reciprocal services or privileges are due to the teenager. This situation demands considerable tact on the part of the clinician/negotiator. A useful start can be made with small relatively non-contentious items. In this way success is achieved and the principles understood before moving on to more difficult topics. For example, 'Feeding the cat each evening is to warrant a free trip to the hair stylist' might be a useful initial contract. Later the real problem might be addressed with the more complicated 'Going out with friends in the evening receives agreement to come in at 10 p.m., not to go on the common alone and not to drink alcohol'. It is important to check repeatedly that the terms of any proposed contract are seen as fair by all parties. To this end it may be necessary to work on the ability of the family members to state their wishes clearly, clarify the wishes of others and provide feedback information on how the behaviour of others affects them. Such skills may well be lacking in families with communication problems.

Fear and Anxiety in Childhood

As most of us can remember, childhood is a time of rapid learning and vulnerability which frequently contains many fearful experiences. Most of these are a normal and natural part of learning which equips us to cope with the dangers of the world. In some cases unreasonable fears can be dealt with by the methods of exposure and anxiety management described in Chapter 5.

There are, however, two problem areas which require special attention — fear of hospital admission and fear of school.

Fear of Hospital Admission

Methods of reducing adults' anxiety before admission to hospital have been covered in Chapter 9. Children are even more vulnerable than adults in this respect, even though free visiting and the admission of parents to hospital with their children has in recent years done much to reduce the potential damage. Several techniques may be useful:

(1) Gradual exposure to the hospital by visits and explanation beforehand. This may be coupled with encouragement of 'the grown-up way the child behaves at the hospital' whilst at the same time allowing fears to be openly discussed.

(2) Films of children going through hospital treatment, meeting the pain and the uncertainties but overcoming them and leaving again better and happy. This presents a *coping model*, dealing with the experience, to the child. This has been shown to be more effective than a mastery model which is one where no difficulty is experienced (Meichenbaum 1971). At present such films are rather hard to find but perhaps in the future they may be made available by health education agencies.

(3) Encouraging and teaching positive self-statements such as 'It will hurt a bit but I can look after myself and I will soon be home better' or 'It is one more bad sore throat but the nurses will help me and soon I'll be home with no more rotten throats.'

Fear of School

Many school phobias are initially reinforced by the parents who readily allow the child to stay at home on the smallest pretext. The GP who is unsure whether the child could be truly ill colludes in this. It follows that the GP is uniquely placed to nip the problem in the bud by being aware of incipient school fears and satisfying himself that there is no unnecessary absence.

Investigation of the established problem must first decide whether the absence is due to true fear of school or the rival attractions of staying away (truancy). The nature of any possible rival attractions is explored and it is established whether the parents know that the child is staying away or not. Truancy can be dealt with rapidly by an explanation of the law concerning school attendance and if necessary referral to the school attendance officer.

True phobias require more delicate handling. The exact nature of the fear is established and explored. It will usually revolve round either anxiety about leaving home or worrying activities at school. Precipitating factors at home might include bereavement, illness of self or others, divorce, separation, moving house or the birth of a new sibling. School factors might be change of school or class, loss of friend, bullying or ridicule, embarrassment at PE or shower time, learning problems or clashes with teacher. A phone call to the school will often throw light on these factors and pave the way for a joint approach.

The main management may be undertaken with the help of the parents alone but cooperation between GP, health visitor, school teachers and educational psychologist is often necessary and desirable. The main tactics of management are:

(1) If possible deal with any problems in the home.
(2) By cooperation with the teachers make sure that the child is attending a school suited to his needs, e.g. not too academic or where the physical demands exceed his capacity.
(3) Arrange for a sympathetic reception at the school when he returns.
(4) Rehearse arrival at school by a gradual approach, perhaps first visiting the school at a week-end when it is empty. Rehearsal of the first conversation with friends is also valuable e.g. 'I wasn't well but I'm better now'. After a long absence it is often valuable to return after a holiday or half term which causes less comment. An arrangement with the teacher for the child to go somewhere quiet, if distressed, without leaving the school may be helpful.
(5) Encourage the parents to remain calm and reward the child for success. At the same time attention should not be given to somatic complaints or 'bad days' at school. If for any reason the child does stay at home, there should be no TV or enjoyable activities.
(6) The child is escorted to school by, if possible, a parent. Failing this a friend or, at the last resort, a professional such as health visitor, social worker, GP or psychologist may act as escort. It is important that the escort should be prepared and able to withstand tears and tantrums.

Follow up is important and particular care should be exercised following illness or any other life event which might act as a precipitating factor for further problems.

Bellyache

Recurrent abdominal pain in the five-to-twelve-year-old is an extremely common problem occurring at some time or another in nearly three-quarters of children. In an important minority it is due to a urinary tract infection and an urinanalysis should always be performed. Most, however, are non-organic and form another example of a somatic reaction to stress similar to those reactions found in adults and described in Chapter 5. Children of this age seldom complain of headache and therefore abdominal pain becomes the chief somatic outlet of anxiety and tension.

Interview and baseline measurements focus on the problem in relation to school (in and out of class), sibling and parent relationships, recent bereavements (e.g. grandparents or pets) and important child life events such as the beginning of the new school year and the approach of Christmas.

Management involves:

(1) Physical examination and urinanalysis
(2) A sympathetic and assured diagnosis to both child and parents
(3) An explanation of how stress can affect muscles, aided by a diagram of the abdomen
(4) An exploration and, if possible, correction of contributory factors
(5) A full discussion with the whole family of misattributions, e.g. appendicitis, twisted bowel or 'something seriously wrong' and a confident explanation that referral is not indicated
(6) Advice about leading as normal a life as possible in spite of the pain
(7) If essential, a prescription for an antispasmodic such as dicyclomine HCl whose effect may be as much placebo as pharmacological

Common pitfalls to be avoided are:

(1) Increasing avoidance of normal life and school by the child 'because of the pain'. Once established this is hard to correct.
(2) A crescendo of family anxiety associated with lack of understanding of the true nature of the problem. This often leads to multiple negative investigations and a series of inconclusive referrals.

Hyperactivity

This takes many forms. The one most likely to present in the primary care is intermittent situation-specific hyperactivity where the child, usually a boy, is overactive and restless in some situations but not in others. This may be seen as a problem in developing an adequate concentration span rather than as a behavioural excess.

Management may be by drugs or diet but these are the province of specialists and lie outside our scope. Behavioural management may include the following elements:

(1) reinforcement of quiet sedentary activities, such as drawing or table games, with praise and attention;
(2) provision of opportunities for structured quiet play — working the energy off by rushing about is ineffective;
(3) the parents responding to overactivity quietly, thus not providing overactive models themselves;
(4) finding and shaping up by praise the smallest amounts of quiet constructive play, thus developing a longer concentration span. It is important to break the cycle of abuse and punishment which is generally the result of these children's unattractive behaviour.

If more unusual types of hyperactivity are suspected or the problem is beyond the resources at hand early referral to a child psychiatrist is advised.

The Elderly

Many of the problems presenting at the GP's consulting room by the elderly population require the same skills and treatment as those of younger patients. However there may be management problems for the family or relatives which are more difficult to deal with and peculiar to this age group, such as confusion or continence problems. This section discusses the handling of such problems.

Assessment of the elderly should preferably be made in the environment in which the difficulties arise, so that the effects of the environment on their behaviour can be seen. Monitoring or time sampling can be set up if necessary. For example, an elderly person who is confused may find that all the doors on the landing look the same and keep wandering into the 'wrong' room. Clear cue cards on the doors and low intensity lighting at night may be all that is required to put matters right.

Elderly people living on their own can become very anxious about minor day-to-day problems. Problem-solving techniques such as listing all potential solutions and finding the most practical and appropriate, can be immensely helpful. For example, a lady was terrified of the dark when alone at night, having read about attacks on elderly people at home. The fear was not irrational and did not amount to a phobia. Finding a lodger and the installation of an alarm solved the problem. In both these cases behavioural assessment helped arrive at solution.

Evidence from research shows that demented elderly people are still able to learn, but compared with non-demented patients they may need even greater consistency in implementing a programme for longer periods of time to maintain new behaviour, or reduce inappropriate behaviour. For example, calling out for the commode at inappropriate times may be reduced by offering the commode after all meals and drinks, and on each occasion explaining when the person last went and when they will be offered the chance to go again. This should be coupled with establishing an appropriate method of calling for assistance in an emergency.

Sleep difficulties may be altered by ensuring stimulus control. Sleep should be reserved as far as possible for bed and for after supper, washing etc. Sleep should preferably be in a different room from daytime activities (see also Chapter 5).

Stimulation during the day can be increased and confusion decreased by using principles of reality orientation in an informal way at home. This means that, during all contact with the person, constant reminders are given about who he is, about the time and about the place. Patients should be encouraged to look after themselves where possible, even if they take a long time, e.g. with dressing and toiletting. Calendars, clocks and newspaper headlines or pictures are useful to help keep the person's attention, and encourage them to be aware of what is going on in their environment.

It will often be the caring relatives who come to the doctor for advice. If difficulties can be foreseen as a result of regular checks with relatives, a preventative approach can be adopted. In this case minor problems are dealt with immediately and general strategies can be adopted to keep the elderly person alert, stimulated and in touch with reality.

For other carers their own stress is the problem. Caring for elderly relatives can be difficult. The constant demands can leave the carer exhausted, guilty and feeling that they are never able to do enough. Stress may be reduced by instructing carers to monitor these demands, to help timetable events and to define limits on both the amount of time which should be reasonably spent and the appropriate level of delegation to outside carers.

Frequently several members of the primary health care team are involved and a concerted effort by the district nurse, health visitor and GP may be needed to solve problems and set appropriate goals. Good communication within the team is particularly important in these cases. In addition it may be worthwhile to consult specialist services early if the locality is adequately served with psychogeriatricians, community psychiatric nurses and specialist clinical psychologists.

References

Douglas, J. and Richman, N. (1982) *Sleep Management Manual*, London, Dept of Psychological Medicine, The Hospital for Sick Children

Hill, P. (1985) Personal communication

Hobbs, S. A. and Forehand, R. (1977) 'Important parameters in the use of time out with children: A re-examination', *Journal of Behaviour Therapy and Experimental Psychiatry, 8*, 365–70

Meichenbaum, D. (1971) 'Examination of model characteristics in reducing avoidance behavior', *Journal of Personality and Social Psychology, 17*, 298–307

Stuart, R. B. (1971) 'Behavioral contracting with families of delinquents', *Journal of Behaviour Therapy and Experimental Psychiatry, 2*, 1–11

Recommended for Further Reading

Hanley, I. and Hodge, J. (eds.) (1984) *Psychological Approaches to the Care of the Elderly*, London, Croom Helm

Herbert, M. (1981) *Behavioural Treatment of Problem Children — a practical manual*, London, Academic Press

Graziano, A. M. and Mooney, K. C. (1984) *Children and Behavior Therapy*, New York, Aldine

Morgan, R. (1981) *Childhood Incontinence*, London, Disabled Living Foundation

Ross, Alan, D. (1981) *Child Behavior Therapy*, New York and Chichester, John Wiley

Woods, R. and Briton, P. (1985) *Clinical Psychology with the Elderly*, London, Croom Helm

Yule, W. and Carr, J. (eds.) (1980) *Behaviour Modification for the Mentally Handicapped*, London, Croom Helm

Books for Patients

Kastenbaum, R. (1979) *Growing Old — Years of Fulfilment*, London, Harper and Row

Patterson, G. R. (1971) *Families: Application of Social Learning to Family Life*, Champaign, Ill., Research Press

Peine, H. A. and Howarth, R. (1975) *Children and Parents*, Harmondsworth, Penguin

Equipment

Enuresis Alarms (as described) available from: Headingly Scientific Services, 45 Westcombe Avenue, Leeds L58 2BS. Telephone number 0532 664222

Useful Addresses

UK: Age Concern England, Bernard Sunley House, 60 Pitcairn Road, Mitcham, Surrey CR2 3LL

USA: Grey Panthers, 3635 Chestnut Street, Philadelphia PA 19104

INDEX